A NORTHUMBERLAND COUNTY BOOKSHELF

or

A Parcel of Old Books

1650-1852

Compiled by
W. Preston Haynie

HERITAGE BOOKS
2007

HERITAGE BOOKS
AN IMPRINT OF HERITAGE BOOKS, INC.

Books, CDs, and more—Worldwide

For our listing of thousands of titles see our website at
www.HeritageBooks.com

Published 2007 by
HERITAGE BOOKS, INC.
Publishing Division
65 East Main Street
Westminster, Maryland 21157-5026

Copyright © 1994 W. Preston Haynie

Other books by the author:

Northumberland County, Virginia Apprenticeships, 1650-1750

Northumberland County, Virginia Apprenticeships, 1750-1852

Records of Indentured Servants and of Certificates for Land, Northumberland County, Virginia, 1650-1795

All rights reserved. No part of this book may be reproduced or transmitted in any form or by any means, electronic or mechanical, including photocopying, recording or by any information storage and retrieval system without written permission from the author, except for the inclusion of brief quotations in a review.

International Standard Book Number: 978-0-7884-0097-1

Table of Contents

Preface v

A Brief Background
To Books Found in Estates
1650 to 1852 1

Books Found in Estates
Northumberland County, Virginia
Between 1650 and 1852 16

Index 116

Preface

The aim of this book is to help one gain an insight into the minds of our ancestors—their beliefs, convictions, and ideals. The titles of books found in estates, probably more than any other single item, provide a clue to those intellectual, religious, political, and social forces that shaped their minds. It is important, in observing titles of books, to note the works in the estates of the rectors, clerks of the court, schoolmasters, professionals, and county officials—all of those who may have had an influence in moulding the minds of individuals—as well as the books in the estates of one's own ancestors.

Although Northumberland County was formed in 1648, the date and title of the first record book is *Deeds Orders 1650–1652*; therefore, the date 1650 has been been used as part of the title for this work even though there are several estates included before 1650. (They are in *Deeds Orders 1650–1652*.) In the compilation of books found in estates, inventories, or accounts of sales, the date used is the date when the inventory was returned to the court to be recorded. In a few cases the dates are out of chronological order. A number of inventories may have been returned to court about the same time, and consequently a few may not have been copied in the record books in the proper order.

If only one word or several words of a book title have been used, the word or words have been put in italics. For example, the complete title of William Sherlock's book is *Practical Discourse Concerning Death*. Most frequently in the estates it is referred to as on *Death*. The complete title of John Locke's work is *Essay Concerning Human Understanding*. The title of Pearson's work is *Exposition of the Creed*; on pages 47 and 56 it is listed as on *The Creed*. On page 47 the author's name is spelled Person; on page 56 it is spelled correctly.

Most frequently in the inventories only one name of the author is listed. By the seventeenth century, Plutarch, Euripides, Virgil, Homer, Ovid, and Cicero had become known by only one name, and our ancestors were familiar with those names just as we are. On the other hand, for us, Gordon, Pearson, Butler, Stackhouse, Harvey, Calamy, and Bailey may have little meaning; however, for those living during the seventeenth and eighteenth centuries, those names would have been as familiar to our ancestors as the names of Sartre, Salinger, Baldwin, Santayana, Faulkner, Updike, and Freeman are to us.

In a few cases both an appraisement and an account of sales have been included. This may have been done to indicate how close the two were in value or how different the two may have been. In several cases both have been included because one contains more titles of books.

At times brackets have been used to identify an author or title or to raise questions. For example, [Edward] followed by Calamy indicates that his name is Edward Calamy. [*The Whole Duty of Man*] following *Duty of Man* indicates that *The Whole Duty of Man* is the complete title of the book. [*Directory?*] following *Darectory* indicates I believe the person taking the inventory meant *Directory*. Another example would be [Ovid?] as opposed to Ovild. If merely a question mark has been placed in the brackets, such as Adition's [?] or Moires [?], this is to indicate I had difficulty in making out the spelling or was not certain of the author or title.

At times items other than books have been included. This has been done in order for one to see the value of the items when books were grouped with other items; thus, one can make a comparison with other estates.

Record Book (RB) and *Order Book* (OB) have been abbreviated for brevity. Because a name may be spelled differently in the index of the record book than in the inventory, one should look at all possible spellings of a name. Examples are Basey, Baisey, Basie, Basye or Barecroft, Bearcroft. In a number of instances, a difference in the spelling of a name has been indicated.

My appreciation goes to the clerk of the circuit court, Steve Thomas, and staff, Linda L. Booth, Eleanor R. Morris, and Emily D. Thomas for their willingness to permit me to occupy a portion of the record room and to Jim and Joanne Foster, who prepared the manuscript.

W. Preston Haynie

A Brief Background To Books Found in Estates 1650 to 1852

Books, probably more than any other single item, provide a clue to the intellectual and social values of those who may have lived during a particular period in history. Thus, to some degree, through the books the people read, we get to know the character or nature of their thinking. Frequent references have been made to the libraries of William Byrd of Westover and Richard Lee of Mount Pleasant, Westmoreland County, but never before has a survey of books found in estates been made of an entire locale or county. Although such a study reveals no final answers about general literacy or literary taste, such a study does provide great insight into one's beliefs, ideas, and convictions. Even more important, through such a study we gain a sense and appreciation of the past, an awareness of the role our ancestors played in the shaping of the colony and later the state. The books found in estates during the colonial and revolutionary periods, the national era, and the antebellum era provide a glimpse into the Northumberland mind as well as a reflection of the period.*

"Throughout the colonial period," according to Louis B. Wright, "the interest in books was a vital and growing manifestation of the American genius for self-improvement."[1] A survey of the inventories of estates in Northumberland County reveals that the Northumberland bookshelf would resemble libraries in farmhouses of England. The inventories prove that most

---

*For purposes of this discussion, the colonial and revolutionary periods have been considered together. Even within the colonial period, one might divide it into the colonial period and the plantation era, the latter being a period in which the colonists enjoyed a reasonable degree of prosperity. However, the nature of the books found in the estates during both the colonial and revolutionary periods remained somewhat the same, with only an increase in the quantity of books and the appearance of new titles as they found their way to the colony. Following the Revolution, one notes a gradual change in the titles of books, and by 1815 the United States probably was at the height of what is known as the national era or the federalist age. The last division is that of the antebellum era; in literature it is referred to as the romantic period.

1. Louis B. Wright, *The Cultural Life of the American Colonies 1607–1763* (New York: Harper and Brothers, 1957), 153.

of the people owned books, and even the poorest and least educated had the *Bible* and several other books. The books in these inventories reveal an interest in religion, the edification of man, history, social conditions or satire, and the classics; however, a large number of inventories do not quote titles but merely refer to the works as "a parcel of old books."

In the estates there are more books on religion than any other category. Nearly every inventory includes one or more *Bibles*. The *New Testament*, which in 1525 was the first printed English translation of any part of the *Bible*, appears in the estates of Col. John Mottrom (1655), widow Bradley (1670), Hancock Lee (1709), and Enoch Hill (1719/20). *The Great Bible*, an English *Bible* published in 1540 and intended primarily for use in churches, appears in the estates of Enoch Hill (1719/20), Thomas Hobson (1726/27), Henry Christopher (1727), Cary Keble (1728), John Wood (1739), and Thomas Dameron (1757). John Waughop's estate (1749) includes a quarto *Bible*; Isaac Edwards's estate includes one *Bible* with *Apocrypha*.

Such value was placed on *Bibles* that they were mentioned in wills. A portion of the will of Robert Bradley reads: "I give and bequeath to my Son John Bradley one large *Bible* and one mare and Bridle and Saddle."[2] Thomas Hughlett left to his "said grandson Thomas Dameron . . . my great *Bible*."[3] Grace Ball in her will left to her "three Daughters Sarah Dameron, Harris Downman and Grace Downman three *Great Bibles* and the said *Bibles* to be in value of three Pounds Current Money in Virginia."[4] John Leland in his will left to his wife Lucy Leland his riding chair and harness and Burkett on the *New Testament*.[5]

Being readily available, the *Bible* was important in the teaching of reading, maybe in some cases providing the only source of instruction, especially among the lower classes and in some cases among other classes as well. Douglas Southall Freeman in volume one of *George Washington* states that "Harrower carried Bathurst Daingerfield through a reading of the entire *Bible* before teaching him to write."[6] Court records often state that when young girls

---

2. *Record Book 1720–1729*, 49.
3. *Record Book 1726–1729*, 144.
4. *Record Book 2*, 78–79.
5. *Record Book 10*, 185.
6. Douglas Southall Freeman, *George Washington*, vol. 1, *Young Washington* (New York: Charles Scribner's Sons, 1948), 132.

were bound out as apprentices, they were to be taught to read the *Bible*. Mary Baker, an orphan eleven years of age, was bound to Samuel Poole who was to teach her "to read ye *Bible* perfectly and to sew with such Christian-like education."[7] Rebecca Maudley, the daughter of Edmund Maudley, was bound to Alexander Wetherstone who was to teach her to read the *Bible* perfectly and give her usable Christian-like education.[8] In 1716 nine-year-old Elizabeth Tignor, orphan daughter of Philip Tignor, was bound to Thomas Hughlett who was to teach her to read the *Bible* perfectly and to educate the said Elizabeth in Christian duties as well as household employment.[9] One is not certain how well they were able to read the *Bible* or how much interpretation was involved; however, the language of the King James version of the *Bible* would have been closer to the language of the time—even though it would have included both formal and colloquial speech patterns—than it would be to the language of people today.

Next to the *Bible*, *The Book of Common Prayer* is the religious work seen most frequently in inventories; however, in all cases it is referred to as *Common Prayer Book*. "Evolved in the 16th. century to meet the popular need for aids to devotion and the demand for the use of the vernacular in church services,"[10] *The Book of Common Prayer* went through several revisions before the final text in 1662; it is probably this book found in the estates of the people of Northumberland. The estate of Hancock Lee (1709) lists four copies as well as two old *Bibles* and one small *Bible*. His is the first inventory to include *The Book of Common Prayer*. Copies are also listed in the estates of Ebenezer Neale (1711) and Peter Hammond (1711). Because the Church of England, the established church of the Virginia colony, remained strong in Northumberland (despite the Baptist and Presbyterian dissenters) until the Revolution, *The Book of Common Prayer* can be found in inventories well into the 1800s; however, the number diminished after 1800.

Sermons and *Psalters* also appear in the inventories of estates. "The main reason for the interest in sermon reading was not theological but devotional and practical: men looked to these divines for wisdom and guidance in both

---

7. *Order Book 1678–1698, Part 2*, 402.
8. Ibid., 408.
9. *Order Book 1713–1719*, 184.
10. Margaret Drabble and Jenny Stringer, eds., *The Concise Oxford Companion to English Literature* (New York: Oxford University Press, 1987), 121.

spiritual and temporal affairs, for help in establishing and following a pattern of life fulfilling their ideas of dignity and honor."[11] According to Louis B. Wright, these sermons "were not the handwork of half-literate fanatics, as we are sometimes led to believe, but of shrewd and intelligent university men, whose piety did not keep them from being practical social thinkers. From them our ancestors learned to follow closely reasoned and logical argument, to discipline their minds to analytical exposition, to appraise questions raised by their authors."[12] Each of the estates of John Hampton (1649) and John Dawson (1711) contains a sermon book; George Dawkins's (1728) includes six as well as two *Psalters*. The estate of Ann Stowell (1723) lists one old sermon book of John Foxe's. His most popular work is his *Book of Martyrs*.

The *Psalter*, or *Book of Psalms* containing the psalms for liturgical or devotional use, was an important part of the religion of the colony. According to Drabble and Stringer, "the Psalms were the basis of the medieval church services, probably the only book in the *Bible* on the use of which, by the laity, the medieval church imposed no veto at all."[13] A number of versions of the *Book of Psalms* have been published. In Northumberland, the *Psalter* is found first in the estate of Robert Wilson (1727). The estate of John Conway (1726/27) includes two. It is found as late as 1792 in the estate of William Barrett.

Works of three other writers—the Rev. William Sherlock, John Bunyan, and John Milton—appear in the inventories of Northumberland. Of the three, the writings of Sherlock appear more frequently. His *Practical Discourse Concerning Death* can be found in the estates of Maj. Charles Lee (1741), Judith Jones (1742), John Dameron (1745), John Taylor (1752), Mosley Mott (1757), and Mrs. Menzies (1775). *Pilgrim's Progress*, an allegorical masterpiece by John Bunyan, is among the books of Hancock Lee (1709), Thomas Burn (1741), and John Taylor (1752). Bunyan in 1653 joined a Baptist church in Bedford and soon began preaching. As a result, he was imprisoned for twelve years. A royal declaration of indulgence released him in 1672. The King's declaration of indulgence permitted dissenters to preach; however, after three years the royal indulgence was withdrawn, and he was imprisoned the second time. It is at this time he produced his masterpiece. Because of the beauty of its language and good characterization, it was read by people other than dissenters.

---

11. Wright, *Cultural Life*, 140.
12. Ibid., 141.
13. Drabble and Stringer, *Concise Oxford Companion*, 458.

Milton, a very religious man, is best known for *Paradise Lost* and *Paradise Regained*, both written after he became blind. Filled with classical references to mythology, *Paradise Lost* deals with the problem of evil, a theme that has concerned writers of all centuries. Why should God permit the destruction of man's body and soul through wars, famine, and man's cruelty to man? For his answer, Milton went to the Hebraic account of Adam and Eve, and produced an epic poem that deals with the wonders of the universe as well as the fall and regeneration of mankind. *Paradise Regained*, the New Testament story of Christ's victory over Satan in the wilderness, points out how the paradise lost can, at least, be partly regained in this world. Milton's reputation was an eighteenth century development in the colony. Copies of *Paradise Lost* are in the inventories of Thomas Smith (1758) and Phebe Menzies (1780).

The estates of many in the county contain books, though somewhat religious in nature, that were aimed primarily at the edification of man. "The theory of conduct and of man's relation with man," according to Louis B. Wright, "was a problem of consuming interest to our soul-searching ancestors. . . ."[14] For one's improvement "they were supplied with books that provided the essentials of instruction in every thing from table manners to the means of attaining a heavenly crown."[15] "The great concern of the colonists, however, was less with the externals of behavior than with deeper problems of conduct that determined reputation and character."[16] By far the book found most frequently in the estates dealing with this traditional rationale of conduct is *The Whole Duty of Man*, published in 1658. It is "a devotional work . . . in which man's duties in respect of God and his fellow men are analysed and discussed in detail."[17] It appears first in the inventory of Hancock Lee (1709). The book was popular for the entire eighteenth century, appearing in the estates of Sarah Jones (1720), Thomas Sandiford (1722), Charles Lee (1746/47), Peter Bearcroft (1746), Robert Boyd (1747), John Taylor (1752), Mosley Mott (1757), Charles Ingram (1760), George Kerr (1761), Samuel Blackwell (1762), Elizabeth Nelms (1762), and Capt. George Ball (1770).

In addition to *The Whole Duty of Man*, there were other works related to devotion and a reverence for God. The estate of William Brent (1737/38)

---

14. Wright, *Cultural Life*, 136.
15. Ibid.
16. Ibid., 137.
17. Drabble and Stringer, *Concise Oxford Companion*, 611.

includes *A Complete Manual of Private Devotion*. Richard Nelms's estate (1737) includes *The Golden Grove* by Jeremy Taylor, a manual of daily prayers. Taylor was bishop of Down and later Droxmore. *Devout Exercises* is among the books listed in the inventory of John Kent (1767), and *Christian Life* is among the books in the estate of Maj. Charles Lee (1741). *The Week's Preparation* is included in the estates of George and Edward Kerr (1761) and Capt. George Ball (1770). Sarah Hill in her will left a copy of the book to her daughter: "... I give my Daughter Sarah Hill the new feather Bed and furniture and all belonging to it my saddle & the book called *The Week's Preparation*...."[18] Titles of books of devotion are not given in the estate of Judith Jones (1742), but the works are referred to as "sundry books of devotion." *The Practice of Piety* by Lewis Bayly, published in 1613, can be found first in the estate of Jane Pery (1650). It is also among the books of Hancock Lee (1709), John Dameron (1743), William Sutton (1755), and Richard Hudnall (1760). Davis speaks of the book as "old-fashioned theology."[19] An *Essay Concerning Human Understanding*, by the English philosopher John Locke, is among the books in the inventories of Judith Jones (1742) and Maj. William Taite (1772).

Next to books on religion and self-improvement, books on history are those found most frequently in inventories. Historical reading, especially of the ancient Greeks and Romans, was highly favored among the Virginia planters and professionals. The educated felt that histories were necessary to one's reading. The estates of John Haynie (1723) and Samuel Blackwell (1762) include Flavius Josephus's *History of the Jews*, a book according to Davis that "every man who wanted to be intelligent about *Old Testament* matters felt he must have a copy. In 1709 William Byrd II read it in the Greek version before breakfast. Jefferson owned several editions in Latin or English."[20] Probably the copies belonging to Haynie and Blackwell were English editions. John Haynie's estate included five other books of Roman history. Maj. Charles Lee's estate (1741) includes two Roman histories and *History of the Turks*; John Taylor's includes three volumes of Roman histories and one volume of *The Antiquities of Rome*. Among the books of Baldwin Matthews Smith (1763) are four volumes of Rapin's *History of England*. A Frenchman, "Rapin felt the necessity of going

---

18. *Record Book 2*, 181.
19. Richard Beale Davis, *A Colonial Southern Bookshelf* (Athens: The University of Georgia Press, 1979), 66.
20. Ibid., 35–36.

back to the Anglo-Saxons to explain English democratic institutions and constitutions. He traces English history from Julius Caesar and brings it through the reign of Charles I."[21] Again one doesn't know whether the volumes owned by Smith are the French or English editions. "Jefferson ... told a friend as late as 1815 that it [Rapin's *History of England*] was still the best history of England, for Hume's tory principles are ... insupportable."[22] The estate of the Rev. Henry Christall (1743/44) contains a work by another Roman biographer, Suetonius, who in his *Lives of the Caesars* aims "to bring out the moral character of his subjects, and he paid attention to their private habits as well as to their imperial policy."[23] The inventory of Hancock Lee (1709) mentions two old histories. The estate of Judith Jones (1742) includes a copy of a Roman history and *The Chronicles of England*.

Richard Lee's inventory (1741) includes a copy of *Plantation Law* and *The History of England*; Benjamin Waddy's (1741) includes a copy of *The Grand Abridgment of the Common and Statute Laws of England*. A *History of Europe* is among the books of Joseph Wildey (1748).

Of the works making social commentaries, *The Spectator* is found in more inventories of Northumberland residents than any other work. A periodical by Addison and Steele, it was published first in 1711 and then revived by Addison in 1714. "It was usually a graceful, entertaining presentation of any sort of subject, including the place of the country gentleman in contemporary society."[24] According to Bernard D. N. Grebanier, "Addison announced that his purpose was to make virtue pleasant through the use of wit, and to bring philosophy out of the schools into homes and coffee houses. In other words, his task was to popularize the learning and good manners that had been practiced at Court during the Restoration, but cleansed of their Restoration indecency."[25] *The Spectator* is listed in estates from 1741 to the end of the century. The fact that it was "popular reading throughout the century in these colonies agrees perfectly with the continuing taste for them in Great Britain."[26] In Northumberland the periodical can be found in the estates of Thomas Burn

---

21. Ibid., 40.
22. Ibid., 41.
23. Drabble and Stringer, *Concise Oxford Companion*, 544.
24. Davis, *Southern Bookshelf*, 114–115.
25. Bernard D. N. Grebanier, *English Literature*, vol. 1 (New York: Barron's Educational Series, Inc., 1959), 325.
26. Davis, *Southern Bookshelf*, 25.

(1741), John Hack (1747), Richard Smith (1748), John Waughop (1749), Thomas Smith (1758), Charles Jones (1737/38), John Kerr (1761), Capt. George Ingram (1798), William Angel (1771), Benjamin Waddy (1783), Phebe Menzies (1780), George Heath (1784), and Charles Copedge (1787).

The Tatler, also a periodical founded by Steele, is among the titles of books in the inventory of John Hack (1747).

The Guardian, also a periodical started by Steele, appears in a number of inventories. Supposedly it was to refrain from political questions, but "Steele soon launched into political controversy"[27] and publication of *The Guardian* ceased in 1713. The periodical is listed in the estates of Richard Smith (1748), Charles Jones (1737/38), John Hack (1747), John Kerr (1761), and Robert Woodrop (1768).

Though classical works listed in the inventories are not as numerous as those in other categories, it is obvious that some of the planters and the members of the clergy were interested in carrying on the tradition of Renaissance learning. Some planters or professionals may have read the works in the original; others may have relied on translations. The inventories do not always make clear what proportion of the books are translations. "The ruling planters," according to Wright, "were eager that their children should be brought up in the old tradition of the Latin grammar schools."[28] "Anyone who went to school ... began the learning process through Latin authors, unless he was an apprentice or a black."[29] The classics and the ancient world provided these men with a cultural anchor.

The inventory of the Rev. Henry Christall (1743/44), in addition to numerous religious works, includes a number of Greek and Roman authors. Classic poetry includes two volumes of *The Odes* of Horace; a Latin version of *Comedies* by Terence, a Roman comic poet; *Aeneid* by Virgil, the greatest of the Roman poets; Homer's *The Iliad*; and Ovid's *Metamorphoses*. Ovid, an early Roman writer, "continued in favour with writers and public so long as Rome was pagan, but the Christian Church disapproved of his immorality. Interest revived with the 11th. century and during the Renaissance Ovid enjoyed great favour."[30] Historians also are amply represented in Christall's inventory and

---

27. Drabble and Stringer, *Concise Oxford Companion*, 241.
28. Wright, *Cultural Life*, 86.
29. Davis, *Southern Bookshelf*, 100.
30. Drabble and Stringer, *Concise Oxford Companion*, 417.

include the Roman writers Cornelius Nepos and Sallustius. Christall owned both English and Latin versions of Sallustius's *The History of the Twelve Caesars*. Justin, an early church historian and philosopher, and Sallust, a Roman historian, are also included. The Greek Stoic philosopher Epictetus and Marcus Tullius Cicero, referred to as Tully, are two other classsic authors listed in the inventory. According to Drabble and Stringer, the writings of Tully "left their mark on ethics, epistemology, and political thought, on men's ideals of conduct, on the development of oratory and letter writing, on literary style, the popularity of paradox, and the viability of Latin as an international language."[31]

The estate of Mrs. Phebe Menzies, the widow of the Rev. Adam Menzies, in addition to numerous religious works and the more recent political and literary writings of the time, includes works of classic authorship. These include Davidson's translations of Virgil as well as a Latin version, Horace's *Delphine*, Euripides, Homer, and Cornelius Nepos. A notation on the inventory of Mrs. Menzies states that the books were "chiefly old and much used," indicating that the books had been used by the Menzies household or neighbors, or they may have been used in the instruction of pupils since the Rev. Menzies was a rector and rectors were often engaged in the education of some pupils.

Though the estates of planters do not indicate as many classical titles as those found in the inventories of the clergy, a number of inventories include at least several works. Thomas Sandiford's (1722) listing includes the Greek minor poets; Joseph Hudnall's estate mentions Francis Meres's *Abridgment* (a work in which the author compared writers of his England to a similar writer in Latin, Greek, or Italian); the Honorable Presly Thornton's (1770) estate includes Virgil and Ovid; David Edenton's (1771) classics include Cicero's *Orations*, Lucian's *Dialogues*, Terence's *Comedies*, and Trap's Virgil. Maj. William Taite (1772) had both Plutarch's *Parallel Lives* and Plutarch's *Morals*. Rodham Kenner's inventory includes Ovid's *Metamorphoses* and *Epistles*.

Too often the titles of books in inventories are not given. An inventory that notes the value of the books, the total number of books, or merely a parcel of old books can be exasperating for one attempting to discover what his ancestors may have read or studied. The value of one library of books for the Rev. Moses Robertson (1747) was £14 17s, for Christopher Neale (1721), £13; surely these

---

31. Ibid., 109.

would have been rather extensive libraries. The value of books in the estate of Isaac Haynie (1726) was £2 5s, the most expensive item in the inventory; for Thomas Cralle (1726) the value placed on the books was £4 2s; for Matthew Neale (1726/27), £1; Ormsby Haynie (1743/44), £1 5s; Thomas Gaskins (1726), £1 15s; and Lindsey Opie (1747), £7 2s 6d.

Equally annoying is an inventory that gives only the total number of books. What books would have been included in the seventy-eight books, good and bad, in the inventory of Sarah Haynie; the thirty-seven works belonging to William Keene (1726); the thirty-six books, a packet of books, and three other books belonging to Capt. Richard Haynie (1725); the forty-one good books and three packets of books belonging to Richard Lattimore (1772); and the fifty titles belonging to Capt. William Eustace (1740)? One at best can only note a person's position in life and the number or value of his books, then look at the titles of books in the inventories of other persons and, in turn, reconstruct a library for that individual.

Even more irritating is when the inventory reads "a parcel of old books." In most cases, more than likely, the total number of books will be fewer than in the estates in which the titles are given. In attempting to determine the number of books (and maybe the titles), one would have to consider the age of the book, old or new; the value and size of the book; and the time period. Books a few years before the Revolution were very expensive. One can look at some inventories and notice the value of books and the titles for that price. In John Dameron's inventory (1753), one old sermon book, one new *Bible*, and one old *Bible* were valued at 14s 6d; Sherlock on *Death*, *The Whole Duty of Man*, and *The Practice of Piety*, 12s; and one *Testament*, one *Psalter*, prayer book, and a parcel of old books, 5s 8d.

Books are found in the estates of Northumberland residents beginning in the 1650s, with the number increasing by the eighteenth century. Though the wilderness was only fifty to a few hundred miles away, Northumberland had become a settled community, and a number of planters, professionals, and small landowners were fairly prosperous. By this time, some of the sons and grandsons of the original settlers were moving westward. Those remaining were secure with their institutions modeled after the British. In Northumberland, and in most of the counties of the Northern Neck, the dominant influence remained the British. Nearly all of the inventories include books. With the exception of a few estates toward the end of the eighteenth century, there is little evidence in Northumberland of the modern languages of the time—German,

Italian, and French. No inventory in Northumberland is as extensive as the three thousand titles in the library of William Byrd, who employed a full-time librarian.[32]

Likewise, in Northumberland those with fairly large numbers of books would have had slaves or indentured servants; thus, they would have had the time or made the time to maintain contact with the past through books. Their reading provided guidance and a way of passing on the amenities of a cultivated life. The estates of those without slaves or servants included at least a few books as well. The person of this period made use of his time. Freeman recounts the tale of a teacher and librarian at the second William Byrd's Westover complaining of the lack of candles. Byrd, half-jesting, replied: "If such [a candle] as you have ... would burn an hour and a half, that is full long enough to read by candle—which is not good for the eyes and after that meditation and devotion might fill up the rest of the winter evening."[33]

And with the preponderance of devotional and religious books in the estates, the Northumberland resident should have been prepared on how to spend time in meditation and devotion. To some there might appear to be a contradiction in the image of a cavalier Virginian who at times attended a cock fight or a horse race.[34] According to Davis, this was not so. "The southern colonial might be reasonable devout, but he took his religion in stride. Its practice was a great reason but not the only reason for human existence."[35] To what extent the titles "southern gentleman" or "Virginia gentleman" can be attributed to the numerous books found in the estates on self-improvement, one's conduct, and man's relation to his fellow man is not certain. Surely they helped to construct a code of behavior by which one should live. Books give us insight into the minds of the seventeenth- and eighteenth-century residents of Northumberland. Their beliefs and wisdom, gained from the readings of the ancients, remain unquestioned in a modern world in which certain aspects of our materialistic society, especially the mass media (primarily television, but also newspapers and magazines), seem, at times, responsible for an erosion of ideas and intellectual pursuit.

---

32. Freeman, *George Washington*, 126.
33. Ibid., 131.
34. J. Motley Booker, "Horse Racing in Northumberland County—Cherry Point 1689," *The Bulletin of the Northumberland County Historical Society*, 52.
35. Davis, *Southern Bookshelf*, 90.

Following the Revolution, one notes a gradual change in the kinds of books found in estates, a change that can be attributed to the loss of the influence of an established church and a spirit of nationalism that swept the country and reached its peak around 1815.

Some years before the Revolution, many people had become disenchanted with the Anglican church, the established church of the colony, and had become members of the Baptist or Methodist persuasions. The Wicomico Anglican Church, built in 1763–67 and demolished about 1840,[36] is a prime example of the decline of influence. Later the present Wicomico Episcopal Church was built on the same site as the Wicomico Anglican Church.

The Book of Common Prayer, so prevalent in earlier periods, is listed in fewer inventories following the Revolution. It can be found in the estates of John Rogers (1810), Charles Dodson (1812), George McAdam Brown (1812), Mrs. Sarah Moore (1815), Walter Anderson (1818), Charles Leland (1820), and William Nicoll (1822). The estate of Anthony Sydnor (1823) contains a *Prayer Book* as well as the *Portraiture of Methodism*. These people may have been members of an Episcopal church or the books may have been handed down from previous generations.

Books of devotions and sermons, found in many estates prior to the Revolution, appear in fewer estates. *Christian Pattern*, a book of devotion, is among the titles in the inventory of Martin Haynie (1804); George McAdam Brown's estate (1812) includes Wilmott's *Devotion*. Sermon books can be found in the inventories of Samuel L. Beacham (1810) and the Rev. Duncan McNaughton (1810). The sermons of John Wesley, who "contributed greatly to the fervent Methodist Spirit,"[37] are listed in the estates of Hopkins Harding (1813) and Thomas Beacham (1823).

"The wave of patriotism and nationalism after the War of 1812"[38] probably caused the greatest change in the kinds of books found in estates. The War of 1812 proved to be a turning point in the history of the United States. The war promoted a feeling of optimism and a trend toward national self-sufficiency. There were challenging opportunities as many moved westward. Every able-

---

36. Carolyn H. Jett, "Wicomico Anglican Church," *The Bulletin of the Northumberland County Historical Society*, 1993, 55.
37. Drabble and Stringer, *Concise Oxford Companion*, 607.
38. John D. Hicks and George E. Mowry, *A Short History of American Democracy* (Boston: Houghton Mifflin Co., 1956), 171.

bodied man could find work, a fact that developed an unrestrained individualism. According to Hicks and Mowry, "Equality of opportunity had much to do with the turn that democracy was taking in America. The equalitarian doctrine of the Declaration of Independence was in its day merely the statement of an ideal: fifty years later it was not far from a correct description of American society. To be sure, an aristocracy still existed in every part of the country, except possibly in the West, but the new aristocracy, whether of industrial New England or of the cotton-planting South, was an aristocracy to which now even the lowliest might aspire."[39]

The ultranationalism of America—love of country and state, patriotism, optimism, and native American subject matter—is revealed in the books found in estates. George Washington was a favorite subject. Marshall's *Life of Washington* can be found in the estates of Charles Leland (1820), David Ball (1816), Henry Lee Gaskins (1819), William H. Nicoll (1822), John Cralle (1823), and John Davenport (1824). *Washington's Letters* is among the works in the inventories of Thomas Hurst (1825) and Willis W. Hudnall (1829). John Miller's estate (1809) includes *Washington's Reports*. Thomas Jefferson was another popular subject. *Jefferson's Manual* is included in the estate of John Miller (1809). *Jefferson's Notes* is among the titles in the inventories of William Davenport (1825), William H. Nicoll (1822), and Thomas Hughlett (1829). *Jefferson's Virginia* is listed among the books of William Claughton (1812). Thomas Hurst's estate (1818) includes *The Life of Franklin;* Peter C. Rice's (1819) includes *The Life of Patrick Henry. History of America,* a popular work of the period, is among the titles of Thomas Hurst (1825), William H. Nicoll (1822), and William Claughton (1812). The inventories of William H. Nicoll (1822) and Thomas Hudnall (1824) list *History of the Late War.* Both John Davenport's (1824) and William Davenport's (1825) estates include *American War.* Other titles that evoke a feeling of pride in the young nation are *American Justice, American Biography, American Negotiation, Laws of Virginia, Virginia Ruins, Laws of the United States, American Farmer, Clay's Speeches,* and *History of the United States.*

One notes a continuation of titles of the classics in estates, especially in the inventories of the Rev. John Leland (1778), Henry Foot (1778), Col. Rodham Kenner (1786), and Thomas Andrews (1794). In some respects, the books in these estates are more typical of those of the colonial period in that they contain

---

39. Ibid., 177.

classics as well as ancient histories, sermons, and books of devotion. Fewer classics are noted after 1810; however, the estate of Thomas Hurst (1818) includes eight volumes of Shakespeare and *Pilgrim's Progress*; the estate of Henry Lee Gaskins (1819), Horace's *Poems*; the estate of William H. Nicoll (1822), Plutarch's *Lives*, Shakespeare's works, Aesop's *Fables*, and *Don Quixote*; and the estate of John Miller (1809), *Paradise Lost* and works of Shakespeare.

From 1830 until 1852, when this study ends, there were many changes in the country. It was an era in which one witnessed the rise of sectionalism, Jacksonian democracy and the rise of the common man, various reform movements, and the Mexican War. In literature, the time has been characterized as the romantic period. New England, because of its high regard for learning, produced such literary greats as Nathaniel Hawthorne, Henry Wadsworth Longfellow, Ralph Waldo Emerson, Henry David Thoreau, Oliver Wendell Holmes, and John Greenleaf Whittier. New York produced Washington Irving and Herman Melville. Virginia produced Edgar Allen Poe, but according to Hicks and Mowry, "The ante-bellum South produced no other writer even faintly comparable to Poe."[40] None of the works of these writers, including those of Poe, are found in the estates of the people in Northumberland. In fact, nearly half of the estates do not include any books at all, despite the fact that many of the inventories are rather extensive, certainly more extensive than those of the period from 1650 to 1800.

There probably are several seasons for the number of estates without books and for the lack of books by well-known writers of the period. Virginia, failing to develop or "enhance its economic and political ties with the emerging west,"[41] drifted into a period of stagnation. The leaders of the state continued to be planters, and they, as leaders, in attempting to hold on to a past way of life, were slow to adapt themselves to the need for schools for everyone. A Literary Fund was established in 1816 "to educate the poor; the notion of public schools for all was out of the question. As late as 1850, Virginia's system of public education combined had the smallest proportion of whites in school of any nonfrontier state in the Union."[42] In addition, the area was rather remote, being surrounded on three sides by the Chesapeake Bay and the Rappahannock and

---

40. Ibid., 249.
41. Louis D. Rubin, Jr., *Virginia—A History* (New York: W. W. Norton & Co., 1984), 94.
42. Ibid., 96.

Potomac rivers.

The period from 1830 to 1852 saw a continuation of book titles that related to the American scene. The estate of Fleming Bates (1831) includes *History of Virginia* and the *American Constitution*. Samuel Blackwell's inventory contains an extensive list of books of a national character: *America, History of the United States, Life of Patrick Henry, Notes on Virginia, Laws of Virginia, Virginia Reports,* Marshall's *Washington,* and *Virginia Convention Debates.* William Sydnor's estate (1837) includes *Life of Franklin;* George Wheatley's (1841), *Memoir of Washington.* The estate of Samuel Cralle (1835) includes *United States Laws;* the estate of Lindsey Barnes (1837), *History of the United States* and *American Biography;* the estate of David T. Ball (1835), *Travels in America.*

Because the people had been brought up in the tradition of the old Latin schools, for some the classics continued to be important. Northumberland Academy, a classical school, existed for those wanting to acquire more than a meager education. It wasn't until 1846 that common schools for the children of indigent parents came into being.[43] For those attending Latin grammar schools, it was still the belief, as during earlier periods, that good lessons could be learned from the ancients. The estate of Fleming Bates (1831) includes the works of Plutarch, Voltaire, Homer's *The Iliad,* Horace, and thirty-six volumes of British classics. Among the works in the inventory of Everard M. Stith (1832) are *Paradise Lost,* Homer's *The Iliad* and *The Odyssey, Lucian, Horace Delphini.* His estate also cites eight volumes of Shakespeare, whose writings by this time could be considered classics. Samuel Blackwell's inventory (1839) includes *Hudibras,* Homer's *Iliad,* and Hume's *England;* George Wheatley's (1841), *Gulliver's Travels;* and William Basye's (1849), Simpson's *Euclid,* Homer's *Odyssey,* and *Paradise Lost.*

The Northumberland County bookshelf reflects the religious, intellectual, political, and social values of its citizens. By observing the books found in estates from 1650 to 1852, we notice the slow transition of a county, with its institutions modeled after the British, transform itself into a county as part of a larger unit seeking its own identity. Hopefully we may also gain an insight into the mind of an ancestor—his beliefs, convictions, and ideals—and a deeper appreciation of the past.

---

43. Miriam Haynie, "Sketch of Public Schools for Northumberland County," *The Bulletin of the Northumberland County Historical Society,* 1973, 3–5.

Books Found in Estates Northumberland County, Virginia Between 1650 and 1852

Robert Sedgrave, 20 March 1649—twenty-four books (small volumes), 120 lbs. tobacco. *Deeds Orders 1650–1652, 48.*

John Hampton, 7 May 1649—one sermon book, 10 lbs. tobacco. *Deeds Orders 1650–1652, 49.*

Jane Pery, 3 March 1650—three Bibles, one *Practice of Piety*, three Latin books. *RB 1652–1658, 7.*

James Claughton, __ April 1647—three books, 10 lbs. tobacco; two books. *RB 1652–1658, 8.*

William Nicholls, 6 May 1651—six books, 60 lbs. tobacco. *RB 1652–1658, 8, 9.*

John Dennis, Junr, 4 Sept. 1652—a *Bible* and seven other books, 50 lbs. tobacco. *RB 1652–1658, 18.*

John Dennis, 28 Jan. 1652—one old *Bible* and looking glass, 15 lbs. tobacco. *RB 1652–1658, 24.*

John Cooke, 20 Sept. 1653—one old *Bible* and five old books, 50 lbs. tobacco. *RB 1652–1658, 36.*

Thomas Walker, 24 Jan. 1656—one *Bible*, 20 lbs. tobacco. *RB 1652–1658, 104.*

Col. John Mottrom, 19 June 1655—Ambrose Parry's *Chyrugery* that was lent to Mr. Speke, French history, Rider's *Dictionary*, *English Housewife*, *Treatise of Y^e Laws*, *Love of God*, *Treatise of Wills and Testament*, a *New Testament*, French *Dictionary*, Rascall Sergeant's Law, *Godly Observations*, Roman history in Latin, *Statute Elizabi Regina*, *Parliament of Christ*, *A Disputation of Y^e Church*, Boulson's *Difference betwixt Religions*, thirty-nine small books. *RB 1652–1658, 118.*

William Nash, 22 July 1657—three Bibles and four small books, 200 lbs. tobacco. *RB 1652–1658, 126.*

Thomas Reade, 22 Sept. 1657—one *Bible*, one small book. *RB 1652–1658, 126.*

Henry Catchmay, 21 Nov. 1657—two Bibles and a smoothing iron, 30 lbs. tobacco. *RB 1652–1658, 130.*

William Bacon, [page worn] 1659—one *Bible* and looking glass, 200 lbs. tobacco. *RB 1658–1666, 24.*

Col. John Trussell, 9 April 1660—two Bibles and a parcel of old books. *RB*

1658–1666, 43.

Thomas Broughton, 22 July 1661—three old books. *RB 1658–1666, 60.*

Robert Smith, 22 July 1661—two brushes and a parcel of old books, 60 lbs. tobacco. *RB 1658–1666, 60.*

William Little, 26 Sept. 1661—a parcel of books. *RB 1658–1666, 67.*

John Earle, 20 May 1662—one *Bible* sold at 60 lbs. tobacco. *RB 1658–1666, 75.*

Symon Overzee, 6 May 1663—a parcel of old books. *RB 1658–1666, 107.*

Capt. Richard Wright, 8 March 1663—a parcel of old books. *RB 1658–1666, 117.*

Elizabeth Symmons, 20 June 1664—a parcel of old books, 64 lbs. tobacco. *RB 1658–1666, 123.*

Jonathan Parker, 8 Feb. 1664—one parcel of old books, 20 lbs. tobacco. *RB 1658–1666, 141.*

Richard Flynt, 14 Sept. 1665—a parcel of old books, one paper book. *RB 1658–1666, 172.*

John Kent, 14 Sept. 1665—three old books. *RB 1658–1666, 172.*

John Shaw, 14 Jan. 1667—seven books. *RB 1666–1672, 33.*

John Pearse, 5 Nov. 1667—one old *Bible* and another small book, 30 lbs. tobacco. *RB 1666–1672, 37.*

John Bennet, 20 Jan. 1667/68—an old *Bible* and an old hat we thought fit to give to ye children. *RB 1666–1672, 39.*

John Bennet, 20 June 1668—one old *Bible* and brush, 20 lbs. tobacco. *RB 1666–1672, 49.*

Thomas Hopkins, 23 May 1669—one *Bible*, 80 lbs. tobacco. *RB 1666–1672, 57.*

Widow Bradley, 1 Jan. 1670—three hornbooks, five books, one *Testament*, one *Bible*, prayer book, two hornbooks. *RB 1666–1672, 86.*

William Bradley, 31 Jan. 1670—five books, 50 lbs. tobacco; three books, 40 lbs. tobacco; three hornbooks. *RB 1666–1672, 92.*

Thomas Steed, 17 Jan. 1671—books and other things, 40 lbs. tobacco. *RB 1666–1672, 122.*

No Record Books Between
1672 and 1706

Thomas Webb, 14 Dec. 1702—a parcel of old books. *RB 1706–1720, 6.*

Thomas Shapleigh, 17 Nov. 1703—one *Bible*, 86 lbs. tobacco. *RB 1706–1720*, 11.

Hancock Lee, [date left blank, will probated 21 July 1709]—four *Common Prayer Books*, 6d; two old *Bibles*, 4s; one small *Bible*, 3d; seven *The Whole Duty of Man* (old), 2s; first, second, and third parts of *Pilgrim's Progress*, 3s; twelve old books, 15s; seven old books, 12s; three old books, 3s; one book of lectures, 7s; one book ditto, 6s; one book entitled *The Disruption of Africa*, 2s; one book written by Purchase, 5s; two old histories, 6s; one *Physic Dictionary*, 10s; three law books, 10s; five Physick books, £1; one *Practice of Piety* and *The Touchstone of Wills and Testament*, 2s 6d. *RB 1706–1720*, 35.

John Webb, 17 May 1711—a parcel of old books, 100 lbs. tobacco. *RB 1706–1720*, 103.

William Sanders, 25 Sept. 1704—a parcel of old books, 60 lbs. tobacco. *RB 1706–1720*, 166.

John Graham, 17 Dec. 1712—a parcel of old books. *RB 1706–1720*, 194.

John Boaze, 19 Jan. 1713/14—a parcel of old books, 60 lbs. tobacco. *RB 1706–1720*, 207.

Peter Coutanceau, 17 Feb. 1714/15—a parcel of old books Viz^t Tulcon's *Of the Statutes*, Y^e *Statutes at Large from 1640 to 1676* by John Keebles, *The Practick Part of the Law*, Shepherd's *County Justice*, *The Clerk's Guide*, and some other old pieces of old books, 480 lbs. tobacco. *RB 1706–1720*, 219.

Simon Thompson, 16 Jan. 1714—nine old books, 100 lbs. tobacco. *RB 1706–1720*, 222.

Capt. John Eustace, 21. Jan. 1718—law books: Cook's *Reports*, twelve parts; Littleton's *Reports*; *The Statutes at Large*, two volumes; Manwood's *Laws of Y^e Forrest*; *Cook Upon Littleton*; Littleton's *Tenures*. *RB 1706–1720*, 246.

Edward Kilpatrick, 21 March 1710—a parcel of old books, 80 lbs. tobacco. *RB 1710–1713*, 14.

Mary Hughlett, 16 May 1711—one old book, 10 lbs. tobacco; some old books, 80 lbs. tobacco. *RB 1710–1713*, 33.

Richard Russell, 16 May 1711—some old books, 45 lbs. tobacco. *RB 1710–1713*, 36.

Robert Boyd, 18 July 1711—a small *Bible* and two other small books, 42 lbs. tobacco. *RB 1710–1713*, 70.

John Corbell, 16 July 1711—three old bottles, some old books, and some lumber, 80 lbs. tobacco. *RB 1710–1713*, 72.

John Husk, 24 June 1711—some old books. *RB 1710–1713*, 82.

Dr. James Rogers, 28 Aug. 1711—a parcel of books. *RB 1710–1713, 102.*

John Dawson, 14 Sept. 1711—a parcel of books, 100 lbs. tobacco; one sermon book, 100 lbs. tobacco; one sermon book, 50 lbs. tobacco. *RB 1710–1713, 104.*

Ebenezer Neale, 9 Jan. 1711/12—a parcel of books, 60 lbs. tobacco; one *Bible*, one *Common Prayer Book*, one knife, 100 lbs. tobacco. *RB 1710–1713, 128, 129.*

Edmund Denny, 20 Feb. 1711—one *Bible*, 40 lbs. tobacco; one little book, 5 lbs. tobacco. *RB 1710–1713, 152.*

Thomas Urguhart, 19 March 1711—one old book and some lumber, 10 lbs. tobacco. *RB 1710–1713, 169.*

William Harcum, 18 Jan. 1712—a parcel of chirurgery books and others, 150 lbs. tobacco. *RB 1710–1713, 170.*

Peter Hammon, 19 March 1711/12—a *Common Prayer Book*, 35 lbs. tobacco. *RB 1710–1713, 186.*

Joseph Hoult, 16 July 1712—a parcel of old books and some old casks, 50 lbs. tobacco. *RB 1710–1713, 205.*

James Oldam, 18 Feb. 1712/13—a parcel of old books, 7s. *RB 1710–1713, 264.*

Hugh Dermott, 19 Feb. 1712/13—old books and a small looking glass, 2s 6d. *RB 1710–1713, 269.*

John Laurence, 18 March 1713—a parcel of books. *RB 1710–1713, 271.*

Hugh Wallis, 18 March 1713—one *Bible*, *Practicall Navigation*, three old Journals, 4s 6d. *RB 1710–1713, 272.*

William Nutt, 17 June 1713—two small *Bibles*, 4s. *RB 1710–1713, 313.*

James Parker, 18 June 1713—one old *Bible*. *RB 1710–1713, 317.*

John Harris, 15 July 1713—seventy-eight books, good and bad. *RB 1710–1713, 324.* [Name of John Harris determined by checking *Order Book*.]

Richard and Ann Nutt, 21 Jan. 1718—an old *Bible* and some other books and a glass, 1s 1d. *RB 1718–1726, 11.*

Richard Hull, 10 Feb. 1718—a parcel of old books, 10s. *RB 1718–1726, 26.*

Thomas Percifull [name listed as Percivall at end of inventory], 18 March 1718—a parcel of old books, 6s. *RB 1718–1726, 34.*

John Coutanceau, 18 March 1718—some books, 10s. *RB 1718–1726, 35.*

John Harris, 14 July 1719—parcel books; one *Bible*, 8s; two books and a parcel of writing paper, 5s. *RB 1718–1726, 44.*

Richard Rush, 20 May 1719—one old *Bible*, an *Old Testament*, and *Common*

Prayer Book, 6s. RB 1718–1726, 47.

William Nelms, 16 Sept. 1719—one large *Bible*, 18s; a parcel of old books, 12s. RB 1718–1726, 55, 56.

James Genn, 16 Sept. 1719—a parcel of books, £1 10s. RB 1718–1726, 57.

John Thomas, 16 Sept. 1719—some books. RB 1718–1726, 58.

William Heath, 17 June 1719—a parcel of books, 4s; two *Bibles*, 5s; one small book. RB 1718–1726, 68.

Capt Peter Presly, 18 Nov. 1719—a parcel of books, a paper book. RB 1718–1726, 78.

William Tapp, 18 Nov. 1719—a parcel old books, 6s. RB 1718–1726, 79.

Mrs Ellenor Oliver, 18 Nov. 1719—some old books, 3s. RB 1718–1726, 80.

Thomas Flynt, 18 Nov. 1719—a parcel of books, 8s. RB 1718–1726, 81.

Enoch Hill, 20 Jan. 1719/20—A *Great Bible*, 15s; a *Testament* and one small book, 2s 6d; a parcel old books, 5s. RB 1718–1726, 83.

Richard Hull's part of his father's estate (Richard Hull), 18 May 1720—a parcel old books. RB 1718–1726, 105.

John Bentley, 18 May 1720—four small books and a razor, 6s. RB 1718–1726, 106.

Sarah Jones, 15 June 1720—one *Bible*, *The Whole Duty of Man*, and a primer, 4s. RB 1718–1726, 116.

John Reason, 15 June 1720—a *Bible* and *Common Prayer Book*, 5s. RB 1718–1726, 117.

Thomas Robinson, 15 June 1720—a parcel of books. RB 1718–1726, 131.

Malachi Burberry, 18 May 1720—a parcel of books, £1 10s. RB 1718–1726, 132.

Mrs Elizabeth Banks, 15 March 1721—twenty-eight books. RB 1718–1726, 168.

Richard Wright, 15 March 1721—two old *Bibles*, 10s; a parcel books, £1; a great sermon book, 18s. RB 1718–1726, 171.

Timothy Sacheveril, 15 March 1721—three old books. RB 1718–1726, 174.

Bartholomew Schrever, 19 July 1721—a large *Bible*, 16s; some other books, 16s 6d. RB 1718–1726, 207.

William Price, 20 July 1721—a parcel books, £2. RB 1718–1726, 209.

Thomas Whitehead, 20 July 1721—a *Bible*. RB 1718–1726, 210.

George Dameron, 20 July 1721—one parcel old books and lumber, 12s. RB 1718–1726, 211.

William Gilbert, 20 Sept. 1721—four old books. RB 1718–1726, 212.

Bartholomew Leazure, 20 Sept. 1721—a parcel books, 10s. *RB 1718–1726, 213.*

Capt Christopher Neale, 20 Sept. 1721—a library of books, £13. *RB 1718–1726, 214.*

Partin Hudnall, 15 Nov. 1721—a parcel old books, 4s. *RB 1718–1726, 229.*

Thomas Taylor, 21 Feb. 1721/22—some old books, 5s. *RB 1718–1726, 256.*

Thomas Downing, 21 March 1721/22—a parcel of books, 7s. *RB 1718–1726, 268.*

Christopher Newton, 21 March 1721/22—a parcel old books. *RB 1718–1726, 272.*

Thomas Sandford, 9 Jan. 1721/22—a parcel of old books, 10s; Salmon's *London Dispensatory*, 3s; Bale's *Dispensatory* by Salmon, 6s; *The Whole Duty of Man*, 2s; an old *Common Prayer Book*, 6d; a *Bible*, 1s 6d; Sydenham's *Practice of Physick*, 2s; Wiseman's *Surgery*, 5s; *London Dispensatory* in Latin, 2s; Dumerbrock's *Anatomy*, 12s; *The Greek Minor Poets*, 2s 6d; Cato's *Disticks, Corderius, and Justin*, 1s 6d; De Le Boe Sylvius his *Practice of Physick*, 1s; Schrevelius his *Lexicon*, 5s; Gibson's *Anatomy*, 3s 5d; *Gradus ad Parnassum*, 1s 6d; *The Art of Memory* and a dictionary, 6s; Shepton's *Dispensatory*, 1s; Bate's *Dispensatory* and Beloste's *Surgery*, 3s; Reverii's *Opera* and Barbette's *Surgery*, 4s. *RB 1718–1726, 277.*

Thomas Webb, 16 May 1722—a parcel books. *RB 1718–1726, 284.*

Dennis Conway, 16 May 1722—a parcel books. *RB 1718–1726, 285.*

John Ingram, 18 July 1722—a parcel of books. *RB 1718–1726, 287.*

Joseph Ball, 16 Dec. 1721—a large new *Bible* and a *Testament*, £1 1s; a parcel of old books, 12s. *RB 1718–1726, 332.*

David Moor, 20 Nov. 1723—parcel old books, 5s. *RB 1718–1726, 369.*

Thomas Ashburn, 17 June 1724—some old books and some trifles, 9s. *RB 1718–1726, 370.*

Elizabeth Richardson, 17 June 1724—one old book, 1s. *RB 1718–1726, 370a.*

William Arledge, 17 Feb. 1724/25—a parcel of old books, 12s 6d. *RB 1718–1726, 375.*

Benjamin Copedge [Coppedge in Index to *Record Book*], 16 June 1725—six sheets of paper and one book, 1s. *RB 1718–1726, 378.*

John Span, 15 July 1724—a parcel of books. *RB 1718–1726, 379.*

Susanna Laurence, 19 May 1725—one small *Bible* and some other small old books, 5s. *RB 1718–1726, 382a.*

Anne Opie, 13 May 1725—a parcel of books and one sugar box, £1 1s. *RB 1718–1726, 383a.*

John Dollin, 19 May 1725—a parcel of old books, 10s. *RB 1718–1726, 384.*

Capt. Richard Haynie, [no date given]—36 books, a packet of books and three other books. *RB 1718–1726, 387.*

William Keene, 20 April 1726—thirty-seven books. *RB 1718–1726, 391.*

John Pope, 15 Jan. 1723/24—six books. *RB 1718–1726, 394a.*

John Haynie, 22 Aug. 1723—five books of Roman history, 15s; a book called *Josephus*, £1; a parcel of books, £1 17s; a violin case and book, £1. *RB 1718–1726, 395a.*

William Berry, 20 Feb. 1722/23—one looking glass, towel, and a parcel of old books, 6s. *RB 1718–1726, 398.*

Andrew Reed, 17 Aug. 1723—an old *Bible*, 1s 6d. *RB 1718–1726, 398a.*

John Blinco, [no date given]—a parcel of old books, 7s. *RB 1718–1726, 399.*

Catherine Butcher, 22 Aug. 1723—one old *Bible*, 3s. *RB 1718–1726, 399.*

Margaret James, 18 March 1723/24—a parcel of books, 6s. *RB 1718–1726, 402a.*

John Appleby, 17 July 1723—some old books and other old things, 2s. *RB 1718–1726, 407.*

Capt John Opie, 17 July 1723—a small parcel of books and one small old looking glass, £1. *RB 1718–1726, 408.*

Richard Thomson [Tomson in Index to *Record Book*], 26 March 1724—one large *Bible* and one small *Common Prayer Book*, 12s. *RB 1718–1726, 410.*

Edmond Basyie, 20 May 1724—a parcel of old books. *RB 1718–1726, 410a.*

John Burn, 17 July 1724—a parcel of old books and two old *Bibles*, 10s 6d. *RB 1718–1726, 421.*

Joseph Knight, 20 Jan. 1724/25—a new *Bible* and some old books. *RB 1726–1729, 5.*

William Wildey, 17 Aug. 1726—a parcel of books, 10s. *RB 1726–1729, 10.*

Benjamin Robinson, 15 Sept. 1725—one horn book, 6d. *RB 1726–1729, 12.*

James Waddey, 16 Feb. 1725/26—a parcel of books. *RB 1726–1729, 14.*

Elinor Welsh, 17 March 1725/26—old books. *RB 1726–1729, 14.*

Richard Cundiff, 17 Aug. 1726—eight old books. *RB 1726–1729, 15.*

Joseph Churchill, 17 Aug. 1726—a parcel of books. *RB 1726–1729, 16.*

Thomas Lucas, 20 Nov. 1723—one new *Bible*, one old *Bible*, and some other books, 9s. *RB 1726–1729, 16.*

Neale O'Daughty, 15 Sept. 1725—some books. *RB 1726–1729, 17.*

Mathew Gater, 20 April 1726—a parcel of old books, 7s. *RB 1726–1729, 17.*

Teag Allen, 20 May 1724—two books, 3s. *RB 1726–1729, 17.*

David Spence, 20 July 1726—a parcel of old books, 7s. *RB 1726-1729, 18.*

Thomas Barecroft, 16 Feb. 1725/26—a large book, £2 5s; some old books, 10s. *RB 1726-1729, 19.*

Henry Aublin, 20 July 1726—two old books. *RB 1726-1729, 19.*

Thomas Harden, 16 Jan. 1722/23—a parcel of old books, 10s 6d. *RB 1726-1729, 19.*

Richard Price, 21 Sept. 1726—one old *Common Prayer Book*, 1s. *RB 1726-1729, 20.*

Henry Lindsey, 20 April 1726—a parcel of old books, £2 5s. *RB 1726-1729, 20.*

Anne Stowell, 18 Sept. 1723—one old *Bible* and one old sermon book; one old sermon book of Foxe's works, 1s. *RB 1726-1729, 21.*

John Clayton, 17 Aug. 1726—a parcel of old books. *RB 1726-1729, 21.*

James Dunlap, 16 Jan. 1722/23—one *Bible* and five other small books, 8s. *RB 1726-1729, 23.*

William Howard, 15 Dec. 1725—three old books, 4s. *RB 1726-1729, 23.*

Jane Parker, 19 Oct. 1726—a parcel of old books, 3s. *RB 1726-1729, 43.*

Mary Price, 19 Oct. 1726—a parcel of books, 7s. *RB 1726-1729, 44.*

John Stanly, 19 Oct. 1726—one *Bible*, 2s 6d. *RB 1726-1729, 44.*

John Hunter, 19 Oct. 1726—a parcel of books and box of iron, 9s 6d. *RB 1726-1729, 44.*

George Dawkins, 21 June 1727—some old books. *RB 1726-1729, 54.*

William Metcalf, 20 Sept. 1727—a parcel of books, 18s. *RB 1726-1729, 55.*

John Hadwell, 10 Oct. 1727—two old books and some pipes, 2s 6d. *RB 1726-1729, 56.*

Thomas Hobson, 15 Feb. 1726/27—one *Great Bible*, 18s. *RB 1726-1729, 56.*

Thomas Cralle, 15 Feb. 1726/27—a parcel of books, £4 2s. *RB 1726-1729, 57.*

Richard Kenner, 15 Feb. 1726/27—two large *Bibles* and some other books, £6 5s 6d. *RB 1726-1729, 57.*

James Garner, 15 Feb. 1726/27—a parcel of books, 16s. *RB 1726-1729, 58.*

Elizabeth Creale [Creal in Index to *Record Book*], 21 June 1729—some old books, 7s. *RB 1726-1729, 59.*

Thomas Gaskins, 15 March 1726/27—a parcel of books, £1 15s. *RB 1726-1729, 59.*

Robert Watts, 15 Feb. 1726/27—two books and fishing line, 5s 8d. *RB 1726-1729, 60.*

John Coppedge, 21 June 1727—two large books, 13s; some old books, one old chest, and some paper, £1 11s. *RB 1726–1729, 61*.

John Allin, 15 March 1726/27—some old books, 6s. *RB 1726–1729, 61*.

Spencer Hack, 17 May 1727—one old looking glass, one *Bible*, one *Common Prayer Book*, one hat brush and box iron and heaters, £1 19s 6d; three books, 3s. *RB 1726–1729, 62*.

Charles Creal [Creel at the end of the inventory], 21 June 1727—some old books, 7s. *RB 1726–1729, 63*.

Patrick Mealey, 17 May 1727—one old *Bible* and *Common Prayer Book*, 3s. *RB 1726–1729, 63*.

Josias Dameron, 19 April 1727—one large *Bible* and two cows and calves and ten geese, £4 2s. *RB 1726–1729, 63*.

Thomas Heath, 17 May 1727—one rug and parcel of old books, £1 1s; one book, 1s 6d; one book, 1s 6d. *RB 1726–1729, 64*.

William Fallin, 15 March 1726/27—a small book not appraised. *RB 1726–1729, 64*.

Robert Banks, 19 July 1727—a parcel of old books, 6s. *RB 1726–1729, 65*.

Matthew Neale, 15 March 1726/27—a parcel old books, £1. *RB 1726–1729, 65*.

Dennis Fallin, 19 April 1727—one old cupboard and some old books, £1 5s. *RB 1726–1729, 66*.

Ephraim Hughlett, 20 Sept. 1727—a parcel of books, 6s. *RB 1726–1729, 66*.

Peter Aublin, 15 Feb. 1726/27—one large *Bible* and some small books, 12s. *RB 1726–1729, 67*.

Thomas Campbell, 17 May 1727—a parcel of old books, 12s. *RB 1726–1729, 67*.

Stephen Hall, 19 April 1727—a parcel of books, 13s. *RB 1726–1729, 68*.

John Cottrell, 15 March 1726/27—a parcel of old books, 17s. *RB 1726–1729, 69*. [Exhibited in court by Sarah Cottrell.]

Christopher Neale, 15 Feb. 1726/27—two large books, £1. *RB 1726–1729, 69*.

Francis Knight, 15 March 1726/27—a parcel of books, 5s. *RB 1726–1729, 69*.

Samuel Winsted, 15 Feb. 1726/27—two *Bibles* and a parcel of other books. *RB 1726–1729, 70*.

Sarah Arledge, 19 April 1727—some old books, 2s. *RB 1726–1729, 70*.

Matthew Neale, 17 May 1727—a parcel of books. *RB 1726–1729, 71*.

John Langsdale, 19 April 1727—a parcel of books, 5s. *RB 1726–1729, 71*.

Thomas Cunningham, 20 Sept. 1727—a parcel of old books, 16s. *RB 1726-1729, 72.*

Robert Bradly, 17 May 1727—a parcel of books, £1 4s. *RB 1726-1729, 72.*

Alexander Love, 19 July 1727—a parcel of old books. *RB 1726-1729, 73.*

Henry Rider, 10 March 1726/27—a parcel of old books, 3s. *RB 1726-1729, 74.*

John Spence, 19 April 1727—*Common Prayer Book*, 2s; some books, 5s. *RB 1726-1729, 74.*

Robert Willson, 21 June 1727—two *Bibles, Testament,* and *Psalter,* 12s. *RB 1726-1729, 75.*

James Claughton, 15 Feb. 1726/27—large *Bible. RB 1726-1729, 75.*

John Cottrell, 15 Feb. 1726/27—a parcel of old books, 2s. *RB 1726-1729, 75.* [Exhibited in court by Elizabeth Cottrell.]

Henry Christopher, 17 May 1727—one *Great Bible* and some other books, 17s. *RB 1726-1729, 76.*

James Burbury, 15 Feb. 1726/27—some books. *RB 1726-1729, 77.*

William Christopher, 17 May 1727—three books. *RB 1726-1729, 78.*

Adam Grinsted, 15 March 1726/27—two old books, 2s. *RB 1726-1729, 78.*

Francis Webb, 17 May 1727—one old *Bible. RB 1726-1729, 79.*

Meredith Mahane, 21 June 1727—a parcel of old books, 8s 6d. *RB 1726-1729, 79.*

John Payne, 17 May 1727—one large *Bible,* 15s. *RB 1726-1729, 80.*

Jeffrey Gouch, 21 June 1727—four old books, 3s 6d. *RB 1726-1729, 80.*

Henry Boggess, 17 Jan. 1727/28—a large *Bible,* two small *Bibles,* seventeen small books, £2 4s. *RB 1726-1729, 83.*

John Conway, 17 Jan. 1727/28—one old *Bible,* one *Testament,* two *Psalters,* one primer. *RB 1726-1729, 85.*

Daniel Neale, 17 Jan. 1727/28—a parcel of books, 9s. *RB 1726-1729, 85.*

Richard Sherley, 18 April 1728—six old books and one looking glass, 10s. *RB 1726-1729, 90.*

John Nichols, 18 April 1728—parcel old books and lumber, 6s. *RB 1726-1729, 90.*

William Cornish, 17 April 1728—a parcel of books, 15s. *RB 1726-1729, 90.*

Anne Conway, 19 June 1728—a parcel of old books, 1s. *RB 1726-1729, 95.*

Richard Foulks, 19 June 1728—one old box with some clothes and old books, 4d. *RB 1726-1729, 96.*

Capt. John Cralle, 19 June 1728—a parcel of books. *RB 1726-1729, 96.*

Richard Chocalat, 17 July 1728—some old books, a small looking glass, and some lines, 2s. *RB 1726–1729, 102.*

John Taylor, 17 July 1728—one *Common Prayer Book*. *RB 1726–1729, 102.*

Nathaniel Walker, 21 Aug. 1728—a small looking glass and some old books, 5s. *RB 1726–1729, 105.*

Capt. Francis Kenner, 21 Aug. 1728—three books, 15s. *RB 1726–1729, 106.*

Capt. Richard Span, 21 Aug. 1728—a parcel of books. *RB 1726–1729, 107.*

Samuel Span, 21 Aug. 1728—one book, £1 9s. *RB 1726–1729, 107.*

Cary Keble, 16 Oct. 1728—one *Great Bible* and frame, £1 15s; a parcel of books, £1; one ink case and a parcel of old broken books, 1s 6d. *RB 1726–1729, 109.*

Richard Lattimore, 20 Nov. 1728—forty-one good books. *RB 1726–1729, 121.*

William Humphris, 20 Nov. 1728—a parcel of books, 12s. *RB 1726–1729, 121.*

Bartholomew Schrever, 19 Feb. 1728/29—one old *Bible, Common Prayer Book,* and *The Whole Duty of Man,* 10s 6d. *RB 1726–1729, 122.*

Benjamin Nutt, 19 Feb. 1728/29—parcel books, 8s; two books, 6s. *RB 1726–1729, 123.*

Joseph Knight, 19 Feb. 1728/29—one *Bible* and slate, 7s 6d; 1 1/2 Quire of writing paper, an old book and grindstone, 2s 6d. *RB 1726–1729, 124.*

Richard Neale, 19 March 1728/29—fourteen books, some old broken books. *RB 1726–1729, 126.*

John Hartly, 19 March 1728/29—an old table and three books, 8s. *RB 1726–1729, 127.*

Richard Warrick, 19 March 1728/29—one raw hide and one old *Bible,* 2s 6d. *RB 1726–1729, 127.*

Robert Cole, 19 March 1728/29—one large *Bible,* £1; one small *Bible* and other books, 4s. *RB 1726–1729, 127.*

George Dawkins, 19 March 1728/29—four old *Bibles,* six old sermon books, two old *Testament* books, two old primers, two old *Psalters,* one old book *The Mariner's Art. RB 1726–1729, 128.*

Peter Neale, 19 March 1728/29—a parcel of books, new and old, £1. *RB 1726–1729, 128.*

George Curtis, 19 March 1728/29—three old books, 1s 6d. *RB 1726–1729, 128.*

William Cornish, 21 May 1729—some books, 5s. *RB 1726–1729, 133.*

William Kesterson, 18 June 1729—some old books. *RB 1726–1729, 135.*

Thomas Reeves, 18 June 1729—an old *Bible* and an old broad axe, 8s. *RB 1726–1729, 136.*

George Eves, 19 Feb. 1728/29—some books and one old warming pan, £1. *RB 1726–1729, 136.*

Maximillian Haynie, 16 July 1729—hornbook, 6d; one old *Bible*, 1s 6d. *RB 1726–1729, 137.*

Jane Toby, 19 Oct. 1729—one *Testament*, 2s. *RB 1726–1729, 142.*

Elizabeth Bradly, 19 Oct. 1729—an old box and some books, 13s. *RB 1726–1729, 143.*

Neale Doarthy [also spelled Dorty, Doherty, and Daughty], 15 Sept. 1729—some books. *RB 1726–1729, 146.*

No Record Books Between
15 Sept. 1729 and 10 April 1738

Thomas Toulson, 10 April 1738—one old *Bible*, a *Psalter*, a primer and trifles, 4s 2d. *RB 1738–1743, 2.*

John Lancaster, 10 July 1738—one book, 3s. *RB 1738–1743, 3.*

Thomas Brown, 10 July 1738—a parcel of books, 5s; one parcel of old books, 4s. *RB 1738–1743, 10.*

Mary Young, 10 July 1738—a parcel of old books, 10s. *RB 1738–1743, 16.*

William Johnson, 14 Aug. 1738—one large book, some earthen ware and funnel, 15s. *RB 1738–1743, 23.*

Edward Turner, 8 May 1738—a parcel of old books, 18s 8d; two prayer books, 4s. *RB 1738–1743, 28.*

John Shurley, 8 May 1738—a parcel of books, 6s. *RB 1738–1743, 29.*

Thomas Hall, 12 June 1738—a parcel of old books, £1; one old book not appraised. *RB 1738–1743, 29.*

William Brent, 12 June 1738—*A Complete Manual of Private Devotion*, 4s; one *Common Prayer Book*, 2s. (One eight part of books belonging to Major Lee's estate.) *RB 1738–1743, 29–30.*

James Walkden, 12 March 1738/39—some old books. *RB 1738–1743, 35.*

Richard Nelms, 12 July 1737—one old *Psalter*, one primer, and some old books, 2s. *RB 1738–1743, 36.*

Elizabeth Schrever, 10 April 1739—*The Golden Grove*, 5s; one old *Bible*, 4s. *RB 1738–1743, 37.*

William Toulson, 9 April 1739—some old books, one *Bible*, one *Testament*. *RB 1738–1743, 37*.

John Rider, 11 June 1739—some old books, 12s. *RB 1738–1743, 41*.

Thomas Waddy, 9 July 1739—one large and one small *Bible*, three *Common Prayer Books*, *The Whole Duty of Man*, a parcel of old books. *RB 1738–1743, 45*.

Edward Downing (division of the estate, one-third to Mrs. Frances Downing), 9 July 1739—a parcel of books, 10s. *RB 1738–1743, 49*.

William Hobson, 8 Oct. 1739—some books, 10s. *RB 1738–1743, 52*.

Francis Gaskins, 8 Oct. 1739—one old *Bible*, two *Testaments*, one *Common Prayer Book*, a *Psalter*, a primer and hornbook. *RB 1738–1743, 52*.

Isaac Basey, 12 Nov. 1739—thirty-four old books. *RB 1738–1743, 54*.

John Wood, 12 Nov. 1739—one *Great Bible*, £1; five good books and two old books, 12s. *RB 1738–1743, 55*.

Richard Booth, 10 Dec. 1739—one large *Bible*, 18s. *RB 1738–1743, 55*.

Thomas Gill, 14 Jan. 1739/40—one large *Bible*, £1; one old *Bible* and three old books, 4s. *RB 1738–1743, 58*.

Samuel Lunsford, 14 Jan. 1739/40—one *Bible* and a parcel of old books, 10s 6d. *RB 1738–1743, 61*.

John Dogget, 10 March 1739/40—a parcel of leather, some cotton, and a parcel of old books, 13s 10d. *RB 1738–1743, 66*.

Joseph Millard, 14 April 1740—one large *Bible*, 20s. *RB 1738–1743, 67*.

Capt. William Eustace, 12 May 1740—fifty books, a parcel of play books. *RB 1738–1743, 78*.

Nathaniel Floyd, 14 Jan. 1739—one *Common Prayer Book*, 2s 6d. *RB 1738–1743, 79*.

Dr. Archibald Johnston, 12 May 1740—nine books, 7s 6d. *RB 1738–1743, 79*.

Francis Vanlandingham, 9 June 1740—two books, 1s 6d. *RB 1738–1743, 80*.

Swanson Prichard, 9 June 1740—a parcel of old books, 12s 2d. *RB 1738–1743, 81*.

Richard Pearce, 9 June 1740—one *Bible* and other books, 14s. *RB 1738–1743, 82*.

Lewis Lamkin, 14 May 1740—one *Common Prayer Book*, 2s. *RB 1738–1743, 85*.

Samuel Garlington, 21 June 1740—four old books, 2s. *RB 1738–1743, 86*.

Samuel Mahane, 14 July 1740—a parcel of old books, 10s. *RB 1738–1743, 87*.

Richard Lee, 14 July 1740—some books. *RB 1738–1743, 88*.

John Colton, 14 July 1740—thirty-five books, 20s; three books, 6s. *RB 1738–*

1743, 89.

Charles Downing, 11 Aug. 1740—one *Common Prayer Book* and two other books. *RB 1738–1743, 89.*

Jervace Elleston, 8 Sept. 1740—two books. *RB 1738–1743, 93.*

Richard Lee, 8 Sept. 1740—to Mrs. Judith Lee, wife of Richard Lee, a parcel of old books, £5 11s; to Peter Conway who married daughter of Richard Lee, a parcel of books, £1 9s 6d. *RB 1738–1743, 95.*

Robert Hunter, 13 Oct. 1740—three old books. *RB 1738–1743, 98.*

James Straughan, 13 April 1741—a parcel of books, £1 6s. *RB 1738–1743, 113.*

Thomas Bonum out of the estate of James Straughan, 13 April 1741—a parcel of books, 16s 4d. *RB 1738–1743, 114.*

Thomas Burn, 13 April 1741—one large *Bible*, Doctor Swift's [Jonathan Swift] works, £1 6s; one *Spectator* (one volume), two *Common Prayer Books*, 5s 6d; six play books, *The Whole Duty of Man*, 4s; *Pilgrim's Progress*, *The Wit and Drollery* and a paper book, 2s; one small book. *RB 1738–1743, 114.*

Benjamin Nutt, 11 May 1741—two old books, 2s. *RB 1738–1743, 119.*

John Edwards, 5 May 1741—a parcel of old books, 2s 6d. *RB 1738–1743, 120.*

Samuel Smith, 11 May 1741—four books. *RB 1738–1743, 121.*

Charles Craven, 8 June 1741—three books, 5s. *RB 1738–1743, 125.*

Jane Miller, 8 June 1741—one large *Bible* and other books, £1. *RB 1738–1743, 127.*

Maj. Charles Lee, 8 June 1741—five volumes *Annals of King George*, 12s 6d; Phillip's English Dictionary [*The New World of English Words*], 10s; one large *Bible*, 7s; two Roman histories, 2s; Sherlock on *Death*, 2s 6d; one small dictionary geography, 2s 6d; one small ditto and Gold's poems, 3s 6d; Scot's *Christian Life*, 1s; *History of the Turks*, 1s; three old books and three old books, 1s 6d. *RB 1738–1743, 128.*

John Hargrove, 13 July 1741—one *Bible*. *RB 1738–1743, 131.*

James Coppedge, 14 Sept. 1741—a parcel of old books, 4s 6d. *RB 1738–1743, 139.*

Thomas Haynie, 14 Sept. 1741—a parcel of books, 3s. *RB 1738–1743, 140.*

James Lamkin, 10 Nov. 1741—one *Bible*, 15s. *RB 1738–1743, 142.*

Thomas Sims, 14. Dec. 1741—one large *Bible*, one *Common Prayer Book*, two *Testaments*, one *Psalter*, 12s; two primers, three hornbooks, 1s 4d. *RB 1738–1743, 146.*

Benjamin Waddy, 14 Dec. 1741—one *Bible*, one old *Bible*, one small *Bible*, £1

3s; three volumes of the *Grand Abridgment of the Common and Statute Laws of England*, £1 1s; *The Acts of Assembly and Contents of Chapters*, £1 6s; *The Complete Collection of the Laws, The Clerk's Guide*, 9s; *A Collection of Precedents*, Judilis's *Dictionary*, 15s; *The Memoirs of What Part of Christendom*, 4s; one old dictionary, Wile's *Practical Editor*, 6s; *Saints Everlasting*, old *Family Prayers*, 3s 6d; one very old *Bible*, old *Testament*, 2s; nine very old books, 3s 6d. *RB 1738–1743, 147.*

William Downing, 14 Dec. 1741—some old books, 4s. *RB 1738–1743, 148.*

John Boyd, 14 Dec. 1741—a parcel of books, 3s 6d. *RB 1738–1743, 149.*

James Moon, 14 Dec. 1741—a parcel of old books and fishing line, 3s. *RB 1738–1743, 150.*

Partin James, 14. Dec. 1741—a parcel of newspapers, 6d. *RB 1738–1743, 151.*

Richard Lee (division of the estate), 14 Dec. 1741—*The Abridgment of the Plantation Law*, 5s; the last volume of *The History of England*, 3s; Braximifiex's *Christianity Reviewed* by Mr. Cave, 3s; Misselany's *John Movces* [?], 2s 6d; an old arithmetick, 6d. *RB 1738–1743, 153.*

John Stepto, 11 Jan. 1741/42—one large new *Bible*, £1 2s; three sermon books. *RB 1738–1743, 154–155.*

Richard Thomas, 11 Jan. 1741/42—a parcel of old books, 4s. *RB 1738–1743, 155.*

John Hill, 12 April 1742—one old *Bible*, 1s 3d. *RB 1738–1743, 166.*

James Straughan, 12 April 1742—a parcel of books, 7s 6d. *RB 1738–1743, 166.*

Tarkle Tarkleson, 10 May 1742—one violin, one small *Bible*, £1 3s; one small *Prayer Book, Psalter*, 2s 3d; one prayer book, 1s 3d. *RB 1738–1743, 177.*

Mary Tolson, 10 May 1742—a parcel of books, 9s. *RB 1738–1743, 178.*

Daniel Beachum, 10 May 1742—books, 5s. *RB 1738–1743, 179.*

John Turner, 10 May 1742—some earthen ware and books, 5s 6d. *RB 1738–1743, 180.*

Judith Jones, 10 May 1742—*Annotations on the Holy Scriptures*, 5s; John Locke on *Human Understanding*, 4s; sundry books of devotion, 3s; Doctor Sherlock's works, 1s 6d; one old small *Bible*, 2s 6d; a large *Common Prayer Book*, 2s; one old *Chronicles of England*, 5s; one old Latin book, 1s; one law book, 6d; one old Roman history, 6d; a parcel of books of medicine, 1s. *RB 1738–1743, 181.*

Hannah Hill, 10 May 1742—one *Bible*, 4s. *RB 1738–1743, 183.*

Thomas Hall, 10 May 1742—one *Testament*. *RB 1738–1743, 183.*

John Shirley, 10 May 1742—a parcel of old books, 1s 6d. *RB 1738–1743, 184.*

Charles Wilkins, 10 May 1742—a parcel of old books, 1s. *RB 1738–1743, 184.*

Joseph Hudnall, 10 May 1742—prayer books, new *Great Bible*, one small *Bible*, Web's *Justice* and Meres's *Abridgment*, one seafaring book. *RB 1738–1743, 185.*

Mary Parker, 10 May 1742—a *Bible* and primer and three other books. *RB 1738–1743, 186.*

Mary Palfry, 10 May 1742—a book and a parcel of wearing linen, 10s. *RB 1738–1743, 186.*

Charles Jones, 14 June 1742—*The Virginia Justice*, 10s; Charles English tutor (two volumes), 11s; *The History of Cold Bathing* by John Floyer, 6s 3d; Bayley's *English Dictionary*, 12s 6d; three volumes of *Spectators*, £1 5s; *Bookkeeping Methodized*, 4s 8d; two volumes of *The Guardian*, 6s. Mrs. Elizabeth Jones's part of her deceased father's estate [Samuel Heath]—a parcel of old books, 3s; Doctor William Beverige's works, two volumes; *Rules of Holy Living* by Jeremia Taylor; *The Careless World* by Josia Woodward; *The Golden _____*, two volumes; one *The Whole Duty of Man*; one spelling book; *The Lady's Calling*; Quincey's *Dispensatory*, £1 8s 1 1/2d. *RB 1738–1743, 190, 191.*

John Sutton, 14 June 1742—a parcel of old books, 4s 6d; two old books. *RB 1738–1743, 191.*

John Power, 15 June 1742—some books. *RB 1738–1743, 192.*

John Wilkins, 14 June 1742—a parcel of old books, 6s. *RB 1738–1743, 193.*

Mary Bell, 14 June 1742—a parcel of old books, 6s. *RB 1738–1743, 193.*

John Keene, 12 July 1742—a parcel of old books, 15s; a parcel of old books in a basket, 1s. *RB 1738–1743, 197.*

Benjamin Waddy, 12 July 1742—one old *Bible*, 1s. *RB 1738–1743, 201.*

Charles Lee (Elizabeth Lee's part of her father's estate), 12 July 1742—two dictionaries, 5s. *RB 1738–1743, 201.*

John Tullos, 9 Aug. 1742—two frying pans and a parcel of old books, 7s. *RB 1738–1743, 206.*

William Wildy, 9 Aug. 1742—old books. *RB 1738–1743, 206.*

Judith Jones, 11 Oct. 1742—a parcel of old books, 12s 9d; a parcel of books, 12s 9d. *RB 1738–1743, 212.*

Lazarus Smith, 8 Nov. 1742—books. *RB 1738–1743, 217.*

Richard Rice, 13 Dec. 1742—some old books, £1 15s. *RB 1738–1743, 218.*

John Donaway, 14 Feb. 1742/43—a *Testament, Common Prayer Book. RB 1738–1743, 226.*

Francis Peart, 14 March 1742/43—a parcel of books, £1 6s. *RB 1738–1743, 228.*

Thomas Wornom, 14 March 1742/43—a parcel of books. *RB 1738–1743, 230.*

James Pew, 14 March 1742/43—a parcel of books, 3s 6d. *RB 1738–1743, 231.*

Samuel Blackwell, 11 April 1743—one old *Bible* and some old books, 7s; one old *Bible* and *Common Prayer Book*, 4s. *RB 1738–1743, 236.*

Thomas Pitman, 11 April 1743—a parcel of books, 11s. *RB 1738–1743, 236.*

Mary Bogges, 11 April 1743—a parcel of old books, 10s. *RB 1738–1743, 237.*

Rev. Francis Peart, 11 April 1743—a parcel of books, 22s 6d; books, 42s. *RB 1738–1743, 239.*

Randolph Mott, 9 May 1743—a parcel of old books, 1s 3d. *RB 1738–1743, 245.*

William Short, 9 May 1743—one large book, 4s; one *Bible* and prayer book, 6s; a parcel of old books, 6s 6d. *RB 1738–1743, 246.*

William Barrat, 13 June 1743—a parcel of old books, £1 3s; one book, 2s. *RB 1738–1743, 252.*

Mrs. Hannah Smith, 11 July 1743—a parcel of old books, 8s; two old books, 2s. *RB 1738–1743, 256.*

Swanson Pritchard, 11 July 1743—fifteen old books, 12s 6d. *RB 1738–1743, 258.*

Abraham Low, 8 Aug. 1743—some old books. *RB 1738–1743, 260.*

James Tomson, 8 Aug. 1743—one old *Bible*, 1s. *RB 1738–1743, 260.*

Rodham Kenner, 12 Sept. 1743—one large *Bible*, £1 15s; four small books, 18s; one book called *Merchant's Magazine*, 2d. *RB 1738–1743, 265.*

John Burch, 10 Oct. 1743—a parcel old books, 3s. *RB 1743–1749, 3.*

Richard Sebree, 14 Nov. 1743—one *Common Prayer Book* and other books, 15s. *RB 1743–1749, 5a.*

Clark Hobson, 14 Nov. 1743—a parcel of old books, 15s. *RB 1743–1749, 6a.*

Thomas Berry, 14 Nov. 1743—one law book, one *Common Prayer Book*, fifteen good books. *RB 1743–1749, 7.*

Thomas and Jane Wornom, __ Dec. 1743—one large *Bible* and a parcel of old books. *RB 1743–1749, 12.*

Dr. Lawrence Alexander, 13 Feb. 1743/44—volumes of *Spectators*, £1 8s; a parcel of books, £1 4s; Thomson's *Seasons*, 4s; Wiseman's *Surgery*, 4s; a parcel of books, £5. *RB 1743–1749, 12a.*

Elias Edmonds, 13 Feb. 1743/44—a parcel of books, £1. *RB 1743–1749, 13.*

Ann Fallin, 12 March 1743/44—some old books, 4s. *RB 1743–1749, 18*.

Capt. Matthew Kenner, 12 March 1743/44—four *Bibles* and some other books, £2. *RB 1743–1749, 19*.

Richard Denny, 13 Feb. 1743/44—a parcel of old books and two pairs spectacles, 10s. *RB 1743–1749, 20a*.

Samuel Gaskins, 12 March 1743/44—a parcel of books, 1s; a parcel of books, 5s. *RB 1743–1749, 21a*.

Ormsby Haynie, 12 March 1743/44—a parcel of books and some other things, £1 5s. *RB 1743–1749, 22a*.

Rev. Henry Christall, 12 March 1743/44—some pamphlets, some news papers & *The History of the Bible* by Stitch^t, and some old papers, 10s; one Greek *Testament*, one Latin *Testament*, 4s 4 1/2d; *The Odes of Horace*, two volumes, 10s 7 1/2d; four volumes of Moires's [?] sermons, £1 2s 6d; two volumes of Foster's sermons, 10s; one volume of Calamy's sermons, 5s 7 1/2d; two volumes of Evense's sermons, 10s; one volume of Stanhope's sermons, 6s 3d; Crudance's [Cruden's?] *Concordance of the Bible*, £1; one volume of Butler's sermons, 2s 6d; Sherlock's *Divine Providence*, 2s 6d; three volumes of Willingfleet's sermons, 7s 6d; Wiseheart's *Theologia*, two volumes, 4s; *The Christian Pattern*, 1s; Dupin's *Church History*, volumes three and four, 4s; Calamy [Edward] *Upon Episeopy*, Henry's *Method for Prayer*, 2s; Sherlock on *The Knowledge of Christ*, 1s 3d; Grocius's *Christian Religion*, 1s 8d; Beveridge's *Church Catechism*, 6d; Penrel's *Concordance*, 2s 3d; Powler's *Christian Liberty*, 1s; *The Confession of Faith*, 1s 3d; *The Gift of Prayer*, 1s; *The Danger of Profane Swearing* and Usher's [Ussher's?] *Imaneul*, 1s 3d; Clement and *The Bishop of London's Directions*, 6d; Vincent's *Catechism*, *The School Wisdom* and one old *Bible*, 2s 7d; seven old books, 2s; *The Elements of Mathematicks*, 2s; Juvenal's *16 Satires in English*, 1s; Monroe's *Anatomy*, 1s; Terence's *Comedies*, 1s; Sallust in English, two books of arithmetick, 4s 8d; Clavis's *Homerica*, Virgil's works, 5s; *Corpus Doctrinae Christiani*, Tully's offices, 3s; Ovid's *Metamorphoses*, *Opera Philosophia*, 2s 6d; Phad Tabula, one Greek grammar, 3s; Suetonius's *History of the Twelve Caesars*, English and Latin, 2s 6d; *Mackii Medula*, *Psalms*, Hebrew and Latin, 1s 6d; Terence's *Comedies*, Latin, Horatius, 2s; Justin and Quintus Curtius, 6s; *Janua Linguarum*, Kerwood's *Grammar*, 6s; Cornelius Nepos, English and Latin, 2s 6d; Virgil's *Aeneid* by Stich^t, 6d; Sallustius, Deonisius's [Dionysius's?] *Rhetorick*, 1s 11d; Homer's *The Iliad* and an old Greek *Testament*, 1s 3d; *Drunken Barnaby* Latin and English, 1s; a parcel of old Latin and Greek books, ten in all, 2s 6d; one Greek Lexicon, one old Latin *Testament*, 2s; one old dictionary, *Theologia Christiani*, second volume,

3s; Tully's *Epistles*, one *Latin Testament*, 1s; Epictetus, 1s. *RB 1743–1749, 23a.*

Alexander Moorhead, 9 April 1744—a parcel of old books, 7s. *RB 1743–1749, 25.*

Thomas Campbell, 9 April 1744—two old books, one primer, 1s 6d. *RB 1743–1749, 25a.*

Samuel Ingram, 9 April 1744—a parcel of old books. *RB 1743–1749, 26a.*

Matthew Neale (division of estate to Sarah Haynie for orphans of Neale), 12 March 1743/44—a parcel of books and some other things, £1 5s. *RB 1743–1749, 27.*

Elias Edmonds, 14 May 1744—one dictionary, a parcel of old books, 7s 6d. *RB 1743–1749, 30.*

Richard Howson, 11 June 1744—three old books, 7s. *RB 1743–1749, 36a.*

Robert Clark, 11 June 1744—one large *Bible*, 17s; a parcel of old books and new books, 15s. *RB 1743–1749, 37a.*

Lazarus Taylor, 11 June 1744—a parcel of books. *RB 1743–1749, 38.*

Joseph Lancaster, 9 July 1744—one large *Bible*, one old sermon book, £1 10s; some old books, 8s 6d. *RB 1743–1749, 40.*

James Waller, 9 July 1744—one old *Bible*, 2s. *RB 1743–1749, 41a.*

Thomas Walker, 9 July 1744—three old books, 2s 6d; a parcel of old books, 8s. *RB 1743–1749, 42.*

John Cockrell (estate division to William Webb), 9 July 1744—two books, 3s 6d. *RB 1743–1749, 42.*

Hannah Howson, 10 Sept. 1744—two *Bibles* and six other books, 16s 6d. *RB 1743–1749, 43.*

Rev. Joshua Nelson, 7 Sept. 1744—a parcel of books, 58s. *RB 1743–1749, 44a.*

William Bell, 10 Sept. 1744—one *Bible* and *Testament*, 4s. *RB 1743–1749, 45a.*

Col. Philip Smith, 10 Sept. 1744—two large *Bibles*, two small *Bibles*, Tillotson's works, Beverege's works, several books of law and physick, books of husbandry, six prayer books, several other sorts of books. *RB 1743–1749, 45a.*

Peter Thomas (Sarahann Thomas orphan of Peter Thomas), 10 Sept. 1744—six old books, 7s 7d. *RB 1743–1749, 46a.*

John Bearcroft, 9 Sept. 1744—some old books, 15s. *RB 1743–1749, 51.*

George Harrison, 12 Nov. 1744—one *Bible* and some old books, 5s. *RB 1743–1749, 57.*

Thomas Williams, 10 Dec. 1744—one old *Bible*, *Testament* and *Prayer Book*, 3s. *RB 1743–1749, 58a.*

John Coleman, 10 Dec. 1744—one good *Bible*, two prayer books and sundry old books, 12s. *RB 1743–1749, 59.*

John Harvey, 14 Jan. 1744/45—a parcel of books, 7s 6d. *RB 1743–1749, 60.*

Division of estate to Mrs. Judith Neale and Mrs. Hannah Howson, 8 April 1745—one *Great Bible,* 6s 9d; one small *Bible,* 4s; one *Testament,* 1s 4d. *RB 1743–1749, 78.*

John Lancaster, 8 April 1745—two books and looking glass, 3s 6d. *RB 1743–1749, 80a.*

Britain Hill, 13 May 1745—one old book, 1s 3d. *RB 1743–1749, 81.*

John Dameron, 13 May 1745—one old sermon book, 10s; one new small *Bible,* one old *Bible,* 4s 6d; one book called Sherlock on *Death,* 2s; *The Whole Duty of Man,* 5s; *The Practice of Piety,* 5s; one *Testament,* one *Psalter,* 1s 8d; one prayer book, a parcel of old books, 4s. *RB 1743–1749, 82.*

Ann Swanson, 13 May 1745—some old books, 2s. *RB 1743–1749, 83.*

Samuel Snow, 13 May 1745—one small *Bible* and prayer book and three old prayer books, 5s. *RB 1743–1749, 83a.*

William Bowley, 14 May 1745—some books, one large trunk, and some things in it, £1 5s. *RB 1743–1749, 84.*

Patrick Fairweather, 13 May 1745—one old *Bible,* 2s. *RB 1743–1749, 85a.*

George Hunt, 10 June 1745—a parcel old books, 3s. *RB 1743–1749, 89.*

John Hurst, 14 Jan. 1744/45—two old books, 2s. *RB 1743–1749, 89a.*

James Stewart, 10 June 1745—some old books and other trifles, 3s. *RB 1743–1749, 91.*

William Hill, 10 June 1745—two old books and one tobacco box, 1s. *RB 1743–1749, 91a.*

William Booze, 8 July 1745—a parcel of old books, 10s. *RB 1743–1749, 94.*

Thomas Tobin, 8 July 1745—one *Common Prayer Book,* 1s 6d. *RB 1743–1749, 95.*

William Ball, 14 Aug. 1745—seven books and other old books, 16s. *RB 1743–1749, 103a.*

Lucretia Barecroft, 12 Aug. 1745—some books, 12s. *RB 1743–1749, 104a.*

John Tolson, 9 Sept. 1745—one *Bible. RB 1743–1749, 109.*

Edward Foster, 9 Sept. 1745—three old books and trifles, 1s 3d. *RB 1743–1749, 110.*

John Cartey, 14 Oct. 1745—one *Testament, Psalter. RB 1743–1749, 114.*

John Whiddon, 13 Jan. 1745/46—a parcel of books, 10s. *RB 1743–1749, 118a.*

Joshua James, 13 Jan. 1745/46—a dictionary, 5s; *The Merchant's Magazine,*

4s; a parcel of books, 9s; one large *Bible*, two large books called *The Annotations on the Bible*, £4. *RB 1743–1749, 119.*

Christopher Neale, 13 Jan. 1745/46—three old books, 2s. *RB 1743–1749, 119a.*

Winifred Straughan, 10 Feb. 1745/46—one book called *Doctor Hall's Works*, a parcel of old books, £3. *RB 1743–1749, 122.*

William Fletcher, 14 April 1746—one *Bible* and some other books, 8s 6d. *RB 1743–1749, 126a.*

John Lewis, 14 April 1746—a parcel of books, 10s. *RB 1743–1749, 128a.*

John Coppedge, 14 April 1746—four law books, £1 16s 6d; a parcel of other books, £1 6s. *RB 1743–1749, 132.*

John Hurst, 14 April 1746—three old books. *RB 1743–1749, 134a.*

Margaret Agnew, 12 May 1746—some old books, 3s. *RB 1743–1749, 139.*

James Moon, 9 June 1746—a parcel of books and fishing lines, 13s. *RB 1743–1749, 146a.*

Edward Mason, 9 June 1746—a parcel of books, £1. *RB 1743–1749, 147a.*

Thomas Mahane, 9 June 1746—one old primer, 3d. *RB 1743–1749, 148.*

Robert Alexander, 9 June 1746—one *Bible* and other books, 8s. *RB 1743–1749, 149.*

Zachariah Efford, 9 June 1746—a parcel of books, 8s. *RB 1743–1749, 149a.*

John Shadock, 9 June 1746—*Testament*. *RB 1743–1749, 150.*

Capt. George Ball, 13 Oct. 1746—a parcel of law books; one large *Bible*; one large *Common Prayer Book*; one sermon book; *The Whole Duty of Man*; a parcel of other books, divine and historical. *RB 1743–1749, 152a.*

Morris Gibbons, 9 Feb. 1746—one good *Bible* and a parcel of other books, £1. *RB 1743–1749, 171.*

John Leland, 9 Feb. 1746—four old books, 4s. *RB 1743–1749, 172a.*

George Turner, 1 Feb. 1746—some old books and old knives and forks, 7s 6d. *RB 1743–1749, 173a.*

Charles Lee, 9 March 1746—*The Week's Preparation*, 2s; seven other books, 10s; one dictionary, 7s 6d; *The Whole Duty of Man* and one large old *Bible*, 7s 6d. *RB 1743–1749, 181.*

Benjamin Forrest, 9 Feb. 1746—one old *Testament* and one prayer book, 2s 6d. *RB 1743–1749, 182a.*

Richard Crute, 9 March 1746—a parcel of old books. *RB 1743–1749, 183.*

James Fontaine, 10 March 1746—one large *Bible*, 15s; one large book for records, 15s; *Virginia Justice*, 8s; a parcel of old books, £1. *RB 1743–1749, 191a.*

Ezekiel Hill, 13 April 1747—some old books, 8s. *RB 1743–1749, 194a.*

Lawrence Parrot, 13 April 1747—a parcel of old books, 8s. *RB 1743–1749, 197.*

Peter Bearcroft, 13 April 1747—things not appraised: one old *Bible, Testament, Common Prayer Book, The Whole Duty of Man. RB 1743–1749, 199.*

Alexander Moorhead, 13 April 1747—a parcel of old books, 3s 6d. *RB 1743–1749, 199a.*

Thomas Short, 13 April 1747—a parcel of good books, 7s. *RB 1743–1749, 200.*

Richard Thomson, 13 April 1747—a parcel of old books, 3s. *RB 1743–1749, 201a.*

Rev. Moses Robertson, 11 May 1747—one library of books, £14 17s. *RB 1743–1749, 208.*

John Singer, 11 May 1747—some old books. *RB 1743–1749, 210.*

Lindsey Opie, 8 June 1747—a parcel of old books, divinity, law, and history, etc., £7 2s 6d. *RB 1743–1749, 213a.*

William Gill, 8 June 1747—one saddle and bridle and some old books, 10s. *RB 1743–1749, 218.*

Robert Boyd, 8 June 1747—*The Whole Duty of Man*, 2s 6d; *A Week's Preparation*, 2s. *RB 1743–1749, 218a.*

William Taylor (his orphans' part of his estate), 8 June 1747—a parcel of books, 7s 6d. *RB 1743–1749, 219a.*

John Hack, 8 June 1747—ten books, *Guardians, Spectators,* and *Tatlers*, £1 5s; one large *Bible* and one small *Bible*, 13s; a parcel of good books, £1 10s. *RB 1743–1749, 221a.*

John Lewis, 11 Aug. 1747—a parcel of old books. *RB 1743–1749, 233.*

Peter Sullevan, 14 Sept. 1747—one large *Bible*, 16s; *The Whole Duty of Man*, 3s; one book, 1s. *RB 1743–1749, 236a.*

John Bowen, 15 Sept. 1747—one large *Common Prayer Book*, 10s; a parcel of old books, 8s. *RB 1743–1749, 237.*

John Hart, 12 Sept. 1747—one *Bible*, 7s 6d. *RB 1743–1749, 237a.*

John Reason, 14 Sept. 1747—a parcel of books, 10s. *RB 1743–1749, 238.*

John Gouch, 15 Sept. 1747—a parcel of old books, 4s. *RB 1743–1749, 240.*

Aaron Taylor, 11 Jan. 1747—ten books. *RB 1747–1749, 16.*

Shapleigh Neale, 11 Jan. 1747—sixteen books, £2 8s. *RB 1747–1749, 18.*

William Webb, 14 March 1747—a parcel of books, 5s. *RB 1747–1749, 62.*

James Lewis, 10 March 1747—books, £1 9s. *RB 1747–1749, 64.*

Lawrence Parrot (allottment to Mr. Richard Haynie of his wife's part of the estate), 11 April 1748—one old *Bible*, 1s 7d. *RB 1747–1749, 79*.

William Knott, 11 April 1748—one large *Bible*, 15s; a parcel of old books, 7s 6d. *RB 1747–1749, 85*.

Thomas Bearcroft, 11 April 1748—a parcel of books, 12s. *RB 1747–1749, 87*.

George Christopher, 9 May 1748—one *Common Prayer Book* and other things, 6d. *RB 1747–1749, 99*.

John Garlington, 13 June 1748—one *Psalter* and one old *Bible*, 1s 6d. *RB 1747–1749, 110*.

John Smith, 13 July 1748—some old books, 3s. *RB 1747–1749, 115*.

Thomas Hickman, 13 July 1748—three books, 4s. *RB 1747–1749, 121*.

William Nutt, 11 July 1748—one prayer book, 2s 6d; one old book, 2s 6d. *RB 1747–1749, 124*.

George Barratt, 11 July 1748—some old books. *RB 1747–1749, 125*.

Joseph Wildey, 11 July 1748—one large *Bible*, 25s; one seafaring book, 1s 6d; Sol-fa Book, *History of Europe*, 4s; Cooke and Littleton, parcel of old books, £1 3s. *RB 1747–1749, 130*.

John Singer, 8 Aug. 1748—some old books. *RB 1747–1749, 153*.

Motley Wildey, 8 Aug. 1748—one small *Bible, Testament, Prayer Book*, and some other books, 7s. *RB 1747–1749, 169*.

Joseph Wildey, 10 Oct. 1748—(William Wildey possessed with his portion of his father's estate) cyphering book, 1s 6d; one *Great Bible*, 25s. *RB 1747–1749, 183*.

Richard Smith, 13 Feb. 1748—a parcel of old books, £1. *RB 1747–1749, 189*.

Henry Miller, 12 Sept. 1748—one *Virginia Justice*, Bailey's *Dictionary*, £1 2s; two volumes of *The Guardian*, 6s; six volumes of *The Spectator*, £1, 6d; one bookkeeping a method, 4s 8d; two volumes of Beverge's *Sermons*, £2; one English dictionary, 5s; *The Ladies' Calling*, 2s; one spelling book and a parcel of old books, 4s. *RB 1747–1749, 213*.

Isaac Palmer, 13 Feb. 1748—one old *Bible* and *Psalter*. *RB 1747–1749, 214*.

Edwin Gaskins, 13 Feb. 1748—two *Common Prayer Books*, one old *Bible*, two volumes of Dr. Hancock's *Sermons, The Religion of a Prince, The Finishing Stroke*, and sundry other books. *RB 1747–1749, 216*.

John Hunt, 13 Feb. 1748—one new *Bible* and *Testament*, 6s; one small book *Duty of Man* [*The Whole Duty of Man*], 1s; three old books, 3s. *RB 1747–1749, 219*.

Robert White, 13 Feb. 1748—two books. *RB 1747–1749, 243*.

William Jones, 13 Feb. 1748—one large *Bible*, 6s 1d; one Latin *Testament*, one

English grammar, 3s; one music book, 6d. *RB 1747–1749, 245.*

George Conway, 13 Feb. 1748/49—a parcel of books, £1 6s; some law books, 15s. *RB 1747–1749, 259.*

William Trussell, 13 March 1748—some old books, 2s 6d. *RB 1747–1749, 262.*

Robert Short, 13 March 1748—*The Duty of Man* and other books, 3s 6d. *RB 1747–1749, 264.*

John Waddey, 13 Feb. 1748—one large old *Bible*, 9s; a parcel of old books, 10s. *RB 1747–1749, 275.*

John Hurst, 10 April 1749—one *Bible*, 5s. *RB 1747–1749, 278.*

Mrs. Sarah Haynie, 8 May 1749—one large *Bible*, 12s 6d; a parcel of old books, 3s. *RB 1747–1749, 281.*

Thomas Yerby possessed with the estate of William Taylor, the orphan of William Taylor deceased, 12 June 1749—a parcel of old books. *RB 1747–1749, 309.*

Thomas Davis, 12 June 1749—a parcel of old books and three chairs, 6s. *RB 1747–1749, 311.*

George Ingram, 12 June 1749—a parcel of old books, 7s 6d. *RB 1747–1749, 312.*

Thomas Quaram, 12 June 1749—a parcel of books. *RB 1747–1749, 315.*

James Farnid, 11 July 1749—one large *Bible*, five old books, £1 1s. *RB 1747–1749, 349.*

Edwin Farnid, 11 July 1749—one large *Bible* and six old books and one old chest above stairs, £1 3s. *RB 1747–1749, 355.* (Edwin Farnid's part of his father's estate [James Farnid].)

John Alexander, 11 Sept. 1749—a parcel of books, £1. *RB 1747–1749, 379.*

Allen Hunter, 11 Sept. 1749—one large *Bible* and some old books, £1 7s. *RB 1747–1749, 382.*

Mrs. Sarah Waddy, 12 Sept. 1749—one large *Bible* and *Common Prayer Book* and book of divinity. *RB 1747–1749, 391.*

Thomas Palmer, 13 Nov. 1749—a parcel of old books. *RB 1747–1749, 404.*

Frances Ann Thomson, 13 Nov. 1749—three books. *RB 1747–1749, 406.*

William Jones, 13 Nov. 1749—one large *Bible*, £1 6d. *RB 1747–1749, 408.*

Edward Barns, 11 Dec. 1749—three *Bibles*, 7s; one large *Bible* and two other books, £1; some old books, 4s; a parcel of old books, 1s. *RB 1747–1749, 416.*

William Barnes, 11 Dec. 1749—William Barnes allotted one sermon book, one *Bible*, and three old books at 4s for his part of his father's estate. *RB 1747–*

1749, 422.

Thomas Watts, 12 March 1750—two old *Bibles*, one old *Psalter*, 5s. *RB 1, 2.*

John Gaskins, 19 March 1749/50—one *Bible*, 20s. *RB 1, 4.*

John Waughop, 23 Nov. 1749—one large Quarto *Bible*, £1 1s 6d; one small Quarto *Bible* and one large *Common Prayer Book*, 5s; seven volumes of *Spectators*, 15s; a parcel of law books, £1; one spelling book. *RB 1, 10, 11.*

Luke Hill, 9 April 1750—some old books, 6s. *RB 1, 11a.*

Peter Lewis, 14 May 1750—three large books, £1 2s; sundry small books, £1. *RB 1, 29.*

Jane Walker, 10 May 1750—a parcel of books, 3s. *RB 1, 46.*

Edwin Smith, 13 Aug. 1750—a parcel of books, 1s. *RB 1, 61.*

Peter Ashburne, 13 Aug. 1750—a parcel of old books and earthen ware, 11s. *RB 1, 70.*

Ambrose Fielding, 13 Aug. 1750—a parcel of books, 17s 6d. *RB 1, 76.*

Frances Ann Thompson, 13 Aug. 1750—some pewter and four old books, 15s 7d. *RB 1, 87.*

John Mayes, 14 Aug. 1750—a parcel of books, 5s. *RB 1, 88.*

William Warrick, 14 Aug. 1750—some old books, 9s 6d. *RB 1, 91.*

William Nash, 10 Sept. 1750—two old books, 2s 6d. *RB 1, 94.*

John Appleby, 10 Sept. 1750—a *Bible*, 5s. *RB 1, 96.*

Richard Haynie, 10 Sept. 1750—one large *Bible*, 7s 6d; some other books, 5s. *RB 1, 100.*

Thomas Ashburn, 10 Sept. 1750—a parcel of old books, 4s. *RB 1, 102.*

John Rider, 21 Oct. 1749—two *Bibles* and two old *Bibles*, 11s; four old books, 4s. *RB 1, 109.*

Maj. Griffin Fauntleroy, 10 Oct. 1750—a parcel of books, £3. *RB 1, 121.*

Richard Cornish, 8 Oct. 1750—three old books, 2s. *RB 1, 139.*

Henry Mayes, 12 Nov. 1750—one old box and some old books, 3s. *RB 1, 172.*

Charles Coppedge, 12 Nov. 1750—two old *Bibles*, a parcel of books, 7s 6d; one *Great Bible*, £1; one *Bible*, 4s; eight *Common Prayer Books*, one *Duty of Man*, 12s 2d. *RB 1, 175.*

Alexander Lunsford, 12 Nov. 1750—three books, 2s. *RB 1, 179.*

William Steptoe, 10 Dec. 1750—*The Body of the Virginia Laws*, one large *Bible*, £1 5s; two *Bibles*, two *Testaments*, *The History of Our Saviour*, £3 11s; *The Lives of the Apostles*, *Prepar^d to the Sacrament*, 4s 6d; sixteen old books, 15s. *RB 1, 188, 189.*

John Beekley, 10 Dec. 1750—two *Bibles*, two *Psalters*, one *Testament*, 8s. *RB 1, 194.*

James Gervis, 11 March 1750/51—some old books. *RB 1, 231.*
John Sutton, 11 March 1750/51—one prayer book. *RB 1, 232.*
William Murphy, 12 March 1750/51—a parcel of old books, 6s. *RB 1, 235.*
Richard Marshall, 11 March 1750/51—a merchant magazine, 2s 6d. *RB 1, 238.*
Thomas Short, 11 March 1750/51—a parcel of old books, 6d. *RB 1, 240.*
Martha Tignor, 11 March 1750/51—looking glass, three books, and six bottles, 6s 6d. *RB 1, 243.*
Samuel Smith, 11 March 1750/51—one *Bible* and *Testament. RB 1, 244.*
Benjamin Waddy, 11 March 1750/51—one old *Dictionary*, 2s; a parcel of old books, 10s. *RB 1, 247.*
Jane Wilson, 8 April 1751—one old book. *RB 1, 286.*
John Garner, 8 April 1751—seven pounds cotton and two old books, 8s 6d. *RB 1, 292.*
Thomas Short, 8 April 1751—(sale of estate) one pan and book, sixteen pounds of tobacco. *RB 1, 294.*
James Lewis, 9 April 1751—one large *Bible*, 10s 3d; two old books, 1s 4d; one book, 9s; one *Common Prayer Book*, 1s; one book, one *Prayer Book*, 6d; books, 3s 7d; parcel books, 9s. *RB 1, 295-297.*
Benjamin Swanson, 13 May 1751—three books, 3s. *RB 1, 308.*
Capt. John Ball, 13 May 1751—large *Bible*, one small *Bible*, a *Prayer Book, Duty of Man* [*The Whole Duty of Man*]. *RB 1, 310.*
Samuel Mahane, 13 May 1751—one large *Bible*, half worn; one small *Bible*, 15s; three books: *The Whole Duty of Man, Practical Discourse,* and *Family Devotion*, 5s; a parcel of old books, 1s. *RB 1, 311.*
Robert Davis, 13 May 1751—seven books, 8s. *RB 1, 313.*
Joseph Stanley, 13 May 1751—a parcel of books, 5s. *RB 1, 316.*
Samuel Denny, 13 May 1751—a parcel of good books, 10s 6d. *RB 1, 318.*
James Booth, 8 July 1751—some old books, 9s. *RB 1, 342.*
Robert Jones, 8 July 1751—a parcel of books, 11s. *RB 1, 345.*
Peter Lewis, 12 Aug. 1751—a parcel of books, £2. *RB 2, 16.*
Aron Williams, 9 Sept. 1751—one old *Bible*, one *Common Prayer. RB 2, 31.*
George Pickren, 9 Sept. 1751—two books, 2s 6d. *RB 2, 32.*
William Garner, 9 Sept. 1751—one *Bible* and some other books, 13s. *RB 2, 33.*
Robert Robuck, 9 Sept. 1751—two old books, 6d; one *Duty of Man*, 3s; one *Week's Preparation*, 1s 6d; three old *Bibles*, 4s. *RB 2, 34-35.*

Mandley Brown, 12 Sept. 1751—a *Bible,* Crush and *Sacrament Book,* 5s. RB 2, *39.*

Edmond Cole, 14 Oct. 1751—two old books, 1s. *RB 2, 58.*

James Garner, 11 Oct. 1751—a parcel of old books, 2s 6d. *RB 2, 59.*

John Austin, 12 Nov. 1751—one parcel of old books, 3s 6d. *RB 2, 68.*

William Betts, 13 Jan. 1752—four books and one *Bible,* 17s; *History of Josephus,* 10s; a parcel of old books, 3s. *RB 2, 80.*

John Claughton, 10 Feb. 1752—a parcel of old books, 10s. *RB 2, 81.*

Henry Turner, 10 Feb. 1752—one *Bible* and prayer book, one box and trifles, 3s 6d. *RB 2, 82.*

John Bransdon, 10 Feb. 1752—a box of iron and some old books, 6s. *RB 2, 94.*

Richard Hudnall, 10 Feb. 1752—a parcel of books, 6s. *RB 2, 95.*

Joseph Lancaster, 9 March 1752—one large *Bible* and some other books. *RB 2, 99.*

Edward Boollock, 13 April 1752—nine books. *RB 2, 108.*

Sarah Hayes, 13 April 1752—one *Testament* and mug, 2s. *RB 2, 109.*

Thomas Dameron, 11 May 1752—one dozen of books. *RB 2, 114.*

John Lamkin, 10 May 1752—two books and his wearing clothes and hat, £2. *RB 2, 124.*

John Swanson, 8 June 1752—a parcel of books, 8s. *RB 2, 125.*

Yarrett Hughlett, 8 June 1752—one old *Bible* and one small book, 4s 6d. *RB 2, 126.*

Travers Colston, 14 July 1752—a parcel of books in bureau as per list, £3 11s; four *Psalters,* two spelling books, one *Testament,* one *Common Prayer Book,* 6s. *RB 2, 129-130.*

John Taylor, 13 July 1752—two old *Bibles, The Whole Duty of Man,* three volumes of Roman histories, one volume *Antiquities of Rome,* two old books, Beverige's *Thoughts on Religion* and Sherlock on *Death, Pilgrim's Progress,* one sermon book, one *Common Prayer Book. RB 2, 129.*

Mary Toulson, 13 July 1752—two books and one old pestle, 2s 6d; one small book, 6s. *RB 2, 130.*

Leonard Walker, 10 Aug. 1752—one old book. *RB 2, 146.*

Joseph Walker, 25 Sept. 1752—some old books and other lumber, 7s. *RB 2, 156.*

John Kesterson, 25 Sept. 1752—two old books, 6d. *RB 2, 157.*

Jane Wilkins, 25 Sept. 1752—books and leather, 3s 2d. *RB 2, 158.*

William Nelms, 9 Oct. 1752—a parcel of books, 2s; one old book and wig, 5s. *RB 2,173,174.*

William Smith, 12 Feb. 1753—a parcel of books, 8s 8d. *RB 2,193.*

Elizabeth Nutt, 12 Feb. 1753—one old *Prayer Book* and some trifles, 1s. *RB 2,194.*

Sarah Hill, 12 Feb. 1753—some old books, 2s 6d. *RB 2,195.*

Charles Fallin, 9 April 1753—one large *Bible* and one small book, 8s. *RB 2, 214.*

Thomas James, 9 April 1753—sundry old books, 3s 6d. *RB 2, 215.*

Aaron Nelms, 9 April 1753—some old books, 7s 6d. *RB 2, 217.*

Francis Vanlandingham, 14 May 1753—a parcel old books and three earthen mugs, 3s. *RB 2, 223.*

Thomas Bonum, 11 June 1753—one large *Bible*, 17s 6d. *RB 2, 232.*

John Gator, 11 June 1753—one old *Bible*, 6d. *RB 2, 233.*

Richard Haynie, 11 June 1753—a parcel of books, £1 2s 6d. *RB 2, 234.*

Grace Ball, 9 July 1753—one large *Bible* and two small books. *RB 2, 238.*

Barbary Thomson, 10 Sept. 1753—three books, 4s. *RB 3, 15.*

Edmond Cole, 10 Sept. 1753—four old books, 4s. *RB 3, 17.*

John Oldham, 10 Dec. 1753—one parcel old books, 12s. *RB 3, 43.*

John Oldham, Jr., 10 Dec. 1753—a parcel old books, 8s. *RB 3, 44.*

Capt. Christopher Garlington, 10 Dec. 1753—seven old books, 7s. *RB 3, 45.*

John Lathrom, 10 Dec. 1753—one *Prayer Book*, 4s. *RB 3, 46.*

Thomas Murphey, 14 Jan. 1754—a parcel of books, 12s. *RB 3, 55.*

John Christopher, 14 Jan. 1754—one large *Bible*, £1 10s; a parcel of old books, 15s. *RB 3, 58.*

William Garner, 11 Feb. 1754—a parcel of books, 2s 6d. *RB 3, 65.*

Hannah Turner, 12 March 1754—one large *Bible* and six small books, 14s. *RB 3, 72.*

Isaac Edwards, 11 March 1754—one *Bible with the Apocrypha*, 10s. *RB 3, 74.*

Silvester Welch, 8 April 1754—four old books, 10s; a parcel of old books, 1s. *RB 3, 89.*

John Ashton possessed with the remaining part of his father's estate (John Ashton), 9 April 1754—a parcel of old books, 2s 6d. *RB 3, 91.*

John Hornsby, 13 May 1754—some old books, 9s. *RB 3, 100.*

John Oldham, 14 May 1754—a parcel of old books, 8s. *RB 3, 103.*

John Oldham, Jr., 9 July 1754—a parcel of old books, 2s. *RB 3, 112.*

John Hudnall, 8 July 1754—one *Common Prayer Book*, five old books, one old book. *RB 3, 115.*

Alexander Moorehead, 8 July 1754—three old books, 1s. *RB 3, 118.*

John Trussel, 12 Aug. 1754—a parcel of old books, 10s. *RB 3, 126.*

Mary Quarom [Quarson in Index to *Record Book*], 12 Aug. 1754—a parcel of books, 19s 6d. *RB 3, 128.*

James Parsons, 12 Aug. 1754—two old books. *RB 3, 132.*

Capt. Cuthbert Span, 9 Sept. 1754—one *Ivory Minute Book*, 2s 6d; a parcel of books, 30s. *RB 3, 139.*

Mrs. Eleanor Haynie, 14 Oct. 1754—one old looking glass and some old books, 8s. *RB 3, 144.*

James Thompson, 12 Nov. 1754—a parcel of old books, 6d. *RB 3, 157.*

John Brown, 13 Jan. 1755—one old *Bible*, 2s; three old books, 1s. *RB 3, 173.*

John James, 10 Feb. 1755—some old books, 2s. *RB 3, 183.*

William Marsh, 10 March 1755—a parcel books, old shoes, and grindstone, 4s 6d. *RB 3, 188.*

Judith Peachey, 12 May 1755—one large *Bible* and three *Prayer Books*, 15s; a parcel of old books, 10s. *RB 3, 209.*

John Hoult, 12 May 1755—five old books. *RB 3, 210.*

Richard Booth, 15 July 1755—a parcel of old books, 2s. *RB 3, 215.*

Dennis Swanson, 14 July 1755—one *Bible*, two old *Bibles*, one *Testament*, 5s 6d; one *Psalter*, one *Common Prayer Book*, 3s 4d; some old books, 2s. *RB 3, 217.*

Charles Jones, 8 Sept. 1755—three old books, 1s. *RB 3, 230.*

William Sutton, 8 Sept.1755—a parcel of old books, one *Practice of Piety*, 14s. *RB 3, 231.*

Edward Rogers, 8 Dec. 1755—one large *Bible*, 20s; four books, 6s; a parcel of old books, 2s. *RB 3, 246.*

John Flint, 8 Dec. 1755—a parcel of old books and two meal tubs and sifter, 5s. *RB 3, 247.*

Richard Haynie, 10 Dec. 1755—one book, 2s 5d; a parcel of books, 12s 8d. *RB 3, 249.*

John Lathrum, 8 Dec. 1755—one *Prayer Book*, 3s 6d. *RB 3, 253.*

John Conway, 13 Jan. 1756—a parcel of old books, 20s; a parcel old books, 8s 6d; one sugar box, *Testament*, and flask bottles, 3s 6d. *RB 3, 261.*

John Christee, 8 March 1756—two books, 5s. *RB 3, 278.*

William Lewis, 8 March 1756—a parcel old books, 8s; nine old books, £1 2s 6d; two old books, 3s 9d. *RB 3, 280.*

John Bean, 12 April 1756—one *Bible*, 3s 6d; a parcel of old books, 5s 6d. *RB*

3, 284.

Joseph Roberson, 12 April 1756—one *Prayer Book* and a parcel of old books, 4s. *RB 3, 288.*

John Leach, 10 May 1756—a parcel of books, 8s. *RB 3, 298.*

Capt. Griffin Fauntleroy, 10 May 1756—four *Bibles*, eight *Spectators*, three *Prayer Books*, Havel's *Sermons*, Biscoe's *Magazine*, two *Week's Preparation*, Webb's *Justice*, *The Whole Duty of Man*, Adition's [?] *Evidence*, eight books. *RB 3, 299.*

George Humphriss, 14 June 1756—three old books, tin canister, and pepper box, 4s. *RB 3, 307.*

Elismond [also spelled Elizmond] Baisey, 12 July 1756—one *Bible* and *Psalter*, 5s; a parcel of old books, 1s. *RB 3, 314.*

George Hunt, 12 July 1756—a parcel of books, 8s. *RB 3, 318.*

George Berry, 12 July 1756—old books, 3s. *RB 3, 319.*

John Harford, 12 July 1756—three old books, 3s. *RB 3, 320.*

William Lewis, 9 Aug. 1756—three old books, 4s. *RB 3, 325.*

John Swanson, 9 Aug. 1756—one *Bible* and some old books. *RB 3, 326.*

Peter Hayes, 8 Nov. 1756—one large *Bible* and four small books, £1 5s. *RB 4, 9.*

Elizabeth Ledford, 8 Nov. 1756—Ambrose's work, 7s 6d; eleven small books, 15s. *RB 4, 10.*

William Betts, 8 Nov. 1756—a parcel of old books, 10s. *RB 4, 12.*

Vincent Garner, 9 Nov. 1756—one pair hinges and one *Testament*, 2s 6d; a parcel of old books, 5s. *RB 4, 12.*

Rebecca Crute, 10 Jan. 1757—a parcel of books. *RB 4, 28.*

Robert More, 14 Feb. 1757—some old books, 6d. *RB 4, 30.*

Wilfrey Bryant, 14 March 1757—four old books. *RB 4, 45.*

John Coles, 2 March 1757—a parcel of old books. *RB 4, 50.*

Joseph Roberson, 14 March 1757—a parcel of books, 7s 6d. *RB 4, 51.*

William Garlington, 9 May 1757—two old books, 6d; one large *Bible*, 9s 6d; one small *Bible*, 3s. *RB 4, 65.*

William Davis, 9 May 1757—one *Bible* and *Testament*, 7s 6d. *RB 4, 69.*

Ann Alexander, 9 May 1757—a parcel of books, 15s. *RB 4, 70.*

Daniel Gaines, 9 May 1757—one book to Kemp Hurst, 6d. *RB 4, 71.*

Vincent Garner, 13 June 1757—one *Great Bible*, 12s 6d. *RB 4, 80.*

Thomas Dameron, 13 June 1757—one fiddle, one *Great Bible* and some other books, 12s. *RB 4, 86.*

Samuel Downing, 13 June 1757—a parcel of books, 20s. *RB 4, 88.*

William Bridgman, 13 June 1757—three books, 3s. RB 4, 89.

Margaret James, 11 July 1757—a parcel of old books, 2s 6d; one large *Bible*, two *Common Prayer Books*, 16s; a parcel of old books, *The Factor's Guide*, 3s 6d; one *Latin Dictionary*, one old ledger, 2s 6d; Mr. Poole's *Annotations on the Old and New Testament*, £1 6s. RB 4, 99.

Mosley Mott, 8 Aug. 1757—one *Great Bible*, 21s 6d; one *Prayer Book*, one *Duty of Man*, and Sherlock on *Death*, 8s; a parcel of old books, 8s. RB 4, 110.

Manuel Walker, 12 Sept. 1757—four old books, 5s. RB 4, 112.

Jesse Gaskins, 12 Sept. 1757—four old books and spectacles, 2s 6d. RB 4, 116.

John Beetley, 12 Sept. 1757—one *Bible*, 3s. RB 4, 125.

Francis Beetley, 12 Sept. 1757—a parcel of books, 3s 6d. RB 4, 129.

Cloe Swanson, 11 Oct. 1757—some old books to Richard Lunsford, 5s 6d. RB 4, 140.

John Swanson, 10 Oct. 1757—some old books and some old bottles, 5s. RB 4, 141.

William Garlington, 14 Nov. 1757—one large *Bible*, 9s 6d. RB 4, 157.

Elizabeth Webb, 14 Nov. 1757—six books, 5s. RB 4, 158.

Robert Hudson, 15 Nov. 1757—one old *Bible*, 2s. RB 4, 160.

Josias Gaskins, 12 Dec. 1757—six books. RB 4, 165.

Stephen Stott, 12 Dec. 1757—old books, knives, 8s 3d. RB 4, 171.

Deborah Mahane, 13 Feb. 1758—a parcel of old books, 5s. RB 4, 187.

Josias Gaskins [in Index to *Record Book*, his name is listed as Josiah], 13 Feb. 1758—three books, 4s. RB 4, 193.

Thomas Taylor, 13 Feb. 1758—a parcel of old books, 6d. RB 4, 195.

Tunsall Hack, 14 Feb. 1758—a parcel of old books and an old trunk, £1 6s. RB 4, 198.

Peter Hayes, 13 March 1758—two books. RB 4, 204.

George Oldham, 13 March 1758—a parcel of old books, 10s. RB 4, 205.

Thomas Bayless, 13 March 1758—a parcel of old books, 4s. RB 4, 215.

William Garlington, Junr, [no date given]—two old books, 4s. RB 4, 215.

James Fitzmorris, 13 March 1758—one old *Bible*, 2s. RB 4, 216.

John Cralle, 10 April 1758—a parcel of old books, 2s 6d. RB 4, 224.

John Mason, 10 April 1758—a parcel of old books, 5s. RB 4, 226.

William Fletcher, 10 April 1758—one small *Bible* and two old books. RB 4, 227.

Moses Champion, 8 May 1758—some old books, 3s 6d. RB 4, 235.

Richard Knott, 8 May 1758—one *Bible,* five old books, 10s. *RB 4, 239.*
William Owens, 8 May 1758—a parcel of old books, 6s 2d. *RB 4, 243.*
John Hall, 12 June 1758—one *Bible* and some old books, 6s. *RB 4, 243.*
William Lattimore, 12 June 1758—nine books. *RB 4, 244.*
Thomas Hurst, 12 June 1758—one large *Bible* and some old books, 10s. *RB 4, 245.*
Joseph Roberson, Jr., 10 July 1758—a parcel of books, 7s 6d. *RB 4, 254.*
Elizabeth Miller, 10 July 1758—*The Whole Duty of Man,* 1s 3d; second *Paradise* of Milton, 2s. *RB 4, 257.*
Mary Hopwood, 14 Aug. 1758—two books, 11s. *RB 4, 267.*
Thomas Smith, 14 Aug. 1758—eight volumes *Spectators,* £1 1s 6d; one small *Bible,* 2s; one *Prayer Book,* 1s 6d; one *Testament,* 6d; one *Christian's Great Interest,* 1s; one *Companion to the Altar,* 1s 6d; Bacon's *Sermons,* 6d; Milton's *Paradise Lost,* 4s; two volumes *Joseph Andrews,* 4s; Henry on *Prayer,* 2s; one volume Tillotson's *Sermons,* £1 7s; one volume Sherlock's *Discourses,* 3s; one volume Puffendoss's *Introduction,* 4s; Evins's *Sermons* (two volumes), 6s; two volumes Bennet's *Oratory,* 5s; one volume *Mark Anthony,* 1s 6d; Kerr's *Grammar,* 1s 3d; two volumes Ruddiman's *Grammar,* 3s; Euclid's *Elements,* 2s 6d; Lucian's *Dialogues,* 3s; Hill's *Arithmetic,* 2s; a *Tractale on Education,* 1s 3d; one Levi, 3s; one Greek *Testament,* 1s; two volumes *Don Cassius,* 5s; one volume *Horace,* 2s 6d; Cyrus's *Travels,* 1s 6d; Synclair's *Hydrosticks,* 6d; one volume Burnet on *39 Articles,* 7s 6d; one volume Person on *The Creed,* one volume Lembroak's *Divinity,* 10s; Gordon's *Georgra Grammar,* 3s; Plato's *Dialogues,* 2s 6d; two volumes *Inusumdelephini,* 2s 6d; two volumes *Virgilin usum Delphem,* 10s; two volumes *Horace,* 10s; *Hudibras,* 2s 6d; Clerk's *Sermons,* 3s 9d; *Coneber Agst Tindal,* 3s; two volumes Locke's *Essays,* 2s; two volumes Abernethy's *Sermons,* 10s; one volume Foster's *Sermons,* 9s; one volume Callemies's *Sermons,* 2s 6d; one volume Dupin, 2s 6d; one volume *Propigation of Christianity,* 5s; Echard's *Gazetteer,* 1s 6d; one Littleton's *Dictionary,* 10s; one Littleton's *Dictionary,* 5s; one Boyer's *Dictionary,* 5s, one volume, 2s; one volume Cruch's *Horace,* 2s 6d; two volumes *Sophocles,* 3s; two volumes Aeschylus's *Tragedies,* 3s; one volume, 1s 6d; one volume, 10s; six Clerk's *Essay on Education,* 1s; two volumes *Virgil,* 4s; *Sacred Dialogues,* 1s; one volume *Horace,* 1s 3d; one Cornelius Nepos, 8d; one Grotius, 1s; Wingate's *Arithmetick,* 2s 6d; Rohault's *Phisick,* 2s; one volume Aristotle, 2s; one, 3s; one Erasmus, 6d; one Tacitus, 6d; one volume Cruches's *Horace,* 3d; one volume Hale's *Thoughts,* 6d; one, 5s; one *Concordance to the Bible,* 5s; one volume Hammond's *Annotations,* 10s; two volumes, 2s; one volume *Guardian,* 1s;

sundry small books, 5s; one large *Prayer Book*, 5s; one folios *Bible*, 10s. *RB 4, 270-272.*

Thomas Bridgman, 14 Aug. 1758—a parcel of old books, 5s. *RB 4, 273.*

John Blundal [also spelled Blundall], 14 Aug. 1758—a parcel of old books, 6s. *RB 4, 279.*

Swanson Lunsford, 14 Aug. 1758—one large *Bible* and a parcel of old books, 16s. *RB 4, 282.*

Sarah Haynie, 11 Sept. 1758—a parcel of books. *RB 4, 289.*

Argail Taylor, 11 Sept. 1758—one large *Bible* and one large *Common Prayer Book*, £1; two volumes Bailey's *Dictionaries*, £1 1s; two volumes Hayey's *Contemporaries* and two volumes *Guardian*, 12s; *The Complete Housewife* and nine old books, £1 5s; some old books, 6s. *RB 4, 293.*

Roger Winter, 11 Sept. 1758—a parcel of old books and a parcel of books with *Duty of Man*, 6s; one old book, three old combs and a cork screw, 1s 6d. *RB 4, 295.*

Adam Booth, 9 Oct. 1758—one large *Bible* and three small books, 10s. *RB 4, 316.*

Thomas Self, 13 Nov. 1758—some old books, 6s. *RB 4, 321.*

William Edmonds, 13 Nov. 1758—five books, 10s. *RB 4, 326.*

Robert Angell, 11 Dec. 1758—some books, 8s; two *Prayer Books, Bible* and grammar, 2s. *RB 5, 28.*

Thomas Wilkins, 11 Sept. 1758—one large *Bible*, 20s; a parcel of old books, 1s 3d. *RB 5, 30.*

John Woods, 8 Jan. 1759—some books, 5s. *RB 5, 42.*

Stephen Haynie, 9 April 1759—a parcel of old books, 10s. *RB 5, 65.*

William Cooke, 9 April 1759—one *Great Bible*, 12s 6d; a parcel of old books, 12s 6d. *RB 5, 68.*

William Morris, 14 May 1759—a parcel old books, 1s. *RB 5, 76.*

Richard Weaver, 9 July 1759—a *Bible* and prayer book, 7s 6d. *RB 5, 89.*

John Gaskins, 9 July 1759—one large *Bible*, 20s. *RB 5, 92.*

John Hammond, 10 Sept. 1759—sundry books, 5s. *RB 5, 113.*

Thomas Harcum, 6 Sept. 1759—a parcel of books, 20s. *RB 5, 117.*

Peter Mason, 10 Sept. 1759—a parcel of books old, 5s. *RB 5, 126.*

John Edward and Edward Ryan, 8 Oct. 1759—a parcel of books and combs, 8s; a parcel of books, 2s 6d. *RB 5, 129, 130.*

John Rout, 11 Sept. 1759—one large *Bible*, 30s; parcel of old books, 1s 3d. *RB 5, 134.*

James Blincoe, 8 Oct. 1759—a parcel of books old, 5s; a parcel of books new, 12s 6d. *RB 5, 138.*

Thomas Pullum, 12 Nov. 1759—a parcel of books, 7s. *RB 5, 144.*

William Wildy, 10 Dec. 1759—a parcel of old books, 22s 6d. *RB 5, 147.*

Rodham Hudson, 11 Feb. 1760—*Bible*, 2s 6d. *RB 5, 180.*

Elinor Gatly, 10 March 1760—one *Bible*, 3s. *RB 5, 183.*

Israel Fogg, 10 March 1760—some old books, 3s. *RB 5, 184.*

John Williams, 12 May 1760—a parcel of old books, 12s 6d. *RB 5, 205.*

Dennis Swanson, 9 June 1760—some old books, 2s 6d. *RB 5, 241.*

Joseph Dameron, 9 June 1760—Bailey's *Dictionary*, second volume, 8s; two *Common Prayer Books*, 4s; one old sermon book, 6s; one *Prayer Book*, 1s 6d. *RB 5, 243.*

Charles Betts, 9 June 1760—one *Bible*, one *Testament* and some other books. *RB 5, 245.*

Aaron Webb, 11 Aug. 1760—a parcel of books, 7s 6d. *RB 5, 251.*

Moses James, 11 Aug. 1760—six prayer books, 6s; a parcel of old books, 5s; two large *Bibles*, one small *Bible*, and one *Testament*, 18s. *RB 5, 254–255.*

Charles Ingram, 13 Oct. 1760—a *Great Bible* and *The Duty of Man*, 12s; a small sermon book, 5s. *RB 5, 272.*

Matthew Bussell, 13 Oct. 1760—one *Bible*, 1s 6d. *RB 5, 277.*

Peter Spencer Hack, 13 Oct. 1760—a parcel of books, £1. *RB 5, 280.*

James Butler, 10 Nov. 1760—one *Bible*, 3s. *RB 5, 286.*

Richard Kennedy, 10 Nov. 1760—a parcel of old books, 10s. *RB 5, 290.*

Richard Hudnall, 8 Dec. 1760—Mercer's *A Bridgement of the Virginia Laws* and Webb's *Justice*, £1; a large *Bible* and three small *Bibles*, 14s 6d; two *Prayer Books*, one *Psalter*, and *Practice of Piety*, 5s 9d; a parcel of old books, 7s 6d; an arithmetick book, 2s 6d. *RB 5, 296.*

John Lork possessed with his wife's part of her father's estate, 8 Dec. 1760—a parcel of books, 9s. *RB 5, 301.*

Thomas Lowther, 9 Feb. 1761—one large *Bible*, three small books, and one old case, £2 5s; one old *Bible*, 7s. *RB 5, 316.*

William Walker, 9 March 1761—a parcel of old books, 5s 6d. *RB 5, 332.*

Jonathan Betts, 9 March 1761—one old *Great Bible*, 12s. *RB 5, 336.*

John Courtney, 9 March 1761—one *Prayer Book*, 3s 6d. *RB 5, 340.*

Andrew Chilton, 9 March 1761—thirteen books, 1s. *RB 5, 357.*

Jane Wildy, 9 March 1761—some old books, 5s. *RB 5, 359.*

Samuel Gouch, 9 Feb. 1761—one *Prayer Book*, 1s 6d. *RB 5, 368.*

William Nelms, 13 April 1761—one book, 1s 3d. *RB 5, 377*.

Elijah Blundall, 13 April 1761—a parcel of books, 12s. *RB 5, 378*.

John Litterell, 13 April 1761—old books, 6d. *RB 5, 379*.

Samuel Nelms, 13 April 1761—a parcel of books and some lumber, £1 5s. *RB 5, 382*.

Capt. Ellis Gill, 13 April 1761—a parcel of old books, 10s; one large *Bible*, 20s. *RB 5, 384*.

Mrs. Ann Fauntleroy, 13 April 1761—a parcel of old books, 15s; one quarto *Bible*, 10s; *The Heads of the Scripture*, 10s; one *Prayer Book*, 3s. *RB 5, 386*.

John Dollins, 13 April 1761—a parcel of old books, 8s. *RB 5, 398*.

Jane Clarke, 8 June 1761—one large *Bible*, 15s; three books, 3s; some old books, 7s. *RB 5, 410*.

John Coan, 8 June 1761—three books, 4s. *RB 5, 427*.

Cornelius Sullivan [also spelled Silivan], 10 Aug. 1761—a parcel old books, 5s; one book and one sword, 5s. *RB 5, 444, 445*.

John Winstead, 10 Aug. 1761—a parcel of old books, 5s. *RB 5, 446*.

Rodham Kenner Cralle, 9 March 1761—one bottle case and some old books, 1s 3d. *RB 5, 448*.

Benjamin Curtis, 14 Sept. 1761—one large *Bible*, three small *Bibles*, one sermon book, £1 5s 3d; seven old books, 3s 6d. *RB 5, 457*.

Jane Hadwell, 14 Sept. 1761—some books. *RB 5, 459*.

Mary Oldham possessed with estate of Thomas Ashburn, 12 Oct. 1761—a parcel of old books, 5s. *RB 5, 487*.

John France, 12 Oct. 1761—a parcel of old books, 6d. *RB 5, 487*.

Elizabeth Nelms, 8 Feb. 1762—one large *Bible*, one book called *The Duty of Man*. *RB 5, 526*.

Mrs. Leanna Lee, 8 Feb. 1762—one old *Bible* and three old books, 13s. *RB 5, 531*.

David Ball, Jr., guardian to Patience Coppedge, possessed with her part of her father's (John Coppedge) estate, 8 Feb. 1762—four old books, 6s 6d. *RB 5, 535*.

David Fluker, 8 March 1762—a parcel of old books, 15s. *RB 5, 542*.

William Baysie, 8 Feb. 1762—a parcel of old books, 12d; one book, 2s 6d. *RB 5, 546*.

Charles Betts, 8 March 1762—one large *Bible*, £1 5s; a parcel of old books, 8s. *RB 5, 547*.

John West, 8 March 1762—one *Prayer Book*, 5s. *RB 5, 552*.

John Hobson, 12 April 1762—wearing clothes and two books, £3 15s. *RB 6, 14.*

George Cox, 12 April 1762—some books, 7s 6d. *RB 6, 17.*

Richard Kellum [also spelled Kellem], 12 April 1762—some old books, 2s. *RB 6, 18.*

Capt. William Haynie, 10 May 1762—one *Testament*, one new *Bible*, two old *Bibles*, two new *Prayer Books*, one *Testament*, one *Psalter*, six old books. *RB 6, 33.*

Onisephorus Dameron, 10 May 1762—one *Bible* and one *Prayer Book*, 4s 6d; one large *Prayer Book* and a parcel of old books, 6s. *RB 6, 34.*

Lemore Jones, 10 May 1762—some old books, 2s 6d. *RB 6, 36.*

Thomas Harding, 10 May 1762—one *Bible*, 12s 6d. *RB 6, 37.*

John Lunsford, 10 May 1762—four books, 6s. *RB 6, 38.*

Charles Betts, 10 May 1762—one large *Bible*, £2 1s. *RB 6, 40.*

William Fossett, 14 June 1762—a parcel of books, 7s. *RB 6, 54.*

John Hill, 15 June 1762—a parcel of books, 3s. *RB 6, 55.*

Samuel Blackwell, 12 July 1762—eight volumes *Spectators*, four volumes *Tatlers*, eight volumes *Turkey Spy*, £2 3s; six volumes *Josephus*, Allen's works, Baylor's *Dictionary*, £1 12s; *Present State of Britain*, two volumes Sherlock on *Death* and *Judgment*, 18s; Thomas Kempis, Gordon's *Geographical Grammar*, parcel books, 12s; *Universal Gazetter*, Burnet *On 39 Articles*, £1 1s; Person on *Creed*, one large *Bible*, one *Bible*, one sermon book, *Duty of Man*, £3 11s; twelve old books, 15s; two old books and one pistole, 3s; Web's *Justice*, Gowges's works and Dodridge's *Progress*, 17s; four volumes *Don Quixote*, 10s. *RB 6, 67, 68.*

William Harcum, 12 July 1762—one large *Bible*, £1; two *Prayer Books* and some old books, 10s. *RB 6, 70.*

Henry Boyer, 12 July 1762—a parcel of books, 8s. *RB 6, 75.*

William Berry, 12 July 1762—one candle stick, pepper box, and old books, 1s 6d. *RB 6, 76.*

Farnefold Nutt, 12 July 1762—some books, 9s. *RB 6, 77.*

William Webb, 13 Sept. 1762—two books, 4s. *RB 6, 114.*

John Lunsford, 14 Sept. 1762—books sold to Joseph More, 3s 3d; books sold to George Angle, 3s 4d. *RB 6, 116.*

Charles McCally [in Index to *Record Book*, the name is McCollis], 11 Oct. 1762—a parcel of books, 3s 6d. *RB 6, 128.*

Andrew Anderson, 8 Nov. 1762—a few old books, 7s. *RB 6, 142.*

Lazerus Coppedge, 8 Nov. 1762—a parcel of old books, 10s. *RB 6, 156.*

Joseph Hester, 10 Dec. 1762—old books, 8s. *RB 6, 158.*

John Rice, 13 Dec. 1762—a parcel of books. *RB 6, 160.*

Baldwin Mathews Smith, 14 Feb. 1763—Rapin's *History of England*, fol° in four volumes, £4; Chamber's *Dictionary*, two volumes, £3; a large *Bible*, £1 10s; a parcel of old books, £5. *RB 6, 166.*

Quilla Kesterson, 14 Feb. 1763—a parcel of books, 5s. *RB 6, 169.*

Wooldridge Smith, 14 March 1763—one large sermon book and parcel of old books, £1 16s. *RB 6, 192.*

Samuel Davis, 14 March 1763—one prayer book, razor and other things, 3s. *RB 6, 193.*

Winder Kenner, 11 April 1763—some old books and one looking glass, 7s 6d. *RB 6, 205.*

Maurice Garlington, 11 April 1763—two pocket books and one *Prayer Book*, 3s 9d. *RB 6, 205.*

William Barrett, 13 June 1763—a parcel of books, 13s. *RB 6, 233.*

William Robuck, 12 July 1763—a parcel of books, 15s. *RB 6, 246.*

Thomas Sims, 10 Oct. 1763—a parcel of old books, 7s 6d. *RB 6, 292.*

Francis Timberlake, 10 Oct. 1763—a parcel of books, 25s. *RB 6, 293.*

John Smith, 14 Nov. 1763—parcel of old books, 10s. *RB 6, 309.*

Thomas Winter, 12 Dec. 1763—a large *Bible*, 10s; Solomon's *Vyneard of the True Church*, 5s; *The True Church*, 5s; *A Dialogue in Discourse*, 2s 6d. *RB 6, 318.*

William Webb, 12 Sept. 1763—a parcel of old books, 5s. *RB 6, 320.*

Mrs. Sarah Harding, 9 Jan. 1764—one large *Bible* and two small books, 15s. *RB 6, 340.*

Rebecca Hudnall, 9 Jan. 1764—seven books. *RB 6, 341.*

Edward White, 13 Feb. 1764—two old books, 2s. *RB 6, Part 2, 358.*

John Gaskins, 9 April 1764—a parcel of old books, 6s. *RB 6, Part 2, 390.*

Mrs. Frances Boyd, 14 May 1764—one large *Bible*, 18s; a parcel of old books, 12s 6d. *RB 6, Part 2, 409.*

George Harvey, 14 May 1764—old and new books, 2s 6d. *RB 6, Part 2, 410.*

Peter Spencer Hack, 16 May 1764—a parcel of old books, 20s. *RB 6, Part 2, 416.*

Thomas Hayes, 11 June 1764—a parcel of old books. *RB 6, Part 2, 428.*

George Winstead, 11 June 1764—a parcel of books, 8s. *RB 6, Part 2, 429.*

William Greenstreet, 9 July 1764—a parcel old books, 5s. *RB 6, Part 2, 437.*

John Cralle, 14 Aug. 1758—parcel books. *RB 6, Part 2, 455.*

Mary Coleman, 25 Sept. 1764—a parcel of old books, 11s 6d. *RB 6, Part 2, 478.*

Gedion Hammond, 12 Nov. 1764—a parcel old books, 5s. *RB 6, Part 2, 488.*

Edward Coles, 11 Feb. 1765—parcel of old books. *RB 6, Part 2, 512.*

William Mott, 11 Feb. 1765—parcel books, 6s. *RB 6, Part 2, 520.*

Mary Ammy Betts, 11 March 1765—parcel old books, 6s. *RB 6, Part 2, 521.*

Nicholas Hughlett, 10 June 1765—a parcel of books, 8s. *RB 6, Part 2, 570.*

Ambrose Fielding, 8 July 1765—a parcel of books, 8s. *RB 6, Part 2, 579.*

Hannah Dollins, 9 July 1765—one *Bible* and *Prayer Book*, 2s 6d. *RB 6, Part 2, 580.*

Spencer Wise, 12 Aug. 1765—a parcel of old books, 6s. *RB 6, Part 2, 586.*

Elizabeth Winstead, 8 Oct. 1764—parcel of old books, 4s. *RB 6, Part 2, 587.*

William Harding, 12 Aug. 1765—large *Bible*, 12s 6d; one black pocket book and *Act of Assembly*, 7s 6d. *RB 6, Part 2, 590, 591.*

Benjamin Doggett, 9 Sept. 1765—one *Bible*, 2s 6d. *RB 6, Part 2, 606.*

George Kirkley, 10 Sept. 1765—a parcel of old books, 5s. *RB 6, Part 2, 622.*

William Palmer, 14 Oct. 1765—some books, 6s. *RB 6, Part 2, 623.*

Hannah Higgins, 9 June 1766—one *Bible*. *RB 6, Part 2, 654.*

Elias Lowry, 14 July 1766—some books. *RB 6, Part 2, 664.*

Joseph Webb, 14 July 1766—one *Bible* and one *Prayer Book*, 6s 6d. *RB 6, Part 2, 664.*

William Lancaster, 14 July 1766—a parcel of old books, 10s. *RB 6, Part 2, 665.*

William Copedge, 14 July 1766—one large *Bible* and other books, 12s 6d. *RB 6, Part 2, 665.*

Thomas Gill, 11 Aug. 1766—a parcel books, 3s. *RB 6, Part 2, 675.*

John Gill, 8 Sept. 1766—a parcel of old books, 8s. *RB 6, Part 2, 690.*

Jane Wilkins, 8 Sept. 1766—some old books, 10s. *RB 6, Part 2, 691.*

George Kesterson, 13 Oct. 1766—a parcel books, 6s 3d. *RB 6, Part 2, 696.*

Nicholas Hughlett, 13 Oct. 1766—one old *Bible*, 2s 6d; some old books, 3s. *RB 6, Part 2, 704.*

Jesse Robinson, 10 Nov. 1766—one large *Bible*, 7s 6d; a parcel of old books, 2s. *RB 6, Part 2, 720.*

Judith Hobson, 10 Nov. 1766—some old books and an old cruet, 2s 6d. *RB 6, Part 2, 720.*

William Troop, 10 Nov. 1766—one large *Bible*, one small *Bible*, and *Spectator*, 10s; two sermon books, 7s 6d; one quadrant, one quadrant case, and book, £2 7s 6d; one arithmetick book, 10s; a parcel of small books, 15s. *RB 6, Part 2, 721.* [An account of the sale of William Troop on page 724 of the same *Record*

Book lists one seafaring book valued at 11s.]

John Betts, 8 Dec. 1766—one *Bible* and *Prayer Book*, 3s. *RB 7, 5.*

Isaac Edwards, 9 Feb. 1767—two books and box of iron, 3s. *RB 7, 10.*

Joseph Nutt, 15 July 1766—a parcel of books, 12s. *RB 7, 14.*

John Kent, Jr., 9 Feb. 1767—two *Prayer Books* and a parcel of old books, 4s. *RB 7, 15.*

John Kent, Sr., 9 Feb. 1767—two *Bibles*, one *Prayer Book* and three other books, 8s. *RB 7, 15.*

George Kerr, 9 Feb. 1767—three blank memorandum books, 6d; twenty-six magazines, 12s; twenty pamphlets, 3s 4d; eight volumes of the *Spectator*, 24s; Pleny's *Letters*, two volumes, 10s; Harvey's *Meditations*, two volumes, 6s; Pope's works, nine volumes, 20s; four volumes of *Jewish Spy*, 6s; *Guardian*, two volumes, first volume of Swift's works, 1s; Parnel's *Poems*, 1s; Locke on *Education*, 2s; Quincey's *Dispensatory*, 5s; *Roxana*, 1s 6d; *Introduction to Trade*, 1s; two *Bibles*, one *Prayer Book* and Watt's *Hymns*, 12s; one volume Tillotson's works, *Introduction to the Lord's Supper, The Whole Duty of Man* and *Devout Exercises*, 2s; *The Compleat Housewife*, Dyches's *Spelling Book* and *Dorashes and Faunia*, 1s 6d; Row's *Letters* and *New Testament*, 3s; collection of magazines, two pamphlets, 6d. *RB 7, 24.*

Division of goods belonging to the estate of George Kerr and Edward Kerr remaining this day on hand. *Bibles*, one at 5d, two at 6d, eight at 13d; two dozen *Prayer Books*, 7s 6d; six *Psalters*, 2s 6d; spelling books, seven at 5s 3d, two at 1s 5d, three at 2s; two histories, 11d; *Week's Preparation*, 1s; twenty-one pamphlets, 3s 6d; two dozen *Hornbooks*, 8d. *RB 7, 28.*

Thomas Dameron, 9 March 1767—six old books and one square table, 8s 6d. *RB 7, 55.*

Stephen Chilton, 9 March 1767—some old books, 2s. *RB 7, 56.*

Joseph Pope, 13 April 1767—parcel of old books, 3s 6d. *RB 7, 69.*

Mary Garner, 13 April 1767—a parcel of books and trifles, 6s. *RB 7, 70.*

William Coppedge, 13 April 1767—one *Bible*, 8s; some books, 4s; one large *Bible* and old books, 12s 6d. *RB 7, 71–73.*

Henry Metcalfe, 13 July 1767—one *Prayer Book*, 3s. *RB 7, 90.*

William Taite, 15 July 1767—Baylie's *Dictionaries*, five volumes in folio; *Laws of Virginia*, two volumes; *Monthly Review*, five volumes large octavio; Foster's *Sermons*, four volumes; South's *Sermons*, five volumes; Tillotson's works, two volumes; Chamberlain's *State of Britain*; Mair's *Bookkeeping*; Shuckford's *Connections of Sacred and Profane; History*, three volumes;

Sacheverell's *Tryall;* Haywood's novels, four volumes; Britain's *True Interest;* Washington's *Abridgment*. [All books listed as being in the back room above the hall.] *RB 7, 94.*

Hugh Watson, 10 Aug. 1767—thirty-four old books, 60s. *RB 7, 100.*

Joshan Champion, 10 Aug. 1767—a parcel of old books, 4s 6d. *RB 7, 103.*

Rev. Adam Menzies, 12 Oct. 1767—Stanhope's *Paraphrase,* four volumes, £1; Rollin's *Ancient History,* ten volumes, £2 5s; Hume's *History of England,* six volumes, £3; Voltaire's *Of Europe,* three volumes, 18s; *Charles of Sweden,* 4s; Stackhouse's *History Of the Bible,* two volumes, £3; Tillotson's *Sermons,* ten volumes, £2 10s; Moser's *Sermons,* eight volumes, £2 10s; Mason's *Sermons,* five volumes, £2; Foster's *Sermons,* four volumes, £1 8s; Sherlock's *Sermons,* four volumes, 16s; Orr's *Sermons,* 8s; Seed's *Sermons,* two volumes, 16s; Abernethy's *Sermons,* four volumes, £1 10s; Tidcomb's *Sermons,* 5s; Butler's *Sermons,* 5s; Barrow *On Contentment,* 3s; Carmichal's *Sermons,* 2s 6d; Clark's *Paraphrase,* two volumes, 15s; *Newton on Daniel,* 5s; Butler's *Analogy,* 10s; *Jewish Spy,* five volumes, £1; *Spectators,* eight volumes, £1 4s; *Tatlers,* four volumes, 14s. *Guardian,* two volumes, 6s; Taylor on *The Romans,* 7s 6d; Locke on *The Epistles,* 8s; *Essay on Sacrifices,* 8s; Groves's *Moral Philosophy,* two volumes, 15s; Harvey's *Meditations,* two volumes, 7s 6d; Anderson's *Remonstrance,* 8s; Anderson on *The Resurrection,* 8s; *Ramblers,* five volumes, 7s 6d; Pope's works, ten volumes, £1 10s; Swift's works, eight volumes, £1 12s; Gay's *Poems,* two volumes, 4s; Gay's *Beggar's Opera,* 2s; Gay's *Fables,* 3s; Milton's *Paradise Lost,* 4s; Milton's *Paradise Regained,* 3s; Scoregal's *Sermons,* 5s; Prior's *Poems,* 4s; Prompet's *Poems,* 2s; Parnel's [Parnell's?] *Poems,* 2s 6d; Addison's *Poems,* 2s 6d; Addison's *Travels,* 3s; Young's *Night Thoughts,* 3s 6d; Caesar's *Commentaries,* 3s; *Critical Reflections,* three volumes, 14s; Brown's *Estimate,* two volumes, 8s; *Travels of Cyrus,* 4s 6d; *Aventure de Telemague,* 2s 6d; *Fingal,* 4s; Sterne's *Sermons,* two volumes, 8s; Gerrard on *Taste,* 5s; *Cicero de Oratora,* 2s 6d; Thomson's *Seasons,* 4s; *Dialogues of the Dead,* 6s; Voltaire's *Letters,* 4s; Shaftsbury's *Characteristicks,* three volumes, 10s; Whitby on the *New Testament,* three volumes, £2 6d; Hammond on the *New Testament,* 17s 6d; Clark on the *Attributes,* 8s; Nichol's *Conference with a Theist,* 4s; Taylor on *Original Sin,* 5s; Epictetus's *Morals,* 5s; *Virtue and Happiness,* 3s; Davidson's *Virgil,* two volumes, 10s; *Virginia Laws Abridged,* 10s; Durham's *Phisico Theology,* 5s; *Testament de Colbert,* 4s; Sydenham's works, 5s; *History of Lewis le Grand,* two volumes, 8s; Lelarid's *View of the Dristical Writers,* two volumes, 8s; Robinson's *History of Scotland,* two volumes, 15s; Down's *Sermons,* two volumes, 10s; *Trinitarian Controversy,* 8s; *Meditations of M. Antoninus,* 2s 6d;

Hume's *Desertations* [*Dissertations*?], 2s 6d; Davis's *Sermons*, three volumes, 12s; Smith's *Theory of Mor.* [*Moral*?] *Sentiment*, 8s; *Josephus*, 2s 6d; Potter's *Antiquities of Greece*, 4s; *Elements on Natural Philosophy*, two volumes, 12s; Watt's *Essay*, 5s; Cote's *Lectures*, 7s 6d; *Voyages de Cyrus*, 2s 6d; Cicero's *Orations Tusculan de finibus & de officiio*, four volumes, 8s; Durham's *Astro Theology*, 2s 6d; *Marcus Antoninus*, 3s; *Elements of Philosophy*, 2s 6d; *Essay on the Nature and Conduct of Y^e Passions*, 2s 6d; Dodridge's *Rise*, etc., 3s; Neilson's *Festivals*, 8s; Hutchison's *Enquiry*, 5s; Ray's *Discourses*, 5s; Bennet's *Memorials*, 4s; Euripides, 3s; Gordon's *Grammar*, 5s; *Revelation Examined*, 4s; *Religion of Nature*, 6s; Limbrock's *Theology*, one volume, 10s; Martial's *Epigrams*, 3s; Temple's *Observations*, 2s 6d; Innis's *Meditations*, 2s 6d; Littleton's *Dictionary*, 15s; Scapulas's *Lexicon*, 10s; *Morale Creticnne*, 2s; Pearson on *The Creed*, 12s 6d; four *Common Prayer Books*, £1 5s; *Answer to White's Letters*, 3s; third and fourth volumes of Hume's essay, 7s; Young's *Satyre* [*Satire*], 1s 3d; Calamy's *Sermons*, 5s; West's *Defence*, 3s 6d; Stephen's *Representation of Popery*, one volume, 4s; Pictitus's *Theology*, two volumes, 8s; one volume *Miscellanea Curiosa*, 4s; second volume *Antiquities of Greece*, 4s; *Horace*, Latin, 5s; Schrivilius's *Lexicon*, 5s; a quarto *Bible*, 18s; a parcel of old books, pamphlets, and magazines, £1 15s. RB 7, 120, 121.

John Denny, 11 Jan. 1768—a parcel of books, 6s. RB 7, 148.

Moses Sullivant, 11 Jan. 1768—Burkit on *The New Testament*, £1; a parcel old books, 7s 6d. RB 7, 149.

Charles Sullivant, 11 Jan. 1768—five good books, 8s; six old books, 2s. RB 7, 150.

James Sebree, 8 Feb. 1768—a parcel of old books, 5s. RB 7, 174.

William Winter, 14 March 1768—some old books, 5s. RB 7, 195.

Daniel Shurley, 14 March 1768—sundry books, candlestick and other trifles, 6s. RB 7, 203.

Daniel Wilkins, 14 March 1768—one *Common Prayer Book*, 2s 6d. RB 7, 205.

John Nutt, 11 April 1768—parcel old books, 3s 9d. RB 7, 212.

Aaron Swanson, 11 April 1768—a parcel of old books, 2s 6d. RB 7, 221.

William Butcher, 11 April 1768—old books, 3s. RB 7, 222.

John Wilkins, 9 May 1768—some books, 7s 6d. RB 7, 232.

Robert Woddrop, 9 May 1768—Chamber's *Dictionary*, two volumes, folio, £5; Johnson's *Dictionary*, two volumes, 10s; Baylies's *Dictionary*, one volume, 6s; Smollet's *History of England*, four volumes, £2; Smollet's *Continuation of England*, four volumes, £1 10s; Salmon's *Geography* and *A State of Britain*, one volume, 15s; *Scotch Proverbs* and Glass's *Act of Bookery*, 7s 6d; Swift's works, eight volumes, £1 10s; Pope's works, six volumes, £1 5s; *Reverie*, two volumes, and Catoe's [Cato's?] *Letters*, two volumes, 12s 6d; Thomson's works, four volumes, 15s; *Tour Through Britain*, two volumes, 5s; Salmon's *Gazetteer*, one volume, 5s; *Guardian*, one volume and one small *Bible*, 5s; thirteen old magazines, 5s. *RB 7, 233, 234.*

John Curtis, 9 May 1768—old books. *RB 7, 236.*

Tygner Fallin, 9 May 1768—a parcel old books, 3s; two old books, 2s. *RB 7, 238.*

Elizabeth Miller, account of sales, 11 July 1768—*Milton's Paradise Lost* sold to David Ball, Jr., 3s. *RB 7, 255.*

Thomas Wornom, 8 Aug. 1768—a parcel of books, 6s. *RB 7, 265.*

George Danks, 8 Aug. 1768—seven old books, 7s. *RB 7, 267.*

Samuel Blackwell, 8 Aug. 1768—parcel of books, 40s. *RB 7, 270.*

Sarah Lowery, 12 Sept. 1768—some old books, 3s. *RB 7, 277.*

John Taylor, 12 Sept. 1768—a parcel of books, 10s. *RB 7, 281.*

James Conway, 11 Oct. 1768—some books. *RB 7, 296.*

Jesse Basye, 12 Dec. 1768—a parcel of old books, 2s. *RB 7, 307.*

John Adams, 12 Dec. 1768—one *Bible, Prayer Book, Testament*, and *Spelling Book*, 5s; one *Bible*, one *Testament*, and *Almanack*, 4s. *RB 7, 310.*

Edward Garner, 13 March 1769—some old books, 2s. *RB 7, 326.*

Job Broughton, 13 March 1769—a parcel of old books and two files, 8s. *RB 7, 329.*

John Alexander, 13 March 1769—some old books, 5s. *RB 7, 330.*

Thomas France, 10 April 1769—some old books, 3s. *RB 7, 343.*

James Marsh, 8 May 1769—old books, 2s 2d. *RB 7, 354.*

William Metcalfe, 12 June 1769—three books and one pocket glass, 6s. *RB 7, 356.*

Thomas Everitt, 14 Aug. 1769—a parcel of old books, 6s. *RB 7, 369.*

Joseph Humphris, 14 Aug. 1769—a parcel of old books, 3s 7d. *RB 7, 377.*

David Lattimore, 11 Sept. 1769—one *Great Bible* (best), £1; one *Bible*, 15s; a parcel of old books, 10s; one *Almanack*, 7 1/2d. *RB 7, 396.*

Col. John Bell, 9 Oct. 1769—a large parcel of old books, £5. *RB 7, 407.*

Charles Hill, 11 Dec. 1769—one *Bible* and other books, 10s. *RB 7, 446.*

James Tapscott, 12 Feb. 1770—one large *Bible*, 12s 6d; two *Prayer Books* and *Week's Preparation*, 4s; one *Testament* and one old book, 1s 6d. *RB 7, 458.*

Capt. John Williams, 14 May 1770—four volumes Chamber's *Dictionary*, 6s; a parcel of books, £1 10s. *RB 7, 493.*

William James, 14 May 1770—a parcel of books, 15s. *RB 7, 500.*
Joseph Wildy, 11 June 1770—three *Prayer Books*, £1 5s; a parcel of old books, 7s 6d. *RB 7, 525.*
Beverly Keeve, 11 June 1770—one large *Bible* and box, £1 6s. *RB 7, 529.*
Robert Ramsey, 15 June 1770—nine divinity books, 15s 6d; eight old history books, 4s 9d; a small paper book, 3d. *RB 7, 532.*
Nargail Sharezer Palmer, 13 Aug. 1770—some books, 5s. *RB 8, 8.*
Honorable Presly Thornton, 13 Aug. 1770—Hogarth's *Midnight Conversation;* Barlow's *Justice* and Nelson's *Justice*, two volumes, £2 5s; Clarke's *Remembrances*, 7s 6d; *The Compleat Attorney*, 5s; Miller's *Gardener's Dictionary*, £3; Rapin's *History of England*, £3; Bailey's *Dictionary*, £1 10s; Hughes's *History of Barbados*, 7s 6d; Littleton's *Dictionary*, £1; Virgil and Ovid's *Will*, 15s; *System of Horsemanship*, two volumes, £1; six *Testamentarius*, 5s; Ward's *Mathematician's Guide*, 5s; fourteen old books of different kinds, £1. *RB 8, 10–17.*
Ewell Alexander, 13 Aug. 1770—three punch bowls, a parcel of books, and one razor, 6s 6d. *RB 8, 27.*
James Crane, 13 Aug. 1770—a parcel of old books. *RB 8, 29.*
Samuel Haydon, 10 Sept. 1770—one table and *Prayer Book*, 3s 3d. *RB 8, 34.*
Isaac Haynie, 10 Sept. 1770—old books, two books. *RB 8, 39.*
David Hammontree, 10 Sept. 1770—some books and trunk, 12s 6d. *RB 8, 54.*
James Courtney, 10 Dec. 1770—three old books, 2s 6d. *RB 8, 83.*
George Payne, 10 Dec. 1770—four books of the first choice, 10s; one *Bible* and two other books, 5s. *RB 8, 85.*
David Lattimore, account of sale, 11 Dec. 1770—to Charles Lattimore one *Great Bible,* 18s 6d; to Charles Lattimore one book, 6d; to Charles Lattimore a parcel of old books, 2s 7d; to Charles Lattimore Bailey's *Dictionary*, 8s 6d; to Joanne Lattimore one *Great Bible*, 10s 2d. *RB 8, 105–109.*
Lewis Lamkin, 14 Jan. 1771—parcel old books, 3s; one large Bible, 12s 6d. *RB 8, 114.*
David Pickren, 14 Jan. 1771—some books, 5s. *RB 8, 120.*
Thomas Edwards, 14 Jan. 1771—books in the bookcase, £10. *RB 8, 125.*
Stephen Crain, 14 Jan. 1771—books. *RB 8, 130.*
Robert Crowther, 11 March 1771—some books, 2s 6d. *RB 8, 157.*
Elizabeth Garlington, appraisement and division of estate, 11 March 1771—a parcel of books to Richard Hudnall, guardian of John Garlington. *RB 8, 160.*

David Morgain, 11 March 1771—six old books, 5s. *RB 8, 164.*

Thomas Hughlett, 11 March 1771—a parcel of books, 18s. *RB 8, 167.*

Thomas Cottrell, 12 March 1771—one *Bible, Testament,* and *Prayer Book,* 7s 6d; some old books and delft bowl, 5s. *RB 8, 179–184.*

William Bailey, 8 April 1771—a parcel of old books, 7s 6d. *RB 8, 201.*

Capt. George Ball, 8 April 1771—Burket on the *New Testament,* £1; five *Prayer Books* and one *Duty of Man,* 11s; two books entitled *The New Year's Gift* and *Week's Preparation,* 3s 9d; one *Great Bible, The Present State of Great Britain* and *The Modern Gazetteer,* £1 1s; one law book and three large histories, 13s 6d; five books and a parcel of books, £1 3s 6d; one book Arnean's [?] *Vozage* [*Voyage*], 7s 6d. *RB 8, 207.*

Bledsoe Dameron, 8 April 1771—one *Bible* and one small *Bible,* 4s 3d. *RB 8, 210.*

David Edenton [also spelled Edington], 9 April 1771—one ivory memorandum book; one box containing ciphering books and translations of ye classics, 1s; one large and two small blank paper books; Ainsworth's *Dictionary,* Hederici's *Lexicon,* Cruden's *Concordance,* £1 10s; Burnet on Y^e 39 Articles, Gregory's *Astronomy,* Henet's *Roman Antiquities,* 15s; Sherwin's *Tables,* Euclid's *Elem,* Horace's *Delph* [*Delphini*?], Hollon's *Arithmetick,* 10s; *Present State of Great Britain,* Cicero's *Orations,* Bayer's *French Grammar, Crucified Jesus,* 7s 6d; Sherlock on *Providence,* Virgil Delph [?], Lucian's *Dialogues,* Rayany's *Wisdom of God,* Leighton's *Sermons,* 12s; Bailey's *Dictionary, Rudimentary Grammar,* Terence's *Comedies,* Buchanan's *Psalms,* 8s; Clarke on Y^e *Attributes,* Livy, Buchanan's *Psalms,* Horace, *Christ A Perfect Pattern,* a *Bible,* Quintus Curtius, 10s; Livy, Cicero's *Orations,* Watt's *Hymns,* a Greek *New Testament,* Eutropius, Quintus Curtius, Cornelius Nepos, 7s 6d; an *English Spelling Book,* Beveridge's *Sermons,* Sallust, Grove on Y^e *Sacrament,* Quintus Curtius, *The Book of Common Prayer,* Worsley on *The Classics,* Eutropies, Vincent's *Catechism,* 8s; Wilson's *Arithmetick,* Salomon's *Gazeteer,* Bishop of Canterbury's *Sermons,* Virgil's *Delphini,* 10s; Mol [?] [Moliere's] *Tracts,* Horace, Buchanan's *Psalms,* Clark's *Introduction, Confession of Faith,* 5s; Sallust, *Rudimentary Grammar,* Arrols [?], Nepos, Horace, Plutarch's *Morals,* Godwin on *Prayer,* Justin, Ovid's *Metamorphoses,* 10s; Justin, two copies, Corderius, two copies, *Forms of Speaking Personal Reformation,* Harrison's [?] *Logick,* Cornelius Nepos, 6s; *The Duty of Man,* Tully's *Offices,* a *Greek Grammar, A Treatise on Trigonometry,* Cato's *Proverbs,* Bennet's *Devotions,* 6s; Ovid's *Metamorphoses, The Worldly Communicant,* a *French Testament,* Horace's *Epodes,* a *Greek Testament,* 6s; Petsim's *Art of Curing, A Discourse of Things, Private*

Devotions, Baxter's *Protestant Religion, Confession of Faith,* Corderey, Euripides, Homer's *Iliad,* Guthrie's *Tryal,* A *Greek Grammar,* Caesar's *Commentaries,* 7s; Boyer's *French Grammar,* Buchanan's *Psalms,* a Latin *New Testament,* David's *Psalms, Grammatical Exercises,* Grotius on *Christian Religion,* Mauovius [?] works, Phaedrus's *Fables,* Clark's *Introduction,* Bennit's *Devotions,* 4s; Livy Owen on *Redeeming Love, Primitive Christianity,* Patter's *Antiquities,* 6s; Solomon's *Grammar, History of Y^e Rebellion,* Love's *Surveying,* Castolios's Latin *Bible,* two volumes, Maynis's *Gauges,* 10s; *History of Y^e Devil,* Burton's *Fourfold State,* Mair's *Bookkeeping,* Trap's *Virgil, The London Dispensatory,* Wingate's *Arithmetick,* Boyer's large quarto *Dictionary,* Doddridge's *Exporita,* volume two, Haupley's *Navigation,* volume two, 6s. *RB 8, 230.*

William Townsend, 13 May 1771—one chest, box, one trunk, and old books, 13s 6d. *RB 8, 249.*

William Angel, 10 June 1771—one *Great Bible,* £1 10s; Salmon's *Geography with the Gazeteer,* 10s 2d; Bayley's *Dictionary,* Johnson's *Dictionary,* both volumes, £1 2s 6d; *Spectators, The Art of Surveying, Nature Delineated, Nature Delineated,* £2 14s; parcel of old books, 5s. *RB 8, 258, 259.*

John Mahanes, 10 June 1771—a parcel of books. *RB 8, 265.*

Michael Taylor, 8 July 1771—Josephus's works, four volumes, 8s; a *Great Bible,* 15s; Wilson's *Navigation,* 1s 6d; Mair's *Bookkeeping,* 1s 6d; a small *Bible* and old books, 2s 6d. *RB 8, 283.*

William Lattimore, 8 July 1771—a large *Bible* and some old books, 12s 6d. *RB 8, 286.*

Spencer Hill, 8 July 1771—a parcel of books, £1 8s. *RB 8, 294.*

Woldridge Smith, 14 May 1771—a large sermon book, £1 10s. *RB 8, 308.*

Elizabeth Brent, 14 Aug. 1771—one *Bible,* 6s; some books, 5s. *RB 8, 309.*

James Daughity, 14 Aug. 1771—books, 10s. *RB 8, 322.*

Spencer Corbell, 14 Aug. 1771—one large book, 10s; a parcel of books, 2s 6d. *RB 8, 323, 324.*

Giles Webb, 9 Sept. 1771—a parcel of books, £1. *RB 8, 345.*

Joseph Blackwell, 9 Sept. 1771—some old books, 15s. *RB 8, 352.*

Thomas Smith, 12 Aug. 1771—four old books, 1s 3d. *RB 8, 360.*

William Chilton, 11 Nov. 1771—one *Bible,* 7s 6d. *RB 8, 366.*

John Wornom, 11 Nov. 1771—parcel of books, £1 15s. *RB 8, 369.*

Thomas Derrick, 11 Nov. 1771—a parcel of books, £1 5s. *RB 8, 372.*

William Self, 14 Oct. 1771—books, 10s. *RB 8, 381.*

William Lattimore, 13 Jan. 1772—some old books, 2s. *RB 8, 386.*

Lazarus Sutton, 9 March 1772—one *Bible*, one *Common Prayer Book*, 7s 6d; old books, 1s 3d. *RB 8, 437.*

John Webb, 9 March 1772—a parcel of books, 5s. *RB 8, 442.*

Maj. William Taite, 13 April 1772—Jacob's *Law Dictionary*, 40s; Fitzherbert's *Natura Brevium*, 10s; Plutarch's *Lives*, one volume, *The Law of Last Wills*, 10s; *The Clerk's English Tutor*, two volumes, 6s; Marshall [Saxe's?] *Reverses*, Nelson's *Justice*, £1 2s 6d; Chamberlayne's *State of Britain*, 3s 6d; *Duhonaruem Rustuum*, two volumes, 10s; Meller's *Gardener's Calendar*, 5s; Gordon's *Grammar*, Rollin's *Belles Letters*, 17s; Dyche's *Dictionary*, Pope's works, nine volumes, £1 11s 6d; *Life etc. of the Late Duke of Wharton*, 8s; Thompson's works, *Betsy Thoughtless*, 16s; Count Saye's *Plan for New Modeling the French Army*, 8s; Locke's *Essay on Human Understanding*, 7s 6d; *The Rambler*, three volumes, *Joseph Andrews*, 13s; two volumes of plays, the *Bible* in two volumes, Watt's *Hymns*, 18s; *Charles XII, Malborough's and Eugene's Lives*, 9s; *Memoirs of Persons of Quality*, 6s; *An Introduction to Geography*, 5s; *Cromwell's and Montrose's Lives* and *A Dissenture's* [*Dissenter's?*] *Letter*, 7s 6d; *The Revolution of Portugal* and *Charles of Lorraine*, 5s 6d; *The Gentleman's Pockey* and *The Farrier's Dictionary*, 6s; one volume *The Conquest of Mexico, A Survey of Trade*, 5s; Salmon's *Gazeteer, An Old Court Calendar*, 8s; *Husbandry Spiritualized, Treatise of the Soul*, 6s; *The Method of Grace, Practical Catechism*, 7s 6d; Scuddur's *Daily Walks, The Rise and Progress of Religion*, 7s 6d; *Sacramental Exercises, A Call to the Unconverted*, 3s; *A Token for Children's Preparation for Suffering, Help and Guide*, 3s 9d; Plutarch's *Morals, Revolutions the Roman* [__?], 5s; *The History Queen Ann's Time, A Tour of Britain*, 5s; two old physical books, *The Art of Surgery*, 5s; *Mental Errors, Private Thoughts of Religion*, 7s 6d; *Thoughtfulness for the Morrow, The Post Boy Robed*, 4s 6d; *Terms of Law*, an old *Abridgment of Virginia Laws*, 1s 6d; *Conquest of Mexico, Dissertation on the Classics*, 3s 6d; *The Snake in the Grass, The Standard of the Quakers*, 5s; *The Merchant's Magazine, The British Opollo*, 7s; two old books, *A Preservation Against Deism, The Practical Part of L* [*Law?*], 10s; a parcel of old books, pamphlets and magazines, 15s. *RB 8, 458–460.*

William Greenwood, 11 May 1772—a large *Bible*, 20s; four old books, 4s. *RB 8, 497, 498.*

Samuel Eskridge, 12 May 1772—a parcel of old books and magazines, 10s. *RB 8, 519.*

John Carter, 8 June 1772—five old books, 7s 6d; one *Prayer Book*, 2s 6d. *RB 8, 537.*

Dennis Fallin, 8 June 1772—*Bible* and pepper box, 3s. *RB 8, 540.*

William Campbell, 13 July 1772—some old books, 4s. *RB 8, 552.*
Phillip C. Brown, 13 July 1772—a parcel of books, 7s. *RB 8, 555.*
John McGoon, 10 Aug. 1772—a parcel of books. *RB 9, 10.*
John Taylor, sale of estate, 10 Aug. 1772—a parcel of old books, 10s. *RB 9, 21.*
Judith Howsen, 14 Sept. 1772—six books, 8s. *RB 9, 42.*
Margaret Watson, 13 Oct. 1772—some books, 30s; two books, one hammer, and punch ladle, 3s 6d. *RB 9, 56, 57.*
Joshua Townsend, 14 Dec. 1772—a parcel of old books, 5s. *RB 9, 68.*
John Boswell, 14 Dec. 1772—*Dictionary*, 10s; a parcel of books, 5s. *RB 9, 74.*
Thomas Haynie, 11 Jan. 1773—seven books, 9s. *RB 9, 78.*
Moses James, sale of estate, 11 Jan. 1773—to Henry Hurst one *Bible* and three small books, 11s. *RB 9, 89.* [On page 88 the same items were appraised at 10s.]
Samuel Steel, 8 March 1773—one large *Bible*, 20s; parcel of old books, 2s 6d. *RB 9, 102.*
Spencer Hill, 8 March 1773—a parcel of books, 13s 6d; some books, 1s. *RB 9, 136.*
Robert Pitman, 9 March 1773—a parcel of old books and one iron pot and hooks, 11s 6d. *RB 9, 147.*
John Cralle, sale of estate, 12 April 1773—to Newton Keene a parcel of books, 2s 6d. *RB 9, 149.*
Isaac Hester, 14 June 1773—a parcel of books, 5s. *RB 9, 176.*
Capt. William Kenner, 9 Aug. 1773—one *Bible*, 12s 6d. *RB 9, 215.*
James Waddy, 13 Sept. 1773—five books, 10s 6d. *RB 9, 261.*
William Dameron, 13 Sept. 1773—a parcel of old books, 1s. *RB 9, 263.*
John Gaskins, account of sale, 13 Sept. 1773—cash paid for books by Mr. Reid, 12s 6d. *RB 9, 264.*
Thomas Norman, 13 Dec. 1773—some books, 4s. *RB 9, 311.*
Mary Chilton, 13 Dec. 1773—one *Prayer Book*, 2s. *RB 9, 313.*
Pemberton Claughton, 13 Dec. 1773—one large *Bible*, 10s; a parcel of books, 18s. *RB 9, 316.*
Vincent Garner, 14 Feb. 1774—a parcel of old books, 7s 6d. *RB 9, 328.*
Charles Fallin, 14 March 1774—a parcel of books, £1; two small *Bibles*, 6s; three volumes of Davis's *Sermons*, 8s; two Benson's *Sermons*, 10s; one *Confession of Faith*, 6s; one Bailey's *Dictionary*, 7s 6d. *RB 9, 342.*
John Leach, 14 March 1774—a parcel of old books, 8s. *RB 9, 356.*

Henry Haynie, 9 May 1774—two books and one old gun, 11s. *RB 9, Part 2, 391.*

Samuel Winstead, 9 May 1774—some baskets and old books, 6s. *RB 9, Part 2, 396.*

John Mahane, 9 May 1774—three books and brush, 5s 1d. *RB 9, Part 2, 398.*

Spencer Corbell, 4 May 1774—one large book, 12s. *RB 9, Part 2, 399.*

John Coles, 3 June 1774—Bailey's *Dictionary*, one Bible, *The Ancient History of Greece*, 16s 6d; a parcel of old books, 10s. *RB 9, Part 2, 405.*

Joanne Coodrak [in Index to Record Book, the name is spelled Coolrick], 8 Aug. 1774—a parcel of books, 7s. *RB 9, Part 2, 430.*

Anthony McQuhae, 16 Dec. 1773—one ivory memorandum book, 1s; five *Bibles*, 9s 2d; eighteen *Testaments*, 12s; twenty-five *Spelling Books*, 16s 8d; six histories, 3s; Wilson's *Darectory* [Directory?], 2s; Smolle's *History of All Nations*, eight volumes, £2 12s; three memorandum books, 7 1/2d; one fine *Prayer Book*, 3s. *RB 9, Part 2, 479.*

Spencer Pickren, 14 Nov. 1774—a parcel of old books, 5s. *RB 9, Part 2, 497.*

Judith Fauntleroy, 9 Jan. 1775—old books, 7s. *RB 9, Part 2, 521.*

George Vanlandingham, 13 Feb. 1775—some old books, 5s. *RB 9, Part 2, 533.*

William Barrett, 13 March 1775—two *Bibles*, *Testament*, and *Prayer Book*, 8s 6d; one old large *Bible*, 5s; some old books, 15s. *RB 9, Part 2, 543.*

John Barrett, 13 March 1775—a parcel of old books, 4s. *RB 9, Part 2, 546.*

Barbee Davis, 14 Aug. 1775—some old books, 12s 6d. *RB 9, Part 2, 564a.*

Richard Walker, 11 Sept. 1775—one large *Bible*, 25s; a parcel of books, 11s. *RB 9, Part 2, 571.*

Mr. Menzies's estate, sundries taken by Mrs. Menzies, the widow of the Rev. Adam Menzies, for her use and the use of her sons, 11 Sept. 1775—Stackhouse's *History of the Bible*, two folio volumes, £3; Clarke's *Paraphrase*, two volumes, Tidcomb's *Sermons*, £1; Calamy's *Sermons*, Orr's *Sermons*, Butler's *Sermons*, 18s; *Dialogues of the Dead*, Seed's *Sermons*, two volumes, £1 2s; Mason's *Sermons*, five volumes, Foster's *Sermons*, four volumes, £3 8s; Sherlock on *Death*, Nelson's *Festivals*, 11s; *Spectators*, eight volumes, *Ramblers*, five volumes, *Guardians*, £1 17s 6d; Harvey's *Meditations*, two volumes, four *Common Prayer Books*, £1 12s 6d; one *Quarto Bible*, Milton, two volumes, *Night Thoughts*, £1 8s 6d; *Beggar's Opera*, Prior's *Poems*, Parnell's *Poems*, 8s 6d; Gay's *Poems*, two volumes, pamphlets, two volumes, Barrow's *Contentment*, 9s 6d; *Virtue and Happiness*, Voltaire's pieces [probably means writings or works], 7s; Addison's *Poems*,

Thomson's *Seasons*, Stem's *Sermons*, 14s 6d; Swift's works, eight volumes, Pope's works, ten volumes, 3s 2d; Down's *Sermons*, two volumes, Littleton's *Dictionary*, £1 5s; Davidson's *Virgil*, two volumes, Horace's *Delphine*, 15s; Scapulas's *Lexicon*, Schrivilius's *Lexicon*, 15s; Clavis's *Homerica*, *Euripides*, 8s; Gordon's *Grammar*, Watt's *Essays*, 10s; Marshal's *Epigrams*, 3s.

The following are books appraised by a lump sum worth about 20s: one small *Bible*, *A Treatise on Education*, *French Grammar*, *French Dictionary*, *Virgil*, *Caesar's Commentaries*, *Erasmus*, *Quintus Curtius*, *Cornelius Nepos*, Kirkwood's *Grammar*, two copies, *Compendium of Rhetorick*, *Greek Testament*, *Homer*, *Minor Poets*, *Greek Rudiments*, *Tryal of Y^e Witnesses*, Buchanan's *Psalms* (chiefly old and much used). *RB 9, Part 2, 574, 575*. [Books included in the account of sales have not been listed since most of these books were listed previously in the inventory of the Rev. Adam Menzies.]

Mark Harding, 9 Oct. 1776—Bailey's *Dictionary*, 6s; a parcel of books, 21s 6d. *RB 9, Part 2, 594*.

Pemberton Claughton, division of estate, 13 Dec. 1776—to Griffethells Claughton some old books, 3s 7d; to John Claughton some books, 3s 7d; to Richard Claughton one *Bible* and *Prayer Book*, 2s 6d; to Jane Claughton some books, 3s 7d. *RB 9, Part 2, 622–624*.

Thomas Blackerby, 15 March 1776—a parcel of books, 2s 6d. *RB 9, Part 2, 632*.

Winefred Berry, 13 May 1776—some old books, 8s. *RB 10, 7*.

John Swift, 13 May 1776—old books, 4s. *RB 10, 8*.

Ellis Hudnall, 13 May 1776—a parcel of old books, 16s. *RB 10, 10*.

Joseph Hardwick [in Index to *Record Book*, the name is spelled Hardige], 8 July 1776—one *Prayer Book* and *Primer*, 2s 3d. *RB 10, 10*.

Judith Taylor, inventory, 9 Sept. 1776—a dozen books. *RB 10, 35*.

William Glascock, 9 Sept. 1776—four books. *RB 10, 46*.

John Waddy, 14 Oct. 1776—five small books, 6s. *RB 10, 47*.

William Kennedy, 9 Dec. 1776—a parcel of books, 10s. *RB 10, 75*.

Charles Nelms, 9 Dec. 1776—one large *Bible*, £1 10s; three *Common Prayer Books*, and *Bible*, 12s; five small books, 5s. *RB 10, 77*.

Phillip Tignor, 9 Dec. 1776—some books, 7s 6d. *RB 10, 96*.

Lewis Lamkin, account of sales, 9 Dec. 1776—to Willoby Churchill one *Great Bible*, £1 5s. *RB 10, 105*.

William Garner, 10 Feb. 1777—some old books and a pocket book, 2s. *RB 10, 113*.

Nancy Blackwell, 10 March 1777—some books, 2s 6d. *RB 10, 139.*
John Knight, 12 May 1777—one *Great Bible*, 12s 6d. *RB 10, 170.*
Thomas Williams, 9 June 1777—one house *Bible*, 25s; one *Dictionary*, 8s; Doddridge's *Rise and Progress*, 3s 9d; two hymn books, 4s; nine old books, 7s 6d; one old *Bible*, 3s. *RB 10, 175, 176.*
William Smith, 9 June 1777—some books, 10s. *RB 10, 178.*
James Self, 9 June 1777—one large *Bible*, £1; three small *Bibles*, 9s; some old books, 6s 9d. *RB 10, 180.*
George Harrison, 11 Aug. 1777—a parcel of books, 5s. *RB 10, 195.*
James Tignor, 11 Aug. 1777—a parcel of old books, 10s. *RB 10, 204.*
John Thomas, 11 Aug. 1777—a parcel of old books, 5s. *RB 10, 205.*
John Walker, 8 Sept. 1777—one old *Bible*, *Testament*, and *Prayer Book. RB 10, 209.*
John Barr, 8 Sept. 1777—a parcel old books, £1 5s; two large *Bibles*, one small *Bible*, and Ambrose's works, £1. *RB 10, 218.*
Richard Edwards, 8 Sept. 1777—five prints with glass covers and a parcel of books, £5 10s. *RB 10, 225.*
Mrs. Anne Keene of Caroline County, Maryland, appraisal of personal estate, 8 Dec. 1777—one *Prayer Book*, 2s. *RB 10, 240.*
Alexander Bearcroft, 8 Dec. 1777—a parcel old books, 7s. *RB 10, 243.*
Richard Hull, 8 Dec. 1777—some books, £4. *RB 10, 248.*
James Claughton, 13 Jan. 1778—some books, 3s 7 1/2d. *RB 10, 257.*
Thomas Hudson, 9 March 1778—a parcel of books, £1. *RB 10, 260.*
Robert Edwards, 14 Aug. 1778—one large *Bible*, one old *Virginia Law Book*, 16s 3d. *RB 10, 262.*
Richard Watts, 9 March 1778—parcel of books, 10s. *RB 10, 269.*
Betty Winter, 13 April 1778—one *Bible*, one *Prayer Book*, a parcel of old books, £1 1s 3d. *RB 10, 271.*
Richard Nutt, 13 April 1778—one small looking glass and a parcel of books, 7s 6d; a parcel of old books, 3s 6d. *RB 10, 273.*
Jonathan Edwards, 14 April 1778—a parcel of books, 5s. *RB 10, 287.*
Elizabeth Kennedy, 11 May 1778—one *Great Bible* and some old books, £1. *RB 10, 301.*
John Hall, 8 June 1778—four old books, 6s. *RB 10, 314.*
Nicholas Pope, 8 June 1778—a parcel of old books, 5s; one *Bible*, 3s. *RB 10, 315.*
Peter Knott, 8 June 1778—books, 10s. *RB 10, 324.*

Rev. John Leland, 10 Aug. 1778—one large *Bible*, 10s; one *Prayer Book*, 15s; Dupin's C. [?] *History*, 10s; Rollin's *Belles Letters*, 5s; Swift's works, 12s 6d; *Cromwell's Life*, 2s 6d; *History of John Bull*, 4s; *Feigned Innocence Detected*, 3s; *The Whole Duty of Man*, 5s; *Confession of Faith*, 3s; Tillotson's works, £5; Rollin's *Ancient History*, £3; Lon^r's [?] *Pastoral Letters*, 4s; Grotius, 5s; Sharp's *Sermons*, 40s; Butler's *Sermons*, 5s; *Religion of Nature*, 10s; Derham, 10s; *View of All the Religion in the World*, 5s; Wake's *Catechism*, 5s; Bacon's *Four Sermons*, 6s; Burnet's *History of the Reformation*, 15s; Sherlock on *Death*, 7s 6d; Sherlock on *Future State*, 7s 6d; Addison's *Evidence*, 5s; Sherlock's *Sermons*, 24s; Whitbey on *The New Testament*, £4; Patrick's *Commentary*, £4; Smith's *Commentary*, 20s; Cruden's *Concordance*, 20s; Cruden's *Concordance*, 10s; Scott's works, 40s; Pearson on *The Creed*, 30s; Stilling Fleet, 30s; Burnet on *Articles*, 30s; *History of Ecclesiastical Writers*, 10s; Leland's *View of the Deists*, 20s; Kettle Well's *Measure of Christian Obedience*, 5s; Homer's *Iliad*, 10s; Bailey's *Dictionary*, 12s 6d; *Book of Maps*, 5s; Pyle's *Paraphrase on the Revelations*, 5s; Hutchison's *Virtue*, 7s 6d; *Nature of Faith*, 10s; Pyle's *Paraphrase on the Acts of the Apostles*, 15s; Clark on *The Attributes*, 5s; Lymborck's *Body of Div^y* [Divinity?], 20s; Clark's *Paraphrase*, 15s; Even's *Sermons*, 15s; *Virginia Law*, 2s 6d; Thomson's *Seasons*, 5s; Fordyce's *Art of Preaching*, 2s 6d; *Instructions to the Indians*, 2s 6d; Calamy's *Sermons*, 5s; Qumiy's *Dispensatory*, 7s 6d; parcel old books, £2; *Prayer Book*, 2s 6d; Boyer's *Dictionary*, 20s; *Present State of Britain*, 10s; *London Magazine*, 5s; Salmon's *Gazeteer*, 5s; Joseph Addison's *Remarks*, 2s 6d; Addison's works, 25s; *Amusem* [?] *of Space*, 4s; Cyrus's *Travels*, 4s; Plato's works, 10s; *Free Thinker*, 12s; *Practice of Piety*, 3s. RB 10, 345, 346.

John Knight, 10 Aug. 1778—one *Great Bible*, 13s 1d. RB 10, 358.

Charles Coleman, account of sales, 14 Sept. 1778—two boxes, books and rasp, 14s. RB 10, 379.

Joseph Norris, 12 Oct. 1778—two books, 10s. RB 10, 398.

Peter Haynie, 13 Oct. 1778—four old books, 7s 6d. RB 10, 401.

Henry Foot, 14 Sept. 1778—two blank books, 12s; one *Greek Dictionary*, £2; one Boyer's *Dictionary*, £2 10s; one *Greek Testament*, one *Greek Elias, Douay Bible, Elijah*, one *Greek Grammar*, one *Rudiment* and one *Lexicon*, £1 10s; one *French Tallamaque*, one *French Testament*, one *French Grammar*, £1 10s; two small French books, 5s; Young's *Latin Dictionary*, £1 10s; one *Latin Virgil*, £1 10s; Watson's *Horace*, two volumes, £1 10s; two *Latin Testaments*, two volumes, £1 4s; one Sallies's and Buckanan's *Psalms*, 12s; three *Cornelius*, Terence's *Plays, The Works of Cicero the Great*, one large Latin book, £1; one Bailey's *Dictionary*, £1 10s; *Preceptor*, two volumes, £1; Warburton's *Sermons*, two volumes, £2; *The Ele-*

ments of Criticism, two volumes, £2; *Sermons for Young Men*, two volumes, 12s; Smith's *Theory*, 15s; *Grave Sanda Phil°*, £1; Salmon's *Grammar*, £1; Simpson's *Euclide*, 15s; Burnett's *39 Articles*, 15s; Battie's *On Truth*, £1; *Thoughts on Cicero*, 5s; one *Bible* and *Testament*, two volumes, 15s; one *Common Prayer Book*, 7s; a parcel old monthly reviews and other books, 6s. *RB 10, 407, 408.*

William Pitman, 14 Dec. 1778—a parcel of books, 16s. *RB 10, 409.*

John Cralle, 8 Feb. 1779—one large *Bible*, £5; one large *Bible*, £3; a parcel of old books, 10s; one Salmon's *Grammar*, and Bailey's *Dictionary*, £2; Stanhope's *Paraphrase*, £1; Fisher's *Arithmetic, Common Prayer Book*, one old volume British *Appollo* [Apollo?], 15s. *RB 10, 417, 418.*

John Corbell, 8 March 1779—some old books, 5s. *RB 10, 430.*

Thomas Smith, 8 March 1779—one *Bible* and *Prayer Book*, 9s. *RB 10, 432.*

Charles Jones, 8 March 1779—one large *Bible* and a parcel of other books, £1. *RB 10, 433.*

William Parrott, 8 March 1779—*Dictionary*, one *Bible*, *Prayer Book*, one large old *Bible*, £2 13s; a parcel of old books, 5s. *RB 10, 435.*

James Alexander, 13 July 1779—some books, 12s. *RB 10, 460.*

Richard Way, 9 Aug. 1779—a parcel of books, £2. *RB 10, 467.*

James Lamkin, 9 Aug. 1779—one large *Prayer Book*, £1; one *Arithmetic Book*, 10s. *RB 10, 467.*

Thomas Routt, 13 Sept. 1779—some old books, 7s. *RB 10, 488.*

Hannah Dameron, 11 Oct. 1779—six old books, 10s. *RB 10, 490.*

Joseph Blackwell, 11 Oct. 1779—a parcel of books, 2s. *RB 10, 499.*

Lowry Oliver, 8 Nov. 1779—three brushes and a parcel of old books, £11. *RB 10, 508.*

William Corbell, 13 March 1780—a parcel of books, 15s. *RB 10, 528.*

Joseph Power, 13 March 1780—one large *Bible* and some old books, £20. *RB 10, 531.*

George Barecroft, 13 March 1780—a parcel of books, £10. *RB 10, 532.*

Anthony Sydnor, 14 March 1780—a parcel of books, £15. *RB 10, 538.*

Samuel Lucas, sale of estate, 10 April 1780—one old book sold to Richard Haynie, 2s 6d. *RB 10, 551.*

Dennis Conway, 10 April 1780—a parcel of old books and slate pencils, £2 10s; two books, £2 10s; one *Dictionary*, £15. *RB 10, 552.*

Joanna Lattimore, 8 May 1780—one large *Bible*, 12s. *RB 11, 3.*

Sally Lattimore, 8 May 1780—one small book, 1s 3d. *RB 11, 4.*

Richard Straughan, 8 May 1780—parcel of books, £5. *RB 11, 5.*

William Blackerby, 12 June 1780—one large *Bible*, 8s; one small *Bible*, 4s; one *Common Prayer Book*, 4s; some old books, 2s. *RB 11, 8.*

William Gill, 12 June 1780—a parcel of books, £6. *RB 11, 17.*

William Blackwell, 11 Dec. 1780—a parcel of books, £2 5s. *RB 11, 43.*

Charles Pritchard, 11 Dec. 1780—one large family *Bible*. *RB 11, 45.*

Willoughby Churchill, 11 Dec. 1780—one large *Bible*, £15; one small *Bible*, *Prayer Book* and *Sermon Book*, £4; some old books, £1 10s. *RB 11, 47.*

Mrs. Phebe Menzies, division of estate between two sons, George and Samuel Peachey Menzies, 8 Jan. 1781. [These books have not been listed since most of the books are the same as those found in the appraisal of the estate of the Rev. Adam Menzies; others can be found in the books taken by Mrs. Menzies for her use and the use of her two sons.] *RB 11, 48–52.*

Peter Presley Thornton, 9 Jan. 1781—two volumes Miller's *Dictionary*, £3; two volumes Rapin's *History of England*, £3; two volumes Gibson on *Horses*, £1; seven volumes *Clarissa Harlowe*, £1; Johnson's *Dictionary*, two volumes, £1; *Life of Mahomet*, £1; one *French and English Dictionary*, £1; *Virgil and Horace Dictionary*, £1; one large *Bible*, *Prayer Book*, £2; seven volumes *Charles Grandison*, £1; Strick'd's *History of Virginia*, £5; *Don Quixote*, £1; *General System Horses*, two volumes, £10; one Latin *Psalmody*, £1; four old books, £2. *RB 11, 58, 59.*

Capt. Matthew Neale, 11 June 1781—Burkett's *Explanation on the New Testament*, £100; one large *Bible*, £100; one old *Bible*, £5; one new *Whole Duty of Man*, £15; Flavel on *The Soul of Man*, £15; Foster's *Sermons*, £8; Baylie's *Dictionary*, £30; Sherlock's *Upon Divine Providence*, £10; Sherlock on *Judgment*, £10; Nelson's *On Christian Perfection*, £5; *The Christian Daily Walk*, £8; one *Testament*, £3; one *Psalter*, £2; some old books (damaged), £2. *RB 11, 93.*

Winnifred Dudley, 11 June 1781—one book, 1s 3d. *RB 11, 95.*

Charles Haynie, 9 July 1781—some old books, 10s. *RB 11, 98.*

Joseph Ball, 8 Oct. 1781—Burkill on *The New Testament*, *The Great Bible*, and several other books, £25; Salmon's *Gazeteer*, and *Grammar*, £4; Johnson's *Dictionary*, £10. *RB 11, 115.*

Ellis Gill, 8 Oct. 1781—all the books, 16s. *RB 11, 117.*

John Cockrell, 10 Dec. 1781—a parcel of books, 15s. *RB 11, 122.*

Thomas Pullen, 11 Oct. 1781—three books, 7s; *Bible*, *Common Prayer Book*, two bottles, *Prayer Book*, and *Testament*, 9s. *RB 11, 128.*

John Christopher, Jr., possessed with the estate of Edwin Conway, 11 Feb. 1782—*Bible*, *Testament*, *Psalter*, and *Phesion* [?], 3s. *RB 11, 142.*

Kendall Lee, 8 April 1782—library books in the back room; over the dining room one book press. *RB 11, 150, 151.*

John Gaskins, 9 April 1782—one *Bible,* three *Prayer Books,* 9s; a parcel of Latin books, £1 17s; *Night Thoughts,* 4s. *RB 11, 153.*

David Boyd, 9 April 1782—Bailey's *Dictionary,* two volumes, 12s 6d; Johnson's *Dictionary,* two volumes, 15s; Smollett's *History of England,* eleven volumes, £4; Voilter's [Voltaire's?] *History of Europe,* three volumes, £1 5s; *History of Charles the Fifth,* three volumes, £1 5s; Pliny's *Letters,* two volumes, £1; Robertson's *History of Scotland,* two volumes, £1; Rollin's *History of Egyptians,* nine volumes, £1 7s; Swift's works, thirteen volumes, £3 1s; Rollin's *Roman History,* twelve volumes, £1 16s; Rollin's *Method,* three volumes, 9s; Sulley's *Memories,* four volumes, £1; *Emellius and Sophia,* four volumes, £1; Thomson's works, three volumes, 12s 6d; Seed's works, two volumes, 10s; Foster's *Sermons,* four volumes, £1; Dodd's *Sermons,* three volumes, 3s 6d; Pope's works, ten volumes, £1 10s; Shakespeare's works, nine volumes, £1 7s; Catoe's [Cato's?] *Letters,* four volumes, 12s; *Spectators,* seven volumes, 15s; Salmon's *Gazeteer,* 15s; Allen on *Physick,* two volumes, 10s; Shaw on *Physick,* two volumes, 6s; *Medical Essays,* two volumes, 6s; *Latin Dictionary,* £1 4s; James on *Guarding,* 10s; Bishop Chester on *The Creed,* 15s; one hundred volumes disorted [dissorted, meaning not sorted?], £15; Jacob's *Law Dictionary,* 15s; Blackstone's *Commentaries,* four volumes, £3 10s; Burrow's *Reports,* two volumes, £2; Strange's *Reports,* two volumes, £2; Puffendorf, £1 5s; *Cook Upon Littleton,* £1 5s; Kible's [?] *Reports,* three volumes, £3; Taylor's *Civil Law,* £2 10s; Wood's *Institute,* £1 10s; *Peer Williams,* three volumes, £6 15s; Carthew's *Reports,* £1 5s; Bird's *Scrivener,* £2; Carlee's *Reports,* 10s; Nelson's *A Bridgement [Abridgment?],* three volumes, £4 10s; Gilbert's *Reports,* £1 5s; Darltor's *Law,* two volumes, £3; Coke's *Reports,* three volumes, £3; Croke's *Reports,* three volumes, £1 10s; Vaughan's *Reports,* two volumes, £2; Finetus's *Reports,* £1 5s; Vernon's *Reports,* two volumes, £3 10s; Shower's *Reports,* two volumes, £1 5s; Coke's *Reports,* seven volumes, £7 10s; *Corse [Course?] of Equitty [Equity?],* 17s 6d; Jacob's *Common Law,* £2; Hawkin's *Pleas of the Crown,* £3 10s; Booth's *Real Actings,* £1 5s; Wingate's *Maxim of Law,* 18s; Hobart's *Reports,* £1 10s; Scrivener's *Guide,* 7s 6d; Salkeld's *Reports,* two volumes, £3; Bathurst *On Trials,* 15s; Bathurst *On Law Evidence,* 17s 6d; Harrison's *Chancery,* two volumes, £1 15s; *Treatise on Wills,* £1 12s; *Attorney's Practice,* two volumes, £1 5s; *Statutes at Large,* £2 10s; *Declarations,* 15s; *Office of Execution,* 15s; Nelson's *Reports,* £1 10s; *Virginia Laws,* four volumes, £1 10s; *Reports and Cases,* three volumes, £1 10s; *Fitz Harbert,* 15s; *Pleadings,* 15s; *Law of Uses and Trust,* 15s; nine small tretices [treatises?]. *RB 11, 155–157.*

Banjamin Waddy, 10 June 1782—five old books, 5s. *RB 11, 197.*

John Efford, 10 June 1782—a parcel of old books, 6s. *RB 11, 199.*

Charles Carter, 8 July 1782—some old books, 6s. *RB 11, 224.*

Elizabeth Sutton, 12 Aug. 1782—a parcel of books, £6. *RB 11, 237.*

John Basye, 12 Aug. 1782—one large *Bible,* four old books. *RB 11, 240.*

Ezekiel Potts, 12 Aug. 1782—one *Bible,* one *Prayer Book* and *Psalm Book,* 10s. *RB 11, 241.*

Robert Potts, 12 Aug. 1782—a parcel of old books, 6s. *RB 11, 243.*

John Blincoe, 9 Sept. 1782—one large *Bible,* 20s. *RB 11, 259.*

Griffith Claughton, 9 Sept. 1782—one old large *Bible,* seven old books, £30. *RB 11, 261.*

Charles Fallin, 14 Oct. 1782—one book, 3s 1d; books, 2s 4d. *RB 11, 287.*

Onesiphorus Dameron, 11 Nov. 1782—a parcel of old books, £1 5s. *RB 11, 305.*

Isaac Richardson, 11 Nov. 1782—four old books, 15s. *RB 11, 307.*

Joseph Taylor, 10 March 1783—one large *Bible* and some old books, £1. *RB 12, 14.*

Joseph Sampson, 11 March 1783—a parcel of old books, 5s. *RB 12, 15.*

William Blackwell, account of sales, 14 April 1783—a parcel of books to George Blackwell, £2 5s. *RB 12, 21.*

Benjamin Waddey, 12 May 1783—three *Spectators* and *Dictionary,* 4s. *RB 12, 33.*

John Easton, 12 May 1783—a parcel of books, 42s. *RB 12, 34.*

David Boyd, additional inventory, 14 July 1783—Burkett on *The New Testament,* £3; one *Bible,* two volumes, Harvey's *Meditations,* two volumes, £1 7s; Harvey's *Letters,* two volumes, Harvey's *Dialogues,* three volumes, £1 10s; Davis's *Sermon's,* three volumes, *Golden Treasure,* Scudder's *Daily Walk,* £1 4s; Willison's *Catechism, Guardians,* two volumes, Shaft's *Character,* three volumes, £1 10s; Smollet's *History of England,* three volumes, one blank book, £2 7s 6d. *RB 12, 42.*

William Taylor, 14 July 1783—one large *Bible,* £1; two small *Bibles* and two *Prayer Books,* 9s; a parcel of old books and a *New Testament,* 7s. *RB 12, 45.*

John Kirk, 14 July 1783—a parcel old books, 2s 6d. *RB 12, 51.*

Joshua Harper, 11 Aug. 1783—a parcel of books, 12s. *RB 12, 57.*

John Partridge, 11 Aug. 1783—some old books, 1s 3d. *RB 12, 62.*

Robert Palmer, 11 Aug. 1783—a parcel of books, 10s; three old books, 1s 6d. *RB 12, 62.*

John Smither, 11 Aug. 1783—one large *Bible,* a parcel books, parcel old books, £1 17s 6d. *RB 12, 64.*

George Hays, 13 Oct. 1783—one large book, £1; parcel very good books, £1. *RB 12, 80.*

Isaac Peed, 13 Oct. 1783—a parcel of books, 5s. *RB 12, 82.*

Stephen Hall, 13 Oct. 1783—one *Bible,* one *Psalm Book,* 10s. *RB 12, 94.*

Penly [also spelled Pendley] Dawkins, 10 Nov. 1783—a parcel of old books, 10s. *RB 12, 100.*

William Lansdell possessed with the estate of William Sutton, orphan of John Sutton, 10 Nov. 1783—a parcel of books, 6s. *RB 12, 101.*

Thomas Webb, 10 Nov. 1783—parcel of books. *RB 12, 102.*

William Downing, 11 Nov. 1783—a parcel of books, £2 10s. *RB 12, 116.*

Thomas Claughton, 8 March 1784—parcel of books, 4s. *RB 12, 148.*

Richard Burton, 12 April 1784—some books and one old glass, 5s. *RB 12, 157.*

William Sebree, 10 May 1784—parcel of books, 12s. *RB 12, 173.*

James Ledford, 10 May 1784—one old *Bible,* 3s. *RB 12, 174.*

Richard Ball, 10 May 1784—a parcel of old books, 4s. *RB 12, 176.*

Joshua Jones, 10 May 1784—a parcel of old books, 8s. *RB 12, 181.*

John Berry, 10 May 1784—old books, 4s. *RB 12, 183.*

Charles Marsh, 10 May 1784—parcel of books, 12s 6d. *RB 12, 185.*

John Mays, 10 May 1784—a parcel of old books, 15s. *RB 12, 188.*

George Humphris, 12 Nov. 1783—small *Bible, Prayer Book,* small book. *RB 12, 202.*

Benedict Short, 15 June 1784—parcel of books, 5s. *RB 12, 206.*

George Rogers, 14 June 1784—side saddle and old books, 6s. *RB 12, 207.*

Anna Ball, 14 June 1784—*Great Bible* and *Prayer Book,* 10s; parcel of books, 5s. *RB 12, 208.*

John Heath, 14 June 1784—eight volumes of *Spectators,* 25s; five volumes *Fool of Quality,* 4s; volume, 15s; one *Great Folio Bible* with Cutts, £1 10s; two volumes of Heter's [?] *Lectures,* £1; two volumes of Johnson's *Dictionary,* 15s; sundry other books, £2 10s. *RB 12, 209.*

Willoughby Churchill, account of sales, 12 July 1784—one large *Bible* to John Thornton, £2 6d; some books to David Dawson, 2s. *RB 12, 236.*

Judith Ollard, 9 Aug. 1784—parcel books, 10s. *RB 12, 239.*

Peter Lamkin, 9 Aug. 1784—spelling book, 1s 6d. *RB 12, 250.*

Joseph Walker, 9 Aug. 1784—three old books, 3s 3d. *RB 12, 254.*

Roysten Betts, 13 Sept. 1784—one large *Bible*, 12s. *RB 12, 258*.

Joseph Spriggs, 13 Sept. 1784—a parcel of old books, 8s. *RB 12, 259*.

Elizabeth Townsend [also spelled Touzen and Tounsend], 13 Sept. 1784—one *Bible* and Testament, 6s. *RB 12, 263*.

William Cole, 13 Sept. 1784—parcel of old books, 8s. *RB 12, 264*.

John Gibbons, 12 Oct. 1784—parcel of old books, 6s. *RB 12, 283*.

William Power, 8 Nov. 1784—one *Testament* and one spelling book, 3s. *RB 12, 293*.

Soloman Billins, account of sales, 13 Dec. 1784—parcel of books to Thomas Webb, 5s 6d. *RB 12, 305*.

Benjamin Lansdell, 14 Feb. 1785—old books, 7s. *RB 12, 318*.

Capt. Thomas Conway, 14 Feb. 1785—*Josephus*, £1; two volumes Burrow's *Discourses*, two volumes *Journals Congress*, Salmon's *Grammar*, £1 8s; sundry books, £2. *RB 12, 327*.

Presley Neale, 14 March 1785—a parcel of books, 12s. *RB 12, 338*.

Risdon Walker, 16 March 1785—*Bible, Prayer Book*, and *Psalter*, 4s 6d. *RB 12, 350*.

Edward Garner, 11 April 1785—some old books, 8s. *RB 12, 351*.

John Webb, 13 June 1785—parcel books, 5s. *RB 12, 367*.

Leanna Webb, 13 June 1785—slate and old books, 2s. *RB 12, 367*.

John Webb, 13 June 1785—parcel of old books, 5s. *RB 12, 391*.

William Denny, 14 June 1785—a parcel of books, 10s. *RB 12, 392*.

William Barecroft, 14 June 1785—two old *Bibles*, 3s; one Bailey's *Dictionary*, 8s; dissorted books, 15s. *RB 12, 393*.

John Bearcroft, 14 June 1785—parcel of books, 12s 6d. *RB 12, 412*.

Benjamin Welch, 11 July 1785—parcel of books, 5s. *RB 12, 413*.

William Curtis [also spelled Curtice], 11 July 1785—some old books, 10s. *RB 12, 416*.

William Dameron, 11 July 1785—one *Bible*, 3s. *RB 12, 416*.

James Winstead, 8 Aug. 1785—a parcel of books, 6s. *RB 13, 8*.

Joseph Hill, account of sales, 12 Sept. 1785—to William Hubbard for one *Bible*, 4s 1d. *RB 13, 43*.

Henry Haynie, 12 Sept. 1785—one large *Bible*, 10s. *RB 13, 44*.

Col. Charles Lee, 13 Sept. 1785—parcel of books, 10s. *RB 13, 52*.

William Cornish, 13 Sept. 1785—two *Bibles*, 3s. *RB 13, 53*.

Richard Neale, 10 Oct. 1785—Burcat's [?] *Explanation on the New Testament*, £2; a parcel of other old books, 25s. *RB 13, 62*.

Lindsey Opie, 10 Oct. 1785—a parcel of books, 15s. *RB 13, 72*.

Robert Clarke, 14 Nov. 1785—one large *Bible*, 10s; Clark's and Brown's *Rig* [?] *Sermons*, 10s; Stone's *Dictionary*, 5s; Porney's *Heruldry*, 3s; Butler's *Sermons*, 3s; sixteen old books, 16s; *The Present State of Great Britain*, 3s; three law books, 12s. *RB 13, 83*.

Benjamin Cundiff, 10 Dec. 1785—Mr. Davis's *Sermons*, 10s; two small *Bibles* and *Prayer Book*, 5s; parcel of books, 2s; religious books, 10s. *RB 13, 112*.

John Neale, 10 Jan. 1786—parcel of old books, 5s. *RB 13, 124*.

Isaac Sutton, 13 March 1786—a parcel of old books, 2s. *RB 13, 148*.

Richard Luttrell, 13 March 1786—three books, 7s 6d. *RB 13, 160*.

Col. Rodham Kenner, 13 March 1786—*The Turkish Spy*, eight volumes, *Spectators*, eight volumes, £4; Shakespeare, eight volumes, *Ramblers*, four volumes, £3; Addison's miscellaneous, three volumes, Gay's *Fables*, £1; Gay's *Poems*, two volumes, Locke's *Conduct*, one volume, 7s; *Modern Gazeteer, Jewish Spy*, two volumes, 17s 6d; Vanbraugh's *Plays*, two volumes, Pardon's *Dictionary*, £1 2s 6d; Rollin's *Bell [Belles?] Letters*, four volumes, Harvey's *Meditations*, two volumes, £1 10s; Gardener's *Kallender [Calendar?], Don Quixote*, four volumes, £1 4s; *Shakespeare's Head* [?], two volumes, *Lewis [Louis] XIV*, £1; *Glass Cookery*, Tessot on *Health*, new *Dispensatory*, £1 11s; large *Bible, Guide to the Devout Christ*, £1 5s; *Whole Duty of Man, Week's Preparation*, 15s; small *Bible, Prayer Book, Comp in the Closett* [?], 14s; *Epistles to the Ladies*, two volumes, Yorick's *Sermons*, two volumes Catesby's *Letters*, £1 5s; Nelson's *Festivals* (old), Ainsworth's *Latin Dictionary*, £1 5s; Ovid's *Metamos [Metamorphoses]*, two volumes, Ovid's *Epistles*, one volume, Caesar's *Commentaries*, Clark's *Introduction*, Salmon's *Grammar, Observations in Husbandry* (mostly old), £2 5s; Gordon's *Grammar*, Builden's *Dictionary*, 17s 6d; Euclid's *Elements, Mathematician's Guide, Art of Surveying*, one volume, £1 4s; Rollin's *Ancient History*, two volumes, Mercer's *Abridgment*, nine volumes of the books, £2 2s; six *Mercatoria [Mercators]*, Saxe's *Reveries*, £2 15s; six bundles of magazines, old ordinances, 14s. *RB 13, 167*.

Elisha Snow, account of sales, 10 April 1786—to William Deacon some old books, 1s. *RB 13, 177*.

John Buckley, 12 June 1786—razors and books, 15s. *RB 13, 186*.

William Rice, account of sales, 12 June 1786—to Henry Christopher a parcel of old books, 3s. *RB 13, 195*.

Col. Winder Kenner, 12 June 1786—a parcel books, £4. *RB 13, 204*.

William Harding, 9 Oct. 1786—*Tatler*, four volumes, 8s; Gordon's *Young*

Man's Companion, Fisker's *Arithmetic,* 4s; one large *Bible, Hymn Book,* 3s 6d; Doddridge's *Progress,* parcel of old books, 6s 6d. *RB 13, 221.*

Benjamin Gough, 9 Oct. 1786—books. *RB 13, 225.*

Thomas Airs, 9 Oct. 1786—one *Great Bible, Prayer Book,* and some other old books, 15s. *RB 13, 227.*

William Mott, 9 Oct. 1786—one large *Bible,* small books, 9s. *RB 13, 230.*

Hannah Knight, 9 Oct. 1786—*Great Bible,* 6s. *RB 13, 231.*

George Smither, 9 Oct. 1786—a parcel of old books, 10s. *RB 13, 271.*

William Haynie, 8 Jan. 1787—a parcel of books, 5s. *RB 13, 294.*

James Ball, 8 Jan. 1787—one *Teaches,* 26s; a parcel of books, £2 5s. *RB 13, 298.*

Isaac Sutton, account of sales, 8 Jan. 1787—to Thomas Coleman a parcel of old books, 2s. *RB 13, 300.*

John Easton, account of sales, 8 Jan. 1787—three books to John Hurst, 6s 6d; a parcel of old books to John Sebree, 7s 6d. *RB 13, 302.*

Jane Steel, 8 Jan. 1787—one large *Bible,* 25s; three small books, 1s. *RB 13, 311.*

Charles Copedge, 9 April 1787—eight *Spectators,* one *Great Bible,* £1 4s; two *Guardians,* parcel old books, 6s; one law book containing the acts of Virginia, £1; Mer [?] book, *Spelling Book, The Compleat Housewife,* 6s. *RB 14, 11.*

Robert Pinkard, 9 April 1787—one *Dictionary* and a parcel of books, £1 6s. *RB 14, 30.*

John Hartley, account of sales, 11 June 1787—five old books to William Neale, 20 lbs. tobacco. *RB 14, 36.*

John Hartley, inventory and appraisement, 11 June 1787—five old books, 4s. *RB 14, 38.*

John Flint, 11 June 1787—a parcel of books, 10s. *RB 14, 41.*

Charles Smoot, account of sales, 11 June 1787—parcel of books, 3s; two small books, 1s 1d. *RB 14, 57.*

Richard Cornish, orphan of William Cornish, to Randolph Mott, 9 July 1787—one *Psalter,* 1s 3d. *RB 14, 78.*

John Rice, 8 Oct. 1787—a parcel of old books, 8s. *RB 14, 111.*

Daniel Betts, 9 Oct. 1787—three books, 3s. *RB 14, 115.*

Joseph Humphris, 11 Dec. 1787—a parcel of books, 4s. *RB 14, 129.*

Elisha Fallin, 13 Oct. 1788—parcel old books, 6s. *RB 14, 191.*

Samuel Airs, 13 Oct. 1788—one large old *Bible,* 6s. *RB 14, 192.*

Norman Applebay, 8 Dec. 1788—a parcel of books, 12s. *RB 14, 201.*

John Span Webb, account of sales, 8 Dec. 1788—a few old books to John Rogers, 10s; one *Quarto Bible* to Hannah Webb, 18s. *RB 14, 204.*

Peter Beane, 8 Dec. 1788—parcel books, 15s. *RB 14, 211.*

William Muse, 5 Jan. 1789—parcel old books and earthenware, 11s 6d. *RB 14, 216.*

Dennis Sullivan, 9 Feb. 1789—parcel books, 7s 6d. *RB 14, 222.*

Moses Sebree, 9 Feb. 1789—parcel books, 4s. *RB 14, 223.*

George Oldham, 9 Feb. 1789—three old books, 3s. *RB 14, 229.*

Samuel Blackwell, 13 April 1789—parcel books, £3. *RB 14, 232.*

William Sebree, 13 April 1789—one *Bible, Prayer Book, Testament,* and brush, 4s. *RB 14, 240.*

James Champion, 8 June 1789—parcel of books, 20s. *RB 14, 250.*

Thomas Russell, 8 June 1789—one half dozen old books, 7s 6d. *RB 14, 262.*

Ezekiel Hayden, 14 Sept. 1789—Johnson's *Dictionary,* one large book *Looking to Jesus,* 14s; parcel more of old books, 5s. *RB 14, 282.*

James Harrison, 14 Sept. 1789—one *Bible,* 2s 6d; three books, 2s 6d. *RB 14, 284.*

Francis Walker, 14 Sept. 1789—a parcel of old books, 1s 6d. *RB 14, 291.*

Randolph Mott, 14 Dec. 1789—a parcel books, 18s. *RB 14, 309.*

William Robuck, 8 Feb. 1790—parcel books, 8s 6d. *RB 14, 320.*

Thomas Beacham, 8 Feb. 1790—one *Bible,* 2s 6d. *RB 14, 324.*

James Maley, 8 Feb. 1790—a parcel of books, 12s. *RB 14, 326.*

John Eustace, 12 April 1790—books, 20s. *RB 14, 346.*

Sarah Ann Lewis, account of sales, 14 June 1790—one iron pot and two books, 7s; one old *Bible,* 1s 6d. *RB 14, 353.*

Thomas Wornom, 12 July 1790—some old books, 2s. *RB 14, 358.*

John Doxey, 11 Oct. 1790—some books, 3s 9d. *RB 14, 375.*

Henry Barns, 13 Dec. 1790—a parcel of old books, 14s. *RB 14, 388.*

Peter Thomas, account of sales, 13 Dec. 1790—to Jesse Dawkins three old books, 2s 7d. *RB 14, 392.*

William Sebree, 10 Jan. 1791—one *Prayer Book,* 2s. *RB 14, 396.*

Nathan Pullin, 10 Jan. 1791—a parcel of books, 10s. *RB 14, 398.*

William Wilkins, 10 Jan. 1791—one *Bible* and two books, 2s 6d. *RB 14, 399.*

Richard Routt, 14 Feb. 1791—one house *Bible,* 20s; sundry books, 20s. *RB 14, 407.*

George Smither, 11 April 1791—a parcel of old books, 10s. *RB 14, 421.*

George Walker, 13 June 1791—old books and claw hammer, 4s 9d. *RB 14, 431.*

John Abbay, 13 June 1791—one *Bible, Testament, Prayer Book,* 4s 6d; two sermon books, sundry old books, 6s. *RB 14, 447*.

John Hall, 13 June 1791—one *Testament*, 1s; one small book, 1s. *RB 14, 448*.

Allen Long Sheverall, 13 June 1791—one *Bible*, 3s. *RB 14, 449*.

Dorothy Wilkins, 11 July 1791—a parcel books, 2s 6d. *RB 14, 468*.

Winefred Crossfield, 11 July 1791—seven books, 10s. *RB 14, 469*.

Moses Lunsford, 11 July 1791—one large *Bible*, £1; a parcel of books, 6s. *RB 14, 470*.

Thomas Haydon, account of sales, 13 Sept. 1791—three old books to Thomas Carter, 1s; three books purchased by Leanah Haydon, 6s. *RB 14, 487*.

Mary Beland, 9 Jan. 1792—a parcel of old books, 1s. *RB 14, 508*.

Neddy Barns, 9 Jan. 1792—three old books, 2s 6d. *RB 14, 508*.

William Lansdell, 13 Feb. 1792—a parcel of old books, 7s 6d. *RB 14, 515*.

Betsy Way's [deceased] dower of her late husband's estate, 13 Feb. 1792—one chest, iron pot, and *Bible*, 16s 6d. *RB 14, 516*.

George Walker, 13 Feb. 1792—one *Bible*, 1s 6d. *RB 14, 519*.

Thomas Walker, 13 Feb. 1792—one large *Bible*, two new books, three *Prayer Books*, £1 1s 9d; sundry books, 13s. *RB 14, 521*.

Joseph Pierce, Jr., 11 June 1792—four law books, one chest, and one side saddle, £6 8s. *RB 14, 544*.

William Oldham, 11 June 1792—one *Bible, Prayer Book,* and *Spelling Book*, 4s. *RB 14, 551*.

William Barrett, 9 July 1792—one *Bible,* two *Prayer Books,* one *Testament* and one *Psalter*, 5s. *RB 14, 563*.

Davenport Way, 9 July 1792—a parcel of old books, 2s 6d. *RB 14, 589*.

Rodham Hudson, 9 July 1792—one *Bible* and *Prayer Book*, 6s. *RB 14, 592*.

William Rice, 8 Oct. 1792—one *Bible* and *Testament*, 5s. *RB 14, 613*.

William Davenport, 8 Oct. 1792—two old books, 2s; one Webb's *Justice*, 2s. *RB 14, 623*.

George Ball, Jr., 10 Dec. 1792—parcel of books, 7s 6d. *RB 14, 638*.

Hillary Curtice, 10 Dec. 1792—one copy Osterwall's Folio *Bible With Notes*, £2; Baylie's *Dictionary*, 9s; a parcel of school books, 6s; two ciphering slates, 4s. *RB 14, 641*.

Elias Hunphris, 14 Jan. 1793—a parcel of books, 19s. *RB 14, 650*.

Kenner Cralle, account of sales, 11 Feb. 1793—old books to John H. Foushee, 14s; old books to John Keene, 3s. *RB 14, 658*.

Nancy Everett [also spelled Everitt], 11 Feb. 1793—parcel of old books, 2s 9d. *RB 14, 659*.

Thomas Whaley, 11 Feb. 1793—a parcel of old books and candlestick, 9s. *RB 14, 664.*

Moses Whealor [in Index to *Record Book*, the name is spelled Whealer], 8 April 1793—three old books and pair old cards, 5s. *RB 14, 668.*

Joseph Swain, 8 April 1793—one *Testament*, 1s 3d. *RB 14, 670.*

Peter Cox, 13 April 1793—(In the Hall) Burkett on *The New Testament*, one large *Bible*, £2 6s; one new *Whole Duty of Man*, Bailey's *Dictionary*, 12s; *Virginia Laws*, Stark's *Justice*, old books, £2 8s. *RB 14, 681.*

Daniel Winstead, 8 July 1793—one *Bible*, 2s 6d. *RB 14, 693.*

William Rains, 8 July 1793—a parcel of books, 6s. *RB 14, 698.*

Edward Douglas, 9 Sept. 1793—slate and books, 3s. *RB 14, 708.*

John Downing, 14 Oct. 1793—fourteen old books, 6s. *RB 14, 712.*

William Moltimore, 14 Oct. 1793—three books and one trunk, 7s. *RB 14, 715.*

Stephen Hall, 13 Jan. 1794—a parcel of old books, 6s. *RB 15, 3.*

William H. Jaques, 13 Jan. 1794—a parcel of books, £1 4s. *RB 15, 7.*

Zachariah Efford, 11 Feb. 1794—a parcel of old books, 2s. *RB 15, 21.*

William Rosson, 14 April 1794—parcel of old books, 12s. *RB 15, 31.*

Isaac Hurst, 15 April 1794—books, 10s. *RB 15, 37.*

William Hudnall, 15 April 1794—one large old book *Hammond*, Pearson on *Bread*, 16s; parcel of books, 5s. *RB 15, 43.*

John Span Webb, 15 April 1794—a few old books, 10s; one large *Bible*, 18s. *RB 15, 46.*

Rodham Palmer, 15 April 1794—five books, 12s. *RB 15, 48.*

John Knight, 9 June 1794—one *Bible* and seaman's monitor, 5s. *RB 15, 57.*

Mary Welch, 9 June 1794—two books, 2s. *RB 15, 64.*

Lewis Lunsford, 14 July 1794—sixty-five religious books and histories, £3 4s; one small box of pamphlets, 5s. *RB 15, 66.*

Charles Coppedge, 8 Sept. 1794—one large *Bible*, 18s; one *Bible* and four other books, 8s; eight volumes of *Spectators*, one volume *Guardian*, £2; *Body of Virginia Laws*, 6s. *RB 15, 76, 77.*

James Self, 8 Sept. 1794—parcel of books, 15s. *RB 15, 80.*

William Graham, 8 Sept. 1794—parcel of books, 15s. *RB 15, 81.*

Thomas Andrews, 13 Oct. 1794—Clarke's *Homer*, Greek and Latin, first volume, 1s; Greek *Testament*, 1s; second and fourth volumes of Levy's *Roman History*, Latin, 1s 6d; Justin in usum [?] *Delphini*, 2s 6d; *Salust* [*Sallust?*] in usum *Delphini*, 2s 6d; *Greek and Latin Testament*, 2s 6d; *Cicero Delphini*, 6s; *Horace*

Delphini, 6s; *Virgil Delphini*, 6s; *Juvenal Delphini*, 6s; Clarke's *Ovid*, 1s; Clarke's *Nepos*, 3s; four Clarke's *Nepos*, 12s; five *Select Sentences from Profane Authors*, Latin, s; three old books French and Latin, 1s; *Help for School Boys*, Latin and English, 1s; four *Help for School Boys* Latin and English, 4s; Euclid's *Elements*, Latin, 1s; *Introduction to Latin Grammar*, 9s; three *Introduction to Latin Grammar*, £2 3s; two *Corderys*, one Ruddunaus's [?] *Rudiments*, 1s 6d; three old Latin books, 1s 6d; Coster's *Orations*, 3d; Cruden's *Concordance*, 12s; fifth volume of Hume's *History of England*, 6s; Kennet's *Antiquities* and Paley's *Philosophy*, 6s; Cicero's *Orations*, English, third volumes, 1s; Ferguson's *Astronomy* and Ferguson's *Lectures*, 8s; Suuson's [?] *Euclid*, 3s; Knox's *Sermons*, 4s; Osseaus's [?] *Poems*, 2s; Gibson's *Surveying* and *Sussous conec Sections* [?], 4s; Knox's *Moral Essays*, second volume, 1s 6d; *Euclid*, 1s 6d; Boyse's *Pantheon* and Eufield's *Speaker*, 4s; McLawreus's *Algebra*, 6s; McEwen's *Grace and Truth*, 2s; *Paradise Lost*, 2s; Row's *Luau*, 2s; *Bible*, 4s 6d; *Prayer Book*, 2s; ten old books, 5s. *RB 15, 86, 87.*

Daniel Haynie, 13 Oct. 1794—a parcel of old books, 2s 6d; one small book, 3s; one small *Hymn Book*, 7d. *RB 15, 100.*

John Turner, 8 Dec. 1794—one *Dictionary*, 4s; one *Bible*, 2s. *RB 15, 110.*

Thomas Yerby, division of personal estate, lot no. 2 drawn by Charles Yerby, 9 Dec. 1794—one large *Bible* and old books, 12s. *RB 15, 148.*

Robert Jones, 14 April 1795—a parcel of old books, 5s. *RB 15, 153.*

John Gibbons, 14 April 1795—seven old books, 3s. *RB 15, 159.*

John Anderson, 8 June 1795—two old books, 9d. *RB 15, 169.*

Samuel Hughlett, account of sales, 8 June 1795—parcel of old books sold to Winny Hughlett, 12s. *RB 15, 170.*

Richard Marsh, 8 June 1795—a parcel of books, 1s 3d. *RB 15, 178.*

John Haynie, Sr., 8 June 1795—one large *Bible*, 15s. *RB 15, 180.*

James Lewis, 8 June 1795—two sermon books, 12s; one *Bible* and *Prayer Book*, 2s 6d; *Truth Vindicated*, 2s; sundry old books, 3s; *Duty of Man* and *Guide for Doubting*, 1s 6d. *RB 15, 181.*

Judith Davis, 13 July 1795—a parcel of books and a parcel of wooden ware, £1 1s. *RB 15, 184.*

William Hughlett, 13 July 1795—a parcel of old books, 7s 6d. *RB 15, 192.*

Richard A. Bearcroft, 14 Sept. 1795—one *Psalm Book*, 3s. *RB 15, 196.*

Luke Headley, 12 Oct. 1795—a parcel of old books, 6d. *RB 15, 207.*

Winter Hughlett, 12 Oct. 1795—parcel of books, 8s. *RB 15, 208.*

Jack Bussell, 12 Oct. 1795—*Bible*, 5s. *RB 15, 212.*

Charles Yerby, 14 Dec. 1795—one large *Bible* and nine small books, 15s. *RB 15, 217.*

George Phillips, 14 April 1795—parcel of books, 6s. *RB 15, 225.*

Nehemiah George, account of sales, 14 Dec. 1795—a parcel of books sold to Edmond Basye, 1s 8d. *RB 15, 234.*

John Wheeler, 14 Dec. 1795—one small sermon book, 1s. *RB 15, 240.*

Thomas Waddy, account of sales, 8 Feb. 1796—parcel of old books sold to Thomas Taylor, 8d; Howard's *Royal Bible*, two volumes, sold to Col. Thomas Gaskins, £2 2s; Stockhouse on the *Bible* sold to Richard Hutchings, £1 16s; *Dictionary on the Bible*, two volumes, sold to Peter Bean, 7s; six old books sold to Col. Thomas Gaskins, 2s. *RB 15, 247.*

Charles Nelms, 8 Feb. 1796—one *Bible* and *Hymn Book*, 4s. *RB 15, 249.*

James Lewis, 8 Feb. 1796—one *Bible* and *Prayer Book*, 1s 6d; two sermon books, book case and books, 1s 6d. *RB 15, 250.*

John Wheeler, account of sales, 8 Feb. 1796—earthen ware and one book sold to James Sutton, 1s 7d. *RB 15, 251.*

John Corbin Hudson, 8 Feb. 1796—parcel books, 2s 6d. *RB 15, 252.*

John Grinstead, 8 Feb. 1796—two books, 1s 3d. *RB 15, 256.*

William Travers, 13 June 1796—five large *Bibles* and five other books, £1. *RB 15, 279.* [Account of sales on page 337.]

John Hughlett, Jr., 13 June 1796—a parcel of books, 17s. *RB 15, 283.*

John R. Harrison, 13 June 1796—a parcel books, 6s. *RB 15, 284.*

William Blundall, 13 June 1796—books, 8s. *RB 15, 288.*

Joseph Hurst, account of sales, 12 Sept. 1796—one large *Bible* sold to Lewis Lunsford, £3 6s; parcel old books sold to Peter Carter, 4s 6d. *RB 15, 307.*

Peter McClanahan, 12 Sept. 1796—a parcel of old books and cloth brush, 7s. *RB 15, 309.*

Nathanael Wilson, 12 Dec. 1796—parcel of books, 4s. *RB 15, 323.*

William Travers, account of sales, 12 Dec. 1796—one large *Bible* sold to John Davis, 5s 6d; two books on Fletcher's works sold to Henry Travers; Wesley's *Notes on the New Testament* sold to Thomas Beacham, 9s. *RB 15, 338, 339.*

Nancy Everitt, 12 Dec. 1796—one spelling book, 1s 6d. *RB 15, 340.*

George Ashburn, 13 Feb. 1797—parcel of books, 6s. *RB 15, 350.*

John Davis, 10 April 1797—parcel of old books and clothes brush, 2s 6d. *RB 15, 375.*

William B. Lewis, 10 April 1797—a parcel of old books, 20s. *RB 15, 377.*

John Turner, 12 June 1797—nine books, 12s. *RB 15, 388.*

Maximilian Haynie, 11 Sept. 1797—parcel of old books and one old *Bible*, 7s. *RB 15, 404.*

William Oldham, 11 Sept. 1797—one *Bible, Prayer Book,* and *Spelling Book,* 4s. *RB 15, 405.*

Yarrott Hughlett, 11 Sept. 1797—one *Bible* and *Hymn Book,* 6s. *RB 15, 415.*

Charles Clarke, 11 Dec. 1797—parcel books, 20s. *RB 15, 431.*

John Claughton, 8 Jan. 1798—parcel of books, 18s. *RB 15, 434.*

John W. Beacham, 9 April 1798—parcel books, 12s. *RB 15, 452.*

Capt. George Ingram, 9 April 1798—one large *Bible,* 9s; Heylyn's *Lectures,* eight volumes *Spectators,* £1; *Fool of Quality,* five volumes, £1; two volumes *Gilblass, Common Prayer,* £1; Bailey's *Dictionary,* parcel of old books, 19s. *RB 15, 455.* [Account of sales on pages 489–491.]

John Wright, 9 July 1798—ninety books, £2 10s. *RB 15, 476.*

David Dawson, 9 July 1798—one parcel of books, 33s. *RB 15, 485.*

John Hughlett, 9 July 1798—one large *Bible* and two *Prayer Books,* 15s; some old Latin books, 3s; some old books, 6s. *RB 15, 488.*

Daniel Beacham, 10 Sept. 1798—parcel of books, 4s 6d. *RB 15, 504.*

William Pickren, 10 Sept. 1798—a parcel of books, 6s. *RB 15, 507.*

Jeadethan Haynie, 8 Oct. 1798—a parcel of books, 6s. *RB 15, 527.*

James McClanahan, 10 June 1799—one large *Bible,* 18s; parcel of books, 12s; parcel of books in closet, 6s. *RB 15, 600, 601.*

Bridgar Haynie, account of sales, 10 June 1799—a parcel of books sold to Capt. Thomas Downing, 9s; one sermon book sold to Bridgar Haynie, 2s; one old book sold to Thomas Downing, 1s 6d. *RB 15, 615.*

Samuel B. Self, 8 July 1799—one *Bible,* 4s. *RB 15, 618.*

Nicholas Brann, 9 Sept. 1799—parcel of books, 5s. *RB 16, 2.*

John Way, 14 Oct. 1799—a parcel of books, 8s. *RB 16, 11.*

William P. Garner, 15 Oct. 1799—parcel of books, £1 9s 3d. *RB 16, 17.*

Richard Walker, 9 Dec. 1799—a parcel of books, 12s. *RB 16, 30.*

Capt. Thomas Downing, 13 Jan. 1800—six volumes Hervey's works, £1 4s; a parcel of old books, 15s. *RB 16, 41.*

Elizabeth Garner, 10 Feb. 1800—*Bible,* 1s 6d. *RB 16, 63.*

William Webb, 10 Feb. 1800—parcel old books, 6s. *RB 16, 65.*

Sarah Downing, 14 April 1800—one large *Bible,* 12s; one large *Prayer Book,* 15s; parcel old books, 7s 6d. *RB 16, 78.*

Griffin Forester, 9 June 1800—a parcel of books, 8s. *RB 16, 115.*

Thomas Williams, 9 June 1800—one pair of flat irons and one *Bible,* 3s. *RB*

16, 116.

John Booth, 9 June 1800—a parcel of books, 6s. *RB 16, 132.*

Richard Morrison, 14 July 1800—a parcel of books, 6s. *RB 16, 144.*

Pryce Campbell, 14 July 1800—*Testament* and *Prayer Book*, 1s. *RB 16, 155.*

William Oldham, 9 Dec. 1800—two old books. *RB 16, 198.*

John Edwards, 9 Oct. 1801—some books, 3s. *RB 16, 223.*

Yarrott Hughlett, 13 April 1801—three books and two other books, 3s 6d. *RB 16, 231.*

John Lewis, 13 April 1801—parcel old books, 6s. *RB 16, 232.*

John Rogers, 8 June 1801—Henning's *Justice*, £1 4s; Morse's *Geography*, 18s; one large *Bible* and *Prayer Book*, 18s; parcel old books, 18s. *RB 16, 245.*

George Lamkin, 9 June 1801—parcel books, £1 4s. *RB 16, 266.*

Thomas James, 13 July 1801—parcel old books, 6d. *RB 16, 274.*

Richard S. Corbell, account of sales, 12 Oct. 1801—a parcel of old books sold to William H. Pickrell, 11s 6d. *RB 16, 286.*

Trussel Beacham, account of sales, 12 Oct. 1801—sundry old books sold to Thomas Beacham, 2s 3d. *RB 16, 291.*

Edwin Barns, 12 Oct. 1801—book case and books, 12s. *RB 16, 297.*

Thomas Harcum, 14 Dec. 1801—a parcel of books and one case, 12s. *RB 16, 305.*

Elisha Harcum, 8 Feb. 1802—one large *Bible* and *Testament*, £1 4s; Burkett on *Testament*, £2 5s; Bailey's *Dictionary*, 9s; two old books, 3s. *RB 16, 339.*

Leroy Edwards, 12 April 1802—a parcel of old books, 9s. *RB 16, 359.*

William Pitman, 14 June 1802—two volumes books to Mr. Norton, 4s; two volumes books to Thomas Taylor, 4s 8d; a parcel books to Burgess Pitman, 1s 9d; three books to Robert Forrester, 8s 9d; two books to William Davenport, 13s 10d; two books to Robert Forrester, 4s 3d; five old books to Henry Hazard, 3s. *RB 16, 387.*

Charles Brown, 14 June 1802—parcel old books, 1s 3d. *RB 16, 405.*

Jesse Dawkins, 12 July 1802—one pair of books, £1 16s. *RB 16, 422.*

Moses Taylor, account of sales, 12 July 1802—seven old books sold to Robert Crockett, 6s. *RB 16, 426.*

Eben Nelms, 11 Oct. 1802—parcel of books, 24s. *RB 16, 463.*

Maj. Catesby Jones, 11 Oct. 1802—four pamphlets. *RB 16, 468.*

George Phillips, account of sales, 11 Oct. 1802—a parcel of books sold to Henry Pullin, 3s; one book sold to William Phillips, 6s. *RB 16, 474.*

Loftis Jones, 13 Dec. 1802—one parcel of books, 18s. *RB 16, 485.*

Thomas Gaskins, 13 Dec. 1802—desk, book case, and books, £15. *RB 16, 499.*

Balaam George, 10 Jan. 1803—one large *Bible*, 3s; one *Bible* and three other books, 5s 6d. *RB 16, 512.*

Jesse Crowder, 11 April 1803—a parcel of books, 9s. *RB 16, 531.*

Capt. Robert Edwards, 12 April 1803—parcel books, 12s. *RB 16, 540.*

William T. Champion, 13 June 1803—a parcel of books, 12s. *RB 16, 554.*

Joseph Power, 13 June 1803—a parcel of old books, 12s. *RB 17, 5.*

William Eustace, 11 July 1803—a parcel of books, £3. *RB 17, 15.*

Moseley Nutt, 12 Sept. 1803—a parcel of old books, 30s. *RB 17, 42.*

Charles Lattimore, 12 Sept. 1803—parcel books, 30s. *RB 17, 45.*

George Edwards, 12 Sept. 1803—a parcel of old books, 3s 6d. *RB 17, 48.*

Mottrom Barecroft, 12 Dec. 1803—three books, 3s; a parcel of old books, 4d; a large *Bible*, 3s. *RB 17, 88.*

Charles Turner, 12 Dec. 1803—a parcel of books, £13 18s. *RB 17, 95.*

Henry Cundiff, 12 Dec. 1803—a parcel of books, 20s. *RB 17, 97.*

William Gaskins, 12 Dec. 1803—one *Bible* and *Prayer Book,* 6s. *RB 17, 100.*

Moses Sutton, account of sales, 10 Jan. 1804—one large *Bible* sold to John H. Fallin, 18s; a parcel of old books sold to Mrs. Catroun Sutton [in other documents her name is listed as Caty], widow, 1s 1 1/2d. *RB 17, 110.*

Richard Hudnall, account of sales, 9 April 1804—one large *Bible* sold to Nanny Hudnall, £1 10s 7d; sundry books on desk sold to Richard Hudnall, 13s. *RB 17, 150.*

Matthias Self, account of sales, 11 June 1804—a parcel of books, 3s 4d. *RB 17, 164.*

Cathran James, 11 June 1804—parcel of books and slate, 6s. *RB 17, 165.*

Dolly Christopher, account of sales, 11 June 1804—one comb and two books sold to Robert Christopher, 1s. *RB 17, 169.*

William Giddings, 9 July 1804—gun, looking glass, and parcel of books, 11s 6d. *RB 17, 185.*

Daniel Muse, 10 Sept. 1804—parcel books, 6s 6d. *RB 17, 200.*

John Hall, 8 Oct. 1804—one *Testament*, 1s; one small book, 1s. *RB 17, 216.*

Martin Haynie, 8 Oct. 1804—one *Bible, Hymn Book, Christian Patttern*, 9s; one large magazine, 9s; one pocket *Dictionary,* 6s; six other books, 18s; six old books, 4s 6d. *RB 17, 219.*

William Pooley, 8 April 1805—a parcel books, 10s. *RB 17, 269.*

Hannah Claughton, 8 July 1805—parcel old books, 6s. *RB 17, 294.*

George Ball, 9 Sept. 1805—one parcel of old books, 12s. *RB 17, 305.*

John Connally, 14 Oct. 1805—a parcel of old books, 1s. *RB 17, 337.*

Thomas Hurst, son to Henry, account of sales, 10 Feb. 1806—a parcel of old books sold to Thomas Hurst, Jr., 6d. *RB 17, 377.*

James C. Knott, 14 April 1806—parcel of books, 9s. *RB 17, 398.*

John Dawson, 14 April 1806—parcel of books, 6s. *RB 17, 399.*

William Waddey, 15 April 1806—a parcel of old books, £1 4s. *RB 17, 403.*

Nancy Claughton, 14 July 1806—a parcel of old books, 12s. *RB 17, 441.*

Richard Grinstead, 14 July 1806—parcel books, 34s. *RB 17, 445.*

Rawleigh Alexander, 14 July 1806—parcel old books, 6s. *RB 17, 447.*

Charles Fallin, 8 Sept. 1806—two books, 9s. *RB 17, 461.*

Thomas McClanahan, 13 Oct. 1806—parcel old books, tub, and casket, 9s. *RB 17, 468.*

John Allen, 14 Oct. 1806—five old books, 1s. *RB 17, 472.*

William Jones, 8 Dec. 1806—a parcel of books, 13s 6d. *RB 17, 487.*

Jesse Swanson, account of sales, 8 June 1807—two books and bell sold to George Haydon, 6s 6d. *RB 17, 530.*

William L. Kellum, 8 June 1807—parcel old books, 7s 6d. *RB 17, 534.*

William G. Langley, 8 June 1807—parcel old books, 3s. *RB 17, 537.*

Winder Kenner, account of sales, 9 June 1807—some books and desk, 9d. *RB 17, 544.*

Cyrus Harding, 9 June 1807—one large *Bible*, 36s; parcel books on desk, 30s. *RB 17, 545.*

John Flint, 12 Oct. 1807—six books, 12s. *RB 17, 581.*

Ann Allmond, account of sales, 11 Jan. 1808—a parcel of books sold to John McCave, 2s. *RB 17, 600.* [In Index to *Record Book*, the name is spelled Almond.]

William Wildy, 11 Jan. 1808—parcel old books, 18s. *RB 17, 603.*

Amos Nicken, 8 Feb. 1808—two old trunks and four old books, 2s. *RB 17, 610.*

William Garlington, account of sales, 13 June 1808—three books sold to Henry L. Gaskins, 8s 6d. *RB 17, 627.*

Mrs. Mary Lackey, 13 June 1808—a parcel of old books, 9s. *RB 17, 632.*

Onesiphorus Harvey, 11 July 1808—a parcel of books on new desk, £3; a parcel of books on old desk, 6s. *RB 18, 4.*

Thomas Hudnall, 11 July 1808—parcel old books, 10s; three books and one jug [no price given]. *RB 18, 12, 13.*

William Blundon, 9 Jan. 1809—one *Bible* and *Hymn Book*, 6s. *RB 18, 90.*

Miss Ann H. Leland, 7 Jan. 1809—a parcel of books, £2 7s 6d. *RB 18, 91*.
Philip Tignor, 13 Feb. 1809—a parcel old books, 4s. *RB 18, 103*.
Betty Downing, account of sales, 13 Feb. 1809—one book Burkett sold to Col. Thomas Downing, 16s 6d; one *Great Bible* sold to Col. Thomas Downing, 3s 6d; parcel books sold to William Fallin, 10s 10d. *RB 18, 105*.
Richard Ball, 10 April 1809—one trunk of books sold to William Hudnall, $4.17. *RB 18, 135*.
William R. Bean, 8 May 1809—one razor and books, 7s 10d. *RB 18, 146*.
George Bean, 8 May 1809—a parcel of books, 3s 6d. *RB 18, 147*.
Gideon Marsh, account of sales, 10 July 1809—one lot of books sold to James Haynie, 6d. *RB 18, 190*.
Shapleigh Waddy, 11 Sept. 1809—one large *Bible*, one pocket *Dictionary*, 6s 6d; six old books, 1s. *RB 18, 218*.
John Miller, Jr., 14 Nov. 1809—Bailey's *Dictionary*, $2; Walker's *Abridged Dictionary*, $1; Pinkerton's *Geography and Atlas*, two volumes, $15; Morse's *Geography and Atlas*, two volumes, $4; Brookes's *Gazeteer*, $3.50; Moore's *Navigation*, $1; Ferguson's *Astronomy*, $1; Gibson's *Surveying*, $1; Harres's *Hermes*, $1; Blair's *Lectures*, three volumes, $4; Kaimes's *Elements Criticism*, two volumes, $2; Rollin's *Ancient History*, ten volumes, $7.50; Raynal's *History*, five volumes, $3; Sydney on *Government*, two volumes, $4; *Constitutions of U. States*, $4; *The Federalist*, two volumes, $4; *Public Carecter* [?], $2; *Virginia Debates*, $2.50; Monroe's *View of the Executive*, $2.75; Bacheton's *Commentaries*, four volumes, $6.75; Bacon's *Abridgment*, six volumes, $27; Reeves's *History of the English Law*, four volumes, $3; Powel on *Contracts and Mortgages*, two volumes, $2; Powel on *Contracts*, $2; Powel on *Mortgages*, $2; Fonblanque's *Equity*, two volumes, $4; Harrison's *Chancery Practice*, two volumes, $2; Fearries on *Ramainders*, two volumes, $4; Kydon on *Bills of Exchange*, $1; Gilbert's *Evidence*, four bound in two, $5; *Peer William Report*, three volumes, $7.50; Call's *Reports*, three volumes, $9; Washington's *Reports*, two volumes, $2; Henning's and Munford's *Reports in Boards*, two volumes, $1; Onslow's *Nin* [?] *Prices*, $1; Espensasses *Prices*, $1; Impeg's *Practice*, $1; Jacob's *Attorney's Practice*, $1; Fitzherbert's *Natura Breveum*, $1; *Revisions of the Laws in 1769*, $4; *Virginia Laws Abridged 1737*, $4.50; Hale's *Summary of Crown Law*, $1; *Acts 3rd Session of 5th Congress*, $1; *Acts 1 Session of 6 Congress*, $1.75; *Revision of Laws* [no price given], Jacob's *Law Dictionary*, $8; *Spectator*, eight volumes, $6.50; *Citizen of the World*, two volumes, $1.70; *Dramatic Works of Shakespeare*, eight volumes, $10; *Paradise Lost*, $1; Thompson's *Seasons*, $1.75; *Terrible Tractoration* [?], $1.75; Moore's *Utopia*, $1.62 1/2; Rennell's

Letters, $1.75; Aken's *Letters*, $1.75; *Letters of* [?], $1.50; Cornaro on *Health*, $1.50; *Beggar Girl* a novel, three volumes, $2; *The Monk* a novel, two volumes, $1.50; *What Has Been* a novel 2 in, $1.75; *Female Review*, $1.75; Ossian's *Poems*, four volumes bound in two volumes, $2; *Literary Leisure*, two volumes [no price given], *Jefferson's Manual*, $2.75; Lemoine's *Art of Speaking*, $2.50; *Life of Cromwell*, $2.62 1/2; Wall's *Latin Grammar*, $2.25; Francis's *Horrace* [*Horace*?], four volumes, $2; six copies *Road to Honour*, six volumes, $2.36; Ash's *Introduction to Lowth's Grammar*, $2.25; *Acts of Assembly 1803 and 1805*, two volumes, $2.50; *Catalogue of Pictures in the Shakespeare's Gallery* a pamphlet, $2.25; *President's Message Concerning Burr's Conspiracy* a pamphlet, $2.06; *Burr's Examination before the Chief Justice* a pamphlet, $2.12 1/2; *Beauties of Shakespeare*, $2.50; *Journals of the Two Houses of Assembly*, two volumes, $2.50; *The Senator of Parliamentary Croncile* [*Chronicle*?], $2.50; *Rights of Man* by T. [Thomas] Paine, $2.12 1/2; *Parliamentary Debates During the Years 1774 and 1775*, pamphlets, ten volumes, $2.75; Goldsmith's *Animated Nature*, four volumes, $6. *RB 18, 257–259.*

Joseph Ball, 8 Jan. 1810—sixteen books at $8. *RB 18, 272.*

George Slacum, 12 Feb. 1810—one old ciphering book, three old books. *RB 18, 323.*

Susanna Pitman, 12 Feb. 1810—a parcel of books, $2. *RB 18, 332.*

Samuel L. Beacham, 12 March 1810—one *Dictionary*, *Every Man's Own Lawyer*, 11s; *Letters on Iceland, Arts and Science*, 12s; Knox's *Sermons*, a parcel of old books, £1 10s. *RB 18, 341.*

Willoughby N. Berryman, 14 March 1810—one large *Bible*, $8; a parcel of books, $1. *RB 18, 356.*

William T. Champion, account of sales, 14 May 1810—parcel of books sold to Henry Hurst, 6s 6d. *RB 18, 384.*

Richard Tropp [spelled Throp in Index to *Record Book*], 14 May 1810—seven old books, case razors, ink stand, and shaving box, 4s 6d. *RB 18, 388.*

Rev. Duncan McNaughton, 15 May 1810—ten volumes *Encyclopedia*, $50; *Biographical Dictionary*, $1.25; Hume's *Plays*, $1.75; *Encyclopedia* and *Festival of Wit*, $2; Swift's works, $24; Ferguson's *Poems*, $1.50; Clerk's *Sermons*, $1.50; Tillotson's works, $2; Sharp's *Sermons*, $2.50; McMillin Stiles, $1; *Form of Writing*, $1; Montague's *Letters*, $1; Sheridan's *Lectures*, 75¢; Newton on *Prophecies*, $3; *Spectator*, eight volumes, $8; Devid [?], 50¢; Knoxe's *Essays*, $2; Talbert's works, 50¢; McEwin on *Tipes* [?], 50¢; *Dialogue*, 50¢; Gee on *Trade*, 75¢; Belfore on *Morality*, 75¢; *Gilblass* [?], four volumes, $3; *Spy and le Herwriter* [?],

75¢; Lucas's *Sermons*, 75¢; Fisher's *Poems*, 50¢; *Pronunciation of Grammar*, 75¢; Paley's *Philosophy*, 75¢; Junius's *Letters*, $3; *Taler* [*Tatler*?], $1.25; *Philosophical Reflections*, 75¢; Miss William's *Letters*, 50¢; *English Grammar*, $3; *Dundee Magazine*, 50¢; Stern's works, $2; *History of the World*, 50¢; *Pheonex*, 50¢; Scott's *Duty*, $1; Abernitha's *Sermons*, $1; Knight's *Thoughts*, 37 1/2¢; Pott's *Observations*, 50¢; Hume's *Essays*, $2; Carven's *Travels*, $1.25; Percey's *Sermons*, $2; *Gallic Bible*, $1; Spratt's works, $1; Hall's *Contemplation*, $4; Lovelasse's [Lovelace?] *Tracts*, 75¢; Berrk's [?] *Reflections*, $1; Prince's *Observations*, 50¢; Freeholder, 50¢; Cummin's *Sermons*, 50¢; Knip's *Lectures*, 50¢; Fuller's *Sisteru*, $1; Gregory on *Nature*, $2.50; *Ladies' Friend*, $1; Hume's *Dialogue*, $1.50; Paley's *Philosophy*, $2; *American Gazeture*, $1.25; *Universal Geography*, $6; Priestly's *Pamphlets*, $1.50; Sheridan's *Dictionary*, $4; Hayley's *Life of Cooper*, $1.50; *Chemistry*, four volumes, $5; *History of Woman*, $2.50; *History of Man*, $2.50; four volumes on medicine, $4; Adkinson's *Sermons*, $1.25; Peter Pinder [Pindar], $1.50; *Survey of Human Understanding*, $1; *Revised Code and Henning's Justice*, $8; seven volumes of novels assorted, $1.50; sundry old books assorted, $8. RB 18, 400, 401.

Samuel L. Beacham, account of sales, 15 Aug. 1810—one floor brush and two volumes Morres's *Geography*, £1 10s; four volumes *Laws U* [*United*] *States*, Knoxe's *Sermons*, 18s 6d; *History of Virginia, Iceland*, 6s 10d; three volumes *Notes on the New Testament, Dictionary*, 13s; a parcel old books, 12s. RB 18, 456.

Richard Ball, 10 Sept. 1810—one large F. [Folio] *Bible*, £2 8s; one parcel of old books, £2 8s. RB 18, 461.

William Sanford, 12 Nov. 1810—one case and some old books, 12 1/2¢. RB 18, 491.

Edward Marsh, 14 Jan. 1811—reading books, 12s. RB 18, 503.

Richard Coles, 10 June 1811—one large *Bible* and five small books, £1 10s. RB 19, 61.

John Fulks, 9 Sept. 1811—one *Bible*, 6s. RB 19, 95.

James Thomas, 14 Oct. 1811—parcel of books, 4s. RB 19, 103.

William Allen, 9 Dec. 1811—one small chest of drawers and some old books, 42¢. RB 19, 136.

Ann Hudnall, account of sales, 9 March 1812—Sheridan's *Dictionary*, two volumes, sold to Henry L. Gaskins, $2; one family *Bible* sold to Thomas Hudnall, $9.65; one lot small books sold to William Lattimore, 25¢. RB 19, 171.

George Slacum, 12 May 1812—a parcel of books, 25¢. RB 19, 184.

Edwin Gaskins, 8 June 1812—a parcel of old books, 25¢. RB 19, 205.

Charles Dodson, 8 June 1812—one large *Bible*, 6s; one *Prayer Book*, 3s. RB

19, 209.

William Morrison, 13 July 1812—one *Bible,* parcel of other old books, and a candle stick, 25¢. *RB 19, 228.*

Mrs. Elizabeth Hughlett, account of sales, 12 Oct. 1812—parcel old books sold to George Edwards, 6¢. *RB 19, 251.*

Ezekiel Haydon, 12 Oct. 1812—one book, 67¢; parcel of old books, $1. *RB 19, 253.*

William Claughton, 12 Oct. 1812—Cook's *Voyages,* $8; *Secret Memoirs,* $1.50; Baccaria on *Crimes,* $1; Salmon's *Grammar,* $1; *Civil Liberty,* $1.75; Smith's *Wealth of Nations,* $2; Martin's *Law of Nations,* $1.25; *Conductor General,* $1; Guthrie's *Grammar,* $2; Locke on *Government,* $1.50; Wilberforce's *View,* $1.50; Pattle's *Law of Nations,* $3; Paine's *Rights of Man,* 50¢; *Elegant Extracts,* 75¢; four volumes of Blackstone, $6.50; *History of America,* four volumes, $8; Montesque's [Montesquieu?] *Spirit of Law,* $2.50; Jefferson's *Virginia,* $2; Morse's *Geography,* $4; a parcel of books and pamphlets, $1; Henning's *Justice,* $2.50. *RB 19, 267.*

Thomas Bearcroft, 14 Dec. 1812—a parcel of old books, $1. *RB 19, 278.*

George McAdam Brown, 17 Nov. 1812—five volumes of Swift's works, broken set; Voltaire's *History of the War of 1741,* complete; Sterne's works, two volumes, broken set; Rolling's *History in French,* four volumes, incomplete; Addison on *Medals, Lay Monastery;* Walter's *Poems,* complete; *Chinese Spy,* fifth volume, incomplete; Phenstone's works, second volume, incomplete; Young's *Night Thoughts,* one volume, complete; Dryden's *Fable,* second volume, incomplete; *The Tatler,* second volume, incomplete; *Tom Jones,* three volumes, incomplete; *History of English Civil Wars,* one volume, incomplete; *Diseases of Women,* one volume, incomplete; Kersley's *Travels,* four volumes, complete; *Weekly Magazine,* twelfth volume, incomplete; *Practice of Physic,* two volumes, complete; *Merchant's Magazine,* one volume, complete; *Fairery,* one volume, complete; *Turkish Spy,* second volume, incomplete; *Institutions of Scottish Law,* one volume, complete; Euclid's *Elements,* one volume, complete; *Sir Charles Grandison,* six volumes, incomplete; Palomon's *Creed,* two volumes, complete; Hill's *Arithmetic,* one volume, complete; *The Guardian,* one volume, incomplete; *Legal Form Book* (without a Name); *Interest Calculations,* one volume, complete; Quincy's *Dispensatory,* one volume, complete; Ferguson's *Astronomy,* one volume, complete; *The Moral Philosopher,* two volumes, incomplete; *Elements of Criticism,* three volumes, complete; *The World,* two volumes, incomplete; Willmott's *Devotion,* one volume, incomplete; *Natural Philosophy,* one volume, complete; *Religious Philosopher,* one volume, incomplete; *Wisdom of God,* one volume, complete; *Method of Studying Divinity,* one volume, complete; *Body of Divinity* by Ridgley, one volume, complete; *Universal Dictionary,* one volume, complete; Cruden's *Concordance,* one volume, complete; *Virginia Gazette from August 1736 to July 1740* bound in one volume and *History of England During the Reigns of the House of Stuart,* one volume, complete; *History of the Reign of Wm. and Mary,* one volume, complete; *Common Prayer,* one volume, complete; *Port Folio,* first volume; *Virtue and Happiness,* one volume, complete; *Poems by Eminent Ladies,* one volume, incomplete; Tully's *Offices,* one volume, complete; *Treatise on the Veneral Disease,* one volume; *Roman Antiquities,* one volume, complete; Plutarch's *Morals,* one volume, incomplete; *Musical Miscellany,* one volume, incomplete; *Confession of Faith,* one volume, complete; *Reality of Knowledge,* one volume, incomplete; *History of Jamaica,* one volume, complete; *Gentleman's Calling,* one volume, complete; *English State Papers,* one volume, complete; *Present State of Britain 1755,* one volume, complete; *Mercantile Penmanship,* one volume, complete; *Treatise on Hawking, Fowling, Fishing etc.,* one volume; *Spelling Book,* one volume; Gay's *Fables,* one volume; five old books much defaced; *History of Justin,* one volume; *Agricultural Enquiries,* one volume, by Judge Peters, thirty volumes Latin and French books mostly calculated for the use of schools; twelve volumes Greek and Hebrew books. RB 19, 318–320.

Mosely Nutt's estate examined and settled by Richard Nutt, 8 March 1813—one *Latin Grammar* for Walter, 3s. RB 19, Part 2, 344.

George P. Waddy, 8 March 1813—one lot of old books, 4s 6d. RB 19, Part 2, 352.

John Clutton, 12 April 1813—one lot old books, $1.50. RB 19, Part 2, 366.

Bartholomew Dameron, 12 April 1813—parcel of books, 10s. RB 19, Part 2, 370.

Elizabeth Pinckard, 10 May 1813—a parcel of books, 1s 6d. RB 19, Part 2, 384.

Hopkins Harding, 14 June 1813—nine volumes Wesley's *Sermons,* $9; balance of library, $50. RB 19, Part 2, 392.

William George, 14 June 1813—one old *Bible* and *Testament,* $15.25. RB 19, Part 2, 393.

Ann Hudnall, 14 June 1813—two books, 50¢. RB 19, Part 2, 394.

Gideon Marsh, 14 June 1813—one lot of books, 75¢. RB 19, Part 2, 407.

William Headley, 14 June 1813—five old books, 20¢. RB 19, Part 2, 409.

Charles Rice, account of sales, 9 Aug. 1813—three books sold to John Dotton, $1.06. RB 19, Part 2, 428.

Thomas Harcum, 9 Aug. 1813—one *Bible*, 75¢. *RB 19, Part 2, 431.*

Charles Rice, Jr., 14 Feb. 1814—one slate and seven books, $1.25. *RB 19, Part 2, 472.*

William Angell, account of sales, 14 Feb. 1814—one *Bible* sold to Roger W. Hughlett, 51¢. *RB 19, Part 2, 478.*

John Cralle, account of sales, 14 Feb. 1814—parcel of old books sold to Samuel McCurdy, $4. *RB 19, Part 2, 486.*

Thomas Miller, account of sales, 14 March 1814—one *Dictionary* sold to Richard Edwards, $1.15; second and third volumes *Moral Philosopher* sold to Thomas Lansdell, 50¢; Ferguson's *Astronomy* sold to William Gordon, 50¢; *Disease of Woman* sold to Mottrom Ball, 25¢; F [folio] volume Farrar [?] sold to John H. Hughlett, 50¢; Euclid's *Elements* sold to Mottrom Ball, 50¢; Pallmon's and *Medical Dispensatory* sold to William Gordon, 20¢; parcel of old books sold to William Gordon, 50¢. *RB 19, Part 2, 514.*

George Cookman, 14 March 1814—parcel of old books, 50¢. *RB 19, Part 2, 532.*

Leroy Pullin, 11 April 1814—a parcel of books, 14s. *RB 19, Part 2, 538.*

Edwin Conway, 9 May 1814—two *Bibles*, 25¢. *RB 19, Part 2, 544.*

Judith Doggett, 11 July 1814—four old books, 50¢. *RB 19, Part 2, 557.*

Stephen Haynie, 11 July 1814—parcel of books, $7. *RB 19, Part 2, 562.*

Edwin Nelms, 12 Dec. 1814—a parcel of books (eighteen volumes), $4. *RB 19, Part 2, 568.*

Edwin Gaskins, account of sales, 9 Jan. 1815—parcel of old books sold to Robert D. Palmer, 25¢. *RB 19, Part 2, 582.*

Joseph Palmer, 9 Jan. 1815—one *Bible* and a lot of old books, $2. *RB 19, Part 2, 598.*

Samuel Low, 9 Jan. 1815—seven old books, $1. *RB 19, Part 2, 600.*

William Wornom, 13 Feb. 1815—eight books, $3; one book, etc., 25¢. *RB 19, Part 2, 610.*

Thomas Ingram, account of sales, 13 Feb. 1815—one large family *Bible* sold to Warner Hudnall, $6.25; one lot of books of sundry sorts sold to Thomas Ball, 50¢. *RB 19, Part 2, 616.*

George Connoley [in Index to *Record Book*, the name is spelled Conolly], 13 Feb. 1815—a parcel of books, $1. *RB 20, 2.*

Mary Conoly [in Index to *Record Book*, the name is spelled Conolly], 13 March 1815—one parcel books, 50¢. *RB 20, 5.*

Shapleigh N. Waddy, account of sales, 13 March 1815—a parcel of old books sold to John Hurst, $1. *RB 20, 20*.

David Ball, 14 March 1815—one *Bible, Prayer* [*Prayer Book*?] and *Hymn Book*, $3; one lot of books, $3. *RB 20, 27*.

Lewis Efford, 14 March 1815—parcel books, 50¢. *RB 20, 30*.

John Cralle, 11 April 1815—a parcel of old books, $2. *RB 20, 61*.

Maj. John Hull, 8 May 1815—one book case and books, $15. *RB 20, 104*.

Jeduthen Moore, 8 May 1815—parcel books, 83¢. *RB 20, 109*.

James Harcum, 8 May 1815—twenty-one books and two old saddles, $4.50. *RB 20, 120*.

Isaac Rice, account of sales, 8 May 1815—one *Bible* and *Testament* sold to Betty George, 37 1/2¢; parcel old books sold to Milley Rice, $1.75. *RB 20, 126*.

Sanford Lowe, 12 June 1815—parcel of old books. *RB 20, 143*.

Jesse Walker, 12 June 1815—old books, $1.25. *RB 20, 150*.

Peter Wilkins, 14 Aug. 1815—a parcel of old books and slate, $1. *RB 20, 167*.

Samuel McCurdy, 14 Aug. 1815—parcel old books. *RB 20, 182*.

Col. James Moore, 15 Aug. 1815—one large *Bible* and lot of old books No. 1, $2.50; lot of books No. 2 and old backgammon box, $2. *RB 20, 196*.

James Forrester, 11 Sept. 1815—six books, 9s. *RB 20, 211*.

Edward Henry, 11 Sept. 1815—three volumes Gill on the *Bible*, $15; two *Bibles* and two *Hymn Books*, $5. *RB 20, 214*.

William Treakle, 11 Sept. 1815—eight books, $1.25. *RB 20, 219*.

Roger W. Hughlett, 11 Sept. 1815—one *Bible* and three old books, $2; three volumes of Cook's *Voyages*, $3; Morse's *Geography*, $1.25; parcel books, 25¢. *RB 20, 224*.

Mrs. Sarah Moore, 9 Oct. 1815—large *Bible* and *Prayer Book*, $4; *Compleat Body of Husbandry, Elegant Extracts*, $3; a lot of old books, $1. *RB 20, 257*. [The word *Husbandry* determined by looking at account of sales on page 262.]

Samuel Blundon, 9 Oct. 1815—a parcel of old books, $3. *RB 20, 278*.

Thomas Littrell, account of sales, 9 Oct. 1815—parcel of books sold to John Hall, 75¢. *RB 20, 283*.

Eli Gill, 13 Nov. 1815—one lamp and three books, $1. *RB 20, 297*.

Caleb Bedmon, 13 Nov. 1815—Pinkertson's *Geography*, two volumes and a chart, $4; Fletcher's *Appeal*, 50¢. *RB 20, 308*.

James Williams, 11 Dec. 1815—four books and case bottles, $1.87. *RB 20, 312*.

William Moon, 11 Dec. 1815—ten old books, coffee mill, pair shoe brushes, and candle stick, $1. *RB 20, 315*.

William Rains, 8 Jan. 1816—four old books, 25¢. *RB 20, 332.*
Robert Clarke, 12 Feb. 1816—two books. *RB 20, 356.*

Richard Edwards, 11 March 1816—*The Jewish Spy*, five volumes, $5; *The Turkish Spy*, $6; *The Spectator*, eight volumes (first and third volumes wanted), $6; Rollin's *Ancient History*, ten volumes (four, six, and seven volumes wanted), $4; Swift's works, eleven volumes, $5.50; Rollin's *Belles Letters*, four volumes, $2; Thompson's works, four volumes (third wanted), $2.25; Homer's *Iliad*, six volumes, $3; Addison's miscellaneous works, three volumes, $1.50; *Travels of Zoroaster*, three volumes, 75¢; *Forensic Eloquence, Geographical, Grammar*, and *Constitution of the U S*, 50¢; *New Testament* and *English Dictionary*, 75¢; Cook's *Gardening*, old almanacks and pamphlets, 12 1/2¢; *Laws of Virginia under Kings*, 12¢; *Tour Through Britain*, four volumes (first volume wanted), $1.50; Locke's *Essay on Human Understanding*, three volumes, $2.25. *RB 20, 371.*

William Coles, Jr., 11 March 1816—ten old books, $1. *RB 20, 383.*

William Harcum, account of sales, 11 March 1816—one family *Bible* and a lot of old books sold to Edward Humphlet, $1.60. *RB 20, 393.*

John Eustice [in Index to *Record Book*, the name is spelled Eustace], 11 March 1816—one *Bible*, $1; Ewell's *Medical Companion*, $2; *Cares in Equity*, $2.26; Murery's [?] *Dictionary*, $2.75. *RB 20, 399.*

John Rice, Sr., account of sales, 8 April 1816—a parcel of old books sold to Richard Headley, $3.20. *RB 20, 417.*

William Mitchell, 8 April 1816—a parcel of old books, $2. *RB 20, 421.*
Joseph Conway, 8 April 1816—books, $575.50. *RB 20, 436.*
Richard Waide, 14 May 1816—one chest, box, and books, $1. *RB 20, 480.*

John Cockarill, 10 June 1816—five *Bibles*, $3.75; three *Testaments*, 75¢; four books, Simpson's *Plea*, $4.50; three books, Simpson's *Plea*, smaller, $2.62; two *Columbian Orators*, $2.62; one *Scotch Lessons*, 87 1/2¢; two blank books, 50¢; three small histories, 37 1/2¢; one small *Hymn Book*, 37 1/2¢. *RB 20, 492.*

Charles Leland, 10 June 1816—one book case and books, $150. *RB 20, 525.*
Ewell Webb, 8 July 1816—parcel of books, $2. *RB 21, 35.*
Thomas Ashburn, 12 Aug. 1816—parcel old books, 25¢. *RB 21, 45.*
Robert Edwards, 14 Oct. 1816—ten old books, 50¢. *RB 21, 90.*
Frances Vanlandingham, 14 Oct. 1816—parcel of books, $1.50. *RB 21, 95.*

David Ball, 11 Nov. 1816—*Circle of Science*, $1; *Ecclesiastical History*, four volumes, $2; Westly's *Philosophy*, five volumes, $3; *Washington's History* by Marshall, five volumes, $20; Westly's *Notes*, two volumes, $2; Fletcher's *Appeal*, two volumes, 75¢; Fletcher's *Life*, one volume, 75¢; Westly's *Life*, 75¢; Henning's

Justice, $1.50; Westly's *Everlasting Rest*, $1.75; Law's *Serious* [?] by Westly; *Euclid's Elements* by Simpson, $1.50; Buckan's *Philosophy*, $1.50; *Immortal Mentor*, 75¢; Walker's *Dictionary*, $1.50; Baily's *Dictionary*, $1.50; *Haminan* [?] *Magazine*, 50¢; Simpson's *Plea*, $1.50; *Historical Compend* by Whipley, $1; two *Bibles*, $8; *Holy War* by John Bunyan, $8.75; *Arts and Sciences*, $8.75; *Vicker of Wakefield*, $8.25; *Practical Piety*, $11.50; *Modern Geography*, $11.75; *Portraiture of Methodism*, $11.75; *Portrait of St. Paul*, $11.75; *Mentoria or the Young Ladies' Friend*, $1.50; *Primitive Physick*, 25¢; lot of old books, $2. RB 21, 103, 104.

William Corbell, 9 Dec. 1816—one lot of books, $1. RB 21, 117.

Haynie Wilkins, 13 June 1817—ten old books, 50¢. RB 21, 130.

John McCave, account of sales, 10 March 1816—a lot of books sold to Elisha Fallin, 51¢. RB 21, 149.

Benjamin Lansdell, account of sales, 14 July 1817—five books sold to Thomas Hughlett, $2. RB 21, 200.

Dr. Walter Jones, 14 July 1817—the library of books, $350. RB 21, 217.

John Lewis, account of sales, 8 Sept. 1817—parcel of books and case sold to John C. Straughan, $1. RB 21, 231.

Miss Winefred Webb, 8 Sept. 1817—one large *Bible*, $8. RB 21, 235.

Col. Thomas D. Downing, 8 Sept. 1817—Howard's *Encyclopedia*, $30; all the other books, $55.50. RB 21, 251.

Winnifred Hurst, 13 Oct. 1817—one large family *Bible*, $5; parcel of old books, $1. RB 21, 262.

William Ball, 11 Nov. 1817—eight volumes of Swift's works, $2.50; a parcel of old *Acts of Assembly*, $2.50; a lot of old books, $2; one lot of old books, $1. RB 21, 288.

Walter Anderson, 12 Jan. 1818—one book, Brook's *Gazetteer*, $1.50; one *Dictionary* and *Prayer Book*, $2; twelve old books, $1.75. RB 21, 318.

William Blackerby, account of sales, 12 Jan. 1818—one Bailey's *Dictionary* sold to John Ingram, $1.30; one large *Bible* sold to Isaac Hurst, $3.80. RB 21, 335.

Thomas Ball, account of sales, 9 March 1818—two old books sold to Isaac Hurst, 31¢; one *Dictionary* and *Gazetteer* sold to Kilkiah Ball, 77¢; *Surveying Book* sold to H. L. Gaskins, $1.36. RB 21, 374.

Peter Carter, 9 March 1818—one lot of old books, $1.50. RB 21, 378.

William Claughton, account of sales, 13 April 1818—four volumes of Cook's *Voyage* sold to Samuel Blackwell, $6.25; one volume of *Secret of Memories* sold to Samuel Blackwell, $1; Baccanil's on *Crimes* sold to Thomas Towles, 87 1/2¢; Salmon's *Grammar* sold to John C. Straughan, 50¢; Swift's *Wealth of*

Nations sold to John Middleton, $1; Martin's *Law of Nations* sold to Col. Thomas D. Downing, $1.75; *Conductors G* sold to Izates Anderson, 50¢; Guthrie's *Grammar* sold to William Middleton, $3; Locke on *Government* sold to Thomas F. Downing, $1.50; Wilberford's *View* sold to John Middleton, $1; Vollet [Voltaire's?] *Law of Nations* sold to Thomas F. Downing, $2.25; Paine's *Rights of Man* sold to Corbin Baker, 80¢; *Elegant Extracts* sold to Thomas D. Downing, $1.50; four volumes of Blackstone's sold to Thomas Towles, $4; four volumes of *The History of America* sold to Thomas F. Downing, $7; Montesquieu's *Spirit Law* sold to Thomas Towles, $1.80; *Jefferson's Virginia* sold to Thomas F. Downing, $2; two volumes Moore's *Universal Geography* sold to Corbin Baker, $3.75; parcel of books and pamphlets sold to Samuel H. Garner, $1.25; three volumes of *Virginia Laws* sold to Samuel Garner, 90¢; Henning's *Justices* sold to Benjamin Turner, $2.60. *RB 21, 402, 403.*

Charles Leland, 8 June 1818—one *Spelling Book* and one *Primer*, 31¢; one *Dictionary*, $1.25; one small Murray's *Grammar*, 33 1/2¢. *RB 21, 431.*

Sarah Rice, 10 Aug. 1818—parcel of books, 12 1/2¢. *RB 21, 467.*

John Davis, 14 Sept. 1818—parcel of old books, $1. *RB 21, 481.*

Thomas Hurst, 14 Sept. 1818—two volumes Morse's *Geography*, $3; Bailey's *Dictionary*, $1.50; Buckan's *Physic*, $1.50; Ruterford's *Letters*, 50¢; eight volumes Shakespeare's works, $2.50; four volumes *Farces*, $1; *Roderick Random [The Adventures of Roderick Random]*, 50¢; *State Trials*, 50¢; eight volumes *Spectators*, $2; *Beauties of Spectator*, 33 1/2¢; *Ready Recknor*, 25¢; two volumes *Present Age*, 25¢; *Life of Franklin*, 25¢; Washington's *Letters*, 25¢; second volume Cook's *Voyages*, 50¢; *History of America*, $1; two volumes Rollin's *History*, 25¢; one *Pilgrim's Progress*, 33¢; Ovild [Ovid?], a Latin book, 50¢; one lot books, $1; one large *Bible*, $8; one small lot books, 50¢. *RB 21, 495, 496.*

Charles Marsh, 12 Oct. 1818—old books. *RB 21, 509.*

Robert Christopher, 9 Nov. 1818—parcel of old books, $1. *RB 21, 535.*

Stephen Haynie, 14 Dec. 1818—one old *Bible*, 12 1/2¢. *RB 21, 566.*

Peter C. Rice, 8 Feb. 1819—Nicholson's *Encyclopedia*, bound, six volumes, $25; *The Naval Monument*, $2; *Dictionary of the Bible*, $2; Warden's *Letters*, 75¢; *Vicar of Wakefield*, 75¢; various other novels, $3. *RB 21, 587.* [The following books are listed in the account of sales of Peter C. Rice, but are not listed in the inventory and appraisement: *Life of P [Patrick] Henry* sold to Griffin H. Foushee, $2.75; Washington's *Letters*, two volumes, sold to Willis W. Hudnall, $1.25; *Life of Marion* sold to Willis W. Hudnall, 25¢; *Sacred Mirror* sold to Samuel Straughan, 50¢; Smith's *View of the Late War*, two volumes, sold to Willis W. Hudnall, 25¢;

Johnson's *Dictionary*, two volumes, sold to Thomas Bell, 60¢; Mosese's [?] *Universal Gro:* [?], two volumes, sold to Samuel Straughan, $2.10; Paine's *Rights of Man* sold to Samuel Straughan, 50¢; *President Com. to Congress* sold to Archibald Dodson, 16¢; *Reign of Grace* sold to Samuel S. Straughan, 50¢; *Self Knowledge* sold to Samuel S. Straughan, 35¢; *Uncle Thomas*, two volumes, sold to Richard Claughton, 25¢; Fraser on *Sanctuary Caveris of Death* and Heck's *Farces* sold to William Way, 60¢; balance of the books sold to Samuel S. Straughan, $1. RB 21, 590, 591.]

Pemberton Claughton, 8 March 1819—one parcel old books, $1. RB 22, 17.

Thomas McClanahan, account of sales, 8 March 1819—a parcel of old books sold to Alexander Rock, 1s 8d. RB 22, 19.

William Wildy, account of sales, 10 May 1819—two books sold to Sarah Wildy, 12 1/2¢. RB 22, 34.

Ellis Edwards, 14 June 1819—ten old books, $1.50. RB 22, 57.

John Bryan, 9 Aug. 1819—parcel books, $2.50. RB 22, 93.

Richard Littrell, 13 Sept. 1819—parcel of old books, 6s 6d. RB 22, 114.

Richard Routt, account of sales, 13 Sept. 1819—a parcel of very old books sold to William Ashburn, 12 1/2¢. RB 22, 118.

Betsy Welch, account of sales, 13 Sept. 1819—three old books sold to Sally Haynie, 50¢. RB 22, 122.

Samuel G. Barnes, 13 Sept. 1819—parcel books, $1.50. RB 22, 124.

William Barnes, account of sales, 13 Dec. 1819—three old books sold to Griffin Lamkin, 40¢. RB 22, 169.

Henry Lee Gaskins, 13 Dec. 1819—one large *Bible*, $1.50; *History of Greece*, 50¢; *History of Greece*, 49¢; eight *History of Rome*, 40¢; two *Polite Learning*, 40¢; one *Polite Learning*, 40¢; three *Polite Learning*, 30¢; one *Psalter*, 17¢; seven *Psalters*, 15¢; two *American Nepos*, 49¢; Goldsmith's *Rome*, 50¢; five *History of Rome*, 37 1/2¢; one Boston's *Fourfold State*, 62 1/2¢; one *Dictionary*, 75¢; one *Dictionary*, 50¢; four *Dictionaries*, Murray's *Grammar and Exercises*, $1.25; one *English Reader*, 37 1/2¢; one abridgment Murray's *Grammar*, six abridgments Murray's *Grammar*, 12 1/2¢; eight volumes Hume's *History of England*, 76¢; Buchan's *Domestic Medicine*, $1; five volumes *Life of Washington*, $16; two volumes Morse's *Geography*, $2.30; Brooks's *Gazetteer*, $1; two Sheridan's *Dictionary*, 50¢; Henning's *Justice*, $1.75; Sampson's *Euclid*, 37 1/2¢; Horace's *Poems*, two *Hebrew Antiquity*, 12¢; two *Swift's Life*, 35¢; Mentagar's *Reflections*, 31¢; Goldsmith's *Greece*, 25¢; *Columbian Orator*, 25¢; Preston's *Masonry*, 55¢; Buchanan's *Researches*, 49¢; one volume Goldsmith's *England*, 55¢; Lee's *Mem-*

oirs, 25¢; four Boling Brooke's works, 52¢; eight *Spectators*, 45¢; two *French Lovers*, 25¢; three old books, 25¢; six old books, 25¢; five old books, 20¢; eight volumes Stern's works, 56¢; four *Gil Blas* [a novel by the French writer Alain Rene Lesage], 50¢; four *Scottish Chiefs*, 25¢; two books for 25¢; one volume Junius's *Letters*, 40¢; four old books and two new, 25¢; one song book, 15¢; two volumes *Roderick Random* [*The Adventures of Roderick Random* by Smollett] [no price given]; twelve books various sorts, 40¢. RB 22, 185–187.

George Barrett, account of sales, 14 Feb. 1820—six volumes Josephus's *History* sold to Leroy Harcum, $3; two *Dictionaries* sold to James Harcum, $3; Clerk's *Magazine* and *History of American Farmers* sold to John Leland, 50¢; one *Bible* sold to Elizabeth Snow, 51¢; one *Bible* and two other books sold to Samuel Jones, 70¢; one lot of old books sold to Haynes Edwards, $1. RB 22, 205.

William Pasquith, 14 Feb. 1820—parcel of old books, 50¢. RB 22, 219.

William Taylor, 14 Feb. 1820—parcel books, $2. RB 22, 222.

Richard Coles, 14 April 1820—one small *Bible*. RB 22, 233.

Peter P. Cockarill, 12 June 1820—eight volumes *British Encyclopedia*, $8; one *Dictionary*, $4; one old *Dictionary*, $1; one family *Bible*, $2; thirteen books of different kinds, $1.50, one medical book (Buckan), $1. RB 22, 303.

John Robinson, account of sales, 12 June 1820—a parcel of old books sold to William Treakle, $1. RB 22, 358.

Charles Leland, 10 July 1820—Marshall's *Life of Washington*, five volumes, $15; Clarendon's *History*, six volumes, $3; old *Dispensatory*, 25¢; *Religion of Nature*, 50¢; Puffendorf's *Introduction*, two volumes, $2; Boyle's *Lectures*, four volumes, $2; Orrery on *Swift*, 50¢; Hume's *Essays*, two volumes, $1.50; Sidney on *Government*, two volumes, $2; Junius's *Letters*, $1; *American Justice* by Cook, 50¢; Beccary [Beccory?] on *Crimson*, $1; *Hudibrass*, 75¢; *American Nepos*, 50¢; Gibbon's *Roman Empire*, six volumes, $10; Rapin's *History of England*, fifteen volumes, $15; Pope's works, six volumes, $3; Moore's *Journal*, two volumes, $1.50; *Immortal Mentor*, 50¢; *Prayer Book*, $1; *World in Miniature*, $1; six volumes Shakespeare's plays, $1.50; *Fifth Lion*, 50¢; Halonius's *Enquiry*, 50¢; Locke's *Understanding*, $2; Clarke on *Attributes*, 50¢; *Nature of Faith*, 50¢; *Law of Executions*, 50¢; Charlon's *France*, $1; Impey's [?] *Practice*, 50¢; Thompson's works, $1; Hutchinson's *Philosophy*, $2; *Medical Companion*, 50¢; Buller's *Nine Prin* [?], $2; Tucker's *Blackstone*, $12; a parcel of books on different subjects consisting chiefly of broken sets, $5. RB 22, 375.

John Hudnall, 17 Dec. 1820—six books, 50¢. RB 22, 444.

John Bell, 12 Feb. 1821—seven knives, nine forks, and a parcel of old books,

50¢. *RB 22, 405.*

Thomas D. Covington, 12 Feb. 1821—seven books, $2. *RB 22, 477.*

Thomas Harvey, Jr., account of sales, 9 April 1821—six volumes by Fletcher [likely John Fletcher], $3.10; two volumes Blair's *Lectures*, $3; three volumes Latin books, $1.25; Gibson's *Surveying*, $1.55; Simsong [?] *Euclids*, $1.15; *Plutarch*, 60¢; Buckan's *Physician*, $2.32; Baxter's *Call*, 50¢; three volumes Pike's *Arithmetic* and M [?] *Exercises*, $1.15; three volumes *Virginia Orator*, $1; Sheridan's *Dictionary*, 61¢; Bailey's old *Dictionary*, 50¢; lot of old books, 12 1/3¢; *Hymn Book* and *Testament*, 53¢; one *Hymn Book*, 42¢; *Bible* and *Concordance*, $3.95. *RB 22,511.*

John C. Kent, 14 May 1821—some old books. *RB 22, 520.*

Thomas J. Haynes, 14 May 1821—nine books, $5. *RB 22, 529.*

Mary Moon, 13 Aug. 1821—one looking glass and some books, 60¢. *RB 22, 603.*

Bridgar Haynie, account of sales, 8 Oct. 1821—one large family *Bible* sold to Edward Oldham, $2.12 1/2; three hymn books sold to Harriet Haynie, 26¢; parcel old books sold to Royston Betts, Jr., 26¢. *RB 23, 15.*

Samuel L. Straughan, 12 Nov. 1821—one book case and books. *RB 23, 34.*

Sarah Ball, 14 Jan. 1822—a parcel of books, $1. *RB 23, 66.*

William H. Nicoll, 14 Jan. 1822—*Encyclopedia*, Dodson's edition, eighteen volumes, $36; *Domestic Encyclopedia*, $5; *Dictionary of Arts and Sciences*, $4; Postlethwaite's *Dictionary*, $2; Abercrombie's *Dictionary*, $1; Johnson's *Dictionary*, $1; Gibbon's *Roman Empire*, $8; Rollin's *Ancient History*, $5; Raspell's [?] *Modern Europe*, $2; Gordon's *American War*, $2; *History of America*, $2.50; *History of Late War*, 50¢; Pinkerton's *Geography with Atlas*, $4; Gathray's *Grammar*, $1; Salmon's *Grammar*, 50¢; Morgan's *France and Queen of France*, 75¢; Wilson's *Egypt*, $1; Marshall's *Life of Washington*, $8; *Life of Sir W. Jones* [Sir William Jones], 50¢; *Life of Darwin*, 25¢; Plutarch's *Lives*, $4; Belknap's *American Biography*, $2; Cook's *Voyages*, $10; Hawksworth's *Voyages*, $4.50; Moor's *Voyages*, $6; McKensie's *Voyages*, two volumes, $1; Dixon's *Voyages*, $1; Young's *Tour*, $1; Young's *Travels*, $2; Whitman's *Travels*, $2.50; Buchanan's *Researches*, $2.50; Jefferson's *Notes*, two copies, $2; Goldsmith's *Animated Nature*, $2; *American Negotiation*, 25¢; Clerk's *Magazine*, $2.25; *Spectator*, $2; *Guardian*, $1; Voltaire's works, $12; Swift's works, $3.25; Sterne's works, $2; Hervey's works, $3; Shakespeare's works, $2; Byron's works, $1; *Pleasures of Hope*, $1; Young's *Agriculture*, $2; Duhamel's *Agriculture*, $2; Taylor's *Arator* [*Orator* ?], $2.50; Wiston's *Gardening*, $2.50; Forsyth on *Fruit Trees*, $2.25; *Bible*, $4; Brown's *Bible*, $3; pocket *Bible*, $1.50; Burket on *Testament*, $2; *Prayer Book*, two copies, $1.50;

Episcopal Manual, $1.50; Blaire's Sermons, $3; Laws of Virginia, $3.25; Laws of United States, $3.50; Journals of Congress, 25¢; Henning's Justice, $2; Chase's Trial, $2.25; Athenian Oracle, $2.25; Buckanan's Family Phyoician, $2.50; James's Dispensatory, $2.50; Perry on Diseases, $2.50; Taplin's Farriery, 50¢; Paine's works, $2.38; Political Justice, $2.37; Smollet's Don Quixote, $1; Smollet's Tom Jones, $2.75; Select Poetry, $2.33; Select Plays, $2.33; Esop's [Aesop's] Fables, $2.34; a parcel of books and pamphlets on different subjects of little value, $1.25; Arrow Smith's Map of the World, $8. RB 23, 73, 74.

John Hall, account of sales, 11 Feb. 1822—a parcel of books sold to James G. Beacham, 50¢. RB 23, 101.

William Treakle, 11 March 1822—three books, $1. RB 23, 114.

James Sutton, account of sales, 11 March 1822—parcel of books sold to Samuel Berry, $1.65; one book (Duane) sold to Richard P. Coles, 75¢. RB 23, 117, 118.

John Clutton, account of sales, 8 April 1822—one lot of books sold to Robert Forrester, 26¢. RB 23, 126.

Mrs. Lucy Haynie, 8 April 1822—a parcel of old books, $1. RB 23, 132.

Elizabeth Ball, 13 May 1822—nine books, $5. RB 23, 137.

William Winstead, account of sales, 12 Aug. 1822—two books sold to Alex: Rock, 12 1/2¢. RB 23, 193.

George Blackwell, 12 Aug. 1822—five old books, $1. RB 23, 200.

P. I. Harcum, 12 Aug. 1822—one lot of books, $4. RB 23, 204.

William Wilkinson, account of sales, 13 Jan. 1823—six books sold to Samuel Harcum, $1; eight books sold to Charles Palmer, $1.12. RB 23, 272.

Thomas Pullin, 10 March 1823—parcel books, 50¢. RB 23, 280.

Griffin Lamkin, 11 March 1823—one parcel of books, 75¢. RB 23, 289.

John Cralle, 12 May 1823—Morse's Universal Geography, $3.50; Life of Washington, $3.25; two old Latin and Greek dictionaries, $3.25; a parcel of old books, $3.50; one Bible, $3.25. RB 23, 299.

Littleton Cockarill, 14 July 1823—three books, 75¢; four old books, 25¢; four old books, 75¢. RB 23, 336.

Anthony Sydnor, account of sales, 12 Aug. 1823—Hymn Book, Prayer Book, Portraiture of Methodism, Bailey's Dictionary. RB 23, 345.

John R. Harcum, account of sales, 11 Aug. 1823—parcel of books sold to James Treakle, $2.55. RB 23, 348.

Elizabeth Kellum, 11 Aug. 1823—basket and books sold to Thomas Hurst, 6 1/4¢. RB 23, 353.

Samuel Clarke, 10 Nov. 1823—parcel of old books, $1. *RB 23, 372.*

Thomas Beacham, 10 Nov. 1823—*Notes on the New Testament,* $5; Wesley's *Sermons,* $2.50; Whitfield's *Sermons,* 50¢; *Portrait of St. Paul,* 75¢; *Family Adviser or Practice of Physic,* $1.25; *Admonition to Unconverted Sinners,* $1.25; *Discipline of the Methodist Church,* $1.25; Laws Know's [?] *Call to a Holy Life,* $1.25; *Letters Containing Some Acct:* [*Account*] *of the Work of God,* $1.25; two *Hymn Books,* one *Dictionary,* $1; parcel of old books, 75¢. *RB 23, 373.*

Mrs. Ann Cralle, account of sales, 12 Jan. 1824—a parcel of books sold to George Ashburne, $1.30. *RB 23, 395.*

David Haynie, 10 May 1824—parcel old books, $1.50. *RB 23, 444.*

Davenport Haynie, 10 May 1824—parcel of books, $1.25. *RB 23, 444.*

Thomas D. Covington, 10 May 1824—one lot of books, 76¢. *RB 23, 470.*

William Nelms, account of sales, 14 June 1824—parcel of books sold to Hiram Nelms, $1.26. *RB 23, 495.*

Thomas Lansdell, account of sales, 14 June 1824—parcel of books sold to Mary Lansdell, $1.12 1/2. *RB 23, 501.*

John Davenport, 14 June 1824—*Life of Washington,* five volumes, and *Atlas,* $15; Stedman's *American War,* one volume, $1; Volney's *View,* one volume, $1; Brook's *Gazetteer,* one volume, $2; Henning's *Justice,* $2; Moore's *Journal,* two volumes, $1.50; Jones's *Dictionary,* $1; *Domestic Medicine,* $2; Cook's *Voyages,* two volumes, $1.50; *Well Bred Scholar,* one volume, $1.50; *Polite Learning,* $1.50; parcel of old English books, $2; parcel of old Latin books, $2.25. *RB 23, 503.*

George Jones, 14 June 1824—one lot of books, $1.75. *RB 23, 512.*

John Haydon, 14 June 1824—one lot of books sold to L. Hammonds, $1.41. *RB 23, 517.*

Jeremiah Robinson, account of sales, 14 June 1824—three books sold to Linszey Davis, 12¢. *RB 23, 525.*

Soloman Evans, 13 Sept. 1824—a parcel of old books sold to Isaac Hurst, 16¢. *RB 24, 43.*

Thomas Hudnall, 13 Dec. 1824—one family *Bible, History of Late War,* lot of books, $4.50. *RB 24, 76.*

Thomas H. Jett, 10 Jan. 1825—one family *Bible,* $3; Henning's *Justice,* $1; one lot old books, $1. *RB 24, 113.*

Alice Demmeritt [also spelled Demerrit and Demerit], 10 Jan. 1825—parcel of old books. *RB 24, 135.*

William Davenport, 10 Jan. 1825—Tucker's *Blackstone,* five volumes, $10; *Life of Washington,* five volumes and *Atlas,* $15; Stedman's *American War,* $1;

Jefferson's *Notes*, $2; Volney's *View*, $1; Brook's *Gazetteer*, $2; Henning's *Justice*, $2; Jones's *Dictionary*, $1; Moore's *Journal*, two volumes, $2.75; *Domestic Medicine*, $2; *History of the Devil*, 38¢; Cook's *Voyages*, two volumes, 75¢; *Well Bred Scholar*, 38¢; lot of old books, $2 [all of the preceding books sold to John Davenport]; *Golden Treasure* sold to Elizabeth S. Davenport, $2.50; Hervey's *Meditations* sold to Elizabeth S. Davenport, $2.75; Whitefield's *Sermons* sold to Elizabeth S. Davenport, $2.40; Archer's *Bible* sold to Elizabeth S. Davenport, $4; Benkett [?] sold to Elizabeth S. Davenport, $2. *RB 24, 135, 136*.

William Walker, 10 Jan. 1825—three old large books, 75¢; two French and Latin books, 25¢; five hymn books, $2.25; five hymn books of different kinds, $1; one large family *Bible*, $2.50; one small *Bible*, 50¢. *RB 24, 141*.

John Hudnall, account of sales, 10 May 1825—a lot old books sold to W. Harvey, $1. *RB 24, 191*.

Samuel Haynie, account of sales, 10 May 1825—parcel of old books sold to Hiram Haynie, $6.12 1/2. *RB 24, 198*.

Mrs. Winefred Hurst, 10 May 1825—one lot of books sold to John Bryant, $3.78; one large family *Bible* sold to Ones. Harvey, $6. *RB 24, 201*.

Sukey Harvey, 10 May 1825—one large *Bible* and old books, $6. *RB 24, 203*.

Thomas Hurst, account of sales, 10 May 1825—eight volumes Shakespeare's works, $3; four volumes *Farces*, $1; two volumes *Roderick Random* [*The Adventures of Roderick Random*], $1.50; *State Trials*, $1.50; eight volumes *Spectator*, $1.50; *Beauties of Spectator*, $2; Cook's *Voyages*, $2.65; Baylie's *Dictionary*, $1.30; two volumes of *Present Age*, $1.30; two volumes *History of America*, $2.90; *Life of Franklin*, $2.06 1/4; *Washington's Letters*, $2.25; Morse's *Geography*, $2.10; Buckan's *Phisick*, $2; *Rutherford's Letters*, $2.25; *Pilgrim's Progress*, $2.25; two volumes Rolin's *History*, $2.12; *Canary and Life*, $2.12; *Ovid*, $2.05; lot of old books, $2.25; one large *Bible*, $5.35. *RB 24, 210, 211*.

Alexander Haynie, 10 May 1825—two old books, $1.50. *RB 24, 224*.

Richard Lee, 13 June 1825—a parcel of old books, $1.12 1/4. *RB 24, 243*.

Thomas Crowder, account of sales, 13 June 1825—books and looking glass sold to James Hurst, $1.05. *RB 24, 249*.

Samuel Jones, 13 June 1825—parcel of old books, $1.25. *RB 24, 257*.

Stephen Haynie, account of sales, 8 Aug. 1825—one *Dictionary*, $1.27; one Clark's *Magazine*, $1.50; *Hymn Book*, $1.08; two books, $1.26; *Bible*, $1.26. *RB 24, 284*.

George Haydon, account of sales, 12 Sept. 1825—old books on the desk sold to Warner Kent, $2.25. *RB 24, 308*.

Frances Holliday, 12 Sept. 1825—parcel of books, $1.75. *RB 24, 320.*

Izates Anderson, 12 Sept. 1825—one large family *Bible*, $4; *Encyclopedia*, twelve volumes, $3; one lot of old books, no. 3, $1; one lot of old books, no. 4, 25¢; one lot of old books, no. 5, 12 1/2¢; one lot of old books, no. 6, 12 1/2¢. *RB 24, 329.*

Holland Haynie, account of sales, 12 Dec. 1825—parcel of old books sold to John George, $1.50. *RB 24, 369.*

Edward Humphlett, 12 Feb. 1826—parcel of old books sold to Samuel Harcum, 25¢; one large *Bible* and other books sold to Nancy Humphlet, $3. *RB 24, 397.*

Thomas Cundiff, 11 April 1826—a lot old books, $2; Brooke's *Gazatteer*, $1.50. *RB 24, 447.*

Jesse Crowder, 10 July 1826—a lot of books, $1.50. *RB 24, 519.*

Hiram Corbell, account of sales, 14 Aug. 1826—books sold to Richard Cockarill, 1¢. *RB 24, 538.*

Ann Hughlett, 14 Aug. 1826—two volumes Heglegn's *Lectures*, $1. *RB 24, 545.*

John Flynt, account of sales, 11 Sept. 1826—two books, Fletcher and Simpson, sold to James Harcum, $2; four old books sold to Edward A. Watts, 51¢. *RB 24, 610.*

William Mitchell, 9 Oct. 1826—a parcel of old books, $1.25. *RB 24, 617.*

Samuel Barnes, account of sales, 8 Jan. 1827—one *Bible* sold to Presly Hudson, 12 1/2¢. *RB 25, 26.*

Elizabeth McClanahan, account of sales, 12 Feb. 1827—parcel of old books sold to Col. W. Henderson, $1.50. *RB 25, 38.*

Thomas Betts, 12 Feb. 1827—one lot old books, 13¢. *RB 25, 52.*

Matthew Lamkin, account of sales, 14 May 1827—a parcel of books sold to Robert Alexander, 44¢. *RB 25, 79.*

Mrs. Mary Cralle, 14 May 1827—a parcel old books, $1.50. *RB 25, 98.*

George C. Ashburn, account of sales, 9 July 1827—one lot of books sold to Linsey F. Barnes, $1.31 1/4. *RB 25, 132.*

Edward Webb, account of sales, 8 Oct. 1827—lot of books sold to Nathan Moore, $1.50. *RB 25, 180.*

Richard P. Coles, account of sales, 10 Dec. 1827—Ewel's *Medical Companion* sold to Edward Coles, $3.05; a parcel old books sold to Max. [Maximillian] Haynie, $3.28. *RB 25, 195.* [Word *Companion* in inventory account.]

John Hayes, account of sales, 10 Dec. 1827—parcel old books sold to Salley

Hayes, 26¢. *RB 25, 202.*

John Cockarill, account of sales, 15 April 1828—parcel old books, 52¢. *RB 25, 278.*

Eli L. Patterson, 12 May 1828—*Biographical Dictionary,* $2; McErven on the *Types,* 75¢; *Reign of Grace,* 75¢. *RB 25, 292.*

George Lee, 12 May 1828—parcel of old books, $1. *RB 25, 304.*

William Rogers, account of sales, 9 June 1828—parcel of old books sold to Henderson Haynie, 26¢. *RB 25, 317.*

Richard Morrison, account of sales, 9 June 1828—old books sold to Richard Flynt, Sr., 5¢. *RB 25, 323.*

William Sutton, 9 June 1828—thirty-six books, $8. *RB 25, 329.*

Edmund R. Jeffries, account of sales, 14 July 1828—old books sold to Elizabeth Sherly [Shirley], 51¢. *RB 25, 345.*

John Coles, 14 July 1828—parcel of books, 50¢. *RB 25, 349.*

William Downman, 14 July 1828—one large family *Bible,* $2; one lot old books, $1. *RB 25, 356.*

John B. Kenner, account of sales, 11 Aug. 1828—one parcel of books sold to John B. Kenner, 35¢. *RB 25, 367.*

Cyrus Pinckard, 8 Sept. 1828—one book case and books, $20. *RB 25, 393.*

Samuel Burgess, 8 Sept. 1828—six books, 60¢; *Orator,* 25¢; two volumes *American Farmer,* $2.10; four books, 25¢; six books, 25¢; seven books, 6¢; a parcel of magazines, 63¢; one volume *Telemachus,* 25¢; four books, 31¢; *Washington Expositler,* 31¢; seven books, 26¢; four books, 40¢; two books, $1.61; three books, 58¢; one volume *Select Plays,* 79¢; two volumes *United States Laws,* 12 1/2¢; three books, 33¢; seven books, 16¢; six books, 34¢. *RB 25, 407, 409.*

William Eskridge, account of sales, 8 Sept. 1828—parcel of books sold to Holland H. Hughlett, 60¢. *RB 25, 419.*

Joseph Ball, account of sales, 13 Oct. 1828—one family *Bible* sold to Fanny Ball, $4; one *Biographical Dictionary* sold to Broadie L. Hull, $1; *Marriage Customs* sold to Edwin Nelms, 12 1/2¢; five old books sold to Fanny Ball, 75¢; Murray's *Exercise and Key* sold to Fanny Ball, 25¢; Pike's *Arithmetic* sold to Kenner Cralle, 6¢; a parcel of old books sold to Thomas Davis, 25¢; Simpson's *Euclid* sold to Samuel Blackwell, 37 1/2¢. *RB 25, 453.*

Richard Hudnall, 13 Oct. 1828—a lot of books, $3. *RB 25, 459.*

Jordan Lewis, 9 Feb. 1829—parcel of old books, $2.25. *RB 26, 11.*

Walter Self, account of sales, 9 Feb. 1829—two books sold to widder [widow?] Self, $1.06; parcel of books sold to Randel Headley, $1.14. *RB 26, 22.*

John Blundon, account of sales, 13 July 1829—one lot of books sold to Joseph H. Jett, 6¢. *RB 26, 96*.

John Lansdell, Sr., 10 Aug. 1829—parcel books sold to John Lansdell, $1.50. *RB 26, 119*.

Willis W. Hudnall, 10 Aug. 1829—*Encyclopedia*, twelve volumes, $5.12 1/2; Brook's *Gazetteer*, 62 1/2¢; *Chesterfield's Letters*, 25¢; *President's Speeches*, $1; *Bookkeeping*, 25¢; *Hudibras*, 16¢; *French Revolution*, 12 1/2¢; *Dictionary*, 14¢; *Washington's Letters*, 37 1/2¢; one lot old books, 12 1/2¢; *Mexican Patriot*, 12 1/2¢; Clay's *Speeches*, 12 1/2¢; Bryon's works, 12 1/2¢; Henning's *Justice*, 16¢; one lot of books, 25¢; one lot of books, 15¢. *RB 26, 125*.

John Williams, Sr., _ Oct. 1828—one lot of books, $2. *RB 26, 159*.

Edmond Lecompt, 9 Nov. 1829—one lot of old books, 25¢. *RB 26, 162*.

John Cottrell, account of sales, 9 Nov. 1829—two volumes Johnson's *Dictionary* sold to William Hughlett, 26¢. *RB 26, 166*.

Thomas Hughlett, 10 Nov. 1829—*S H. [Short History ?] of Virginia*, 22¢; *Biographical Dictionary*, 75¢; *V. [Virginia ?] Ruins*, 13¢; one old book, 7¢; one old book, 13¢; three old books, 7¢; four old books, 28¢; two monick [?] books, 50¢; *History of the United States*, 37¢; *Jefferson's Notes*, 50¢; one *Federalist*, 50¢; C. *Chemistry*, 26¢; *Encyclopedia*, six volumes, $10. *RB 26, 168, 169*.

Thomas Conway, 14 Dec. 1829—*Revised Code*, one volume, $1.50; Henning's *Justice*, $1; Stark's *Virginia Justice*, $1; Walker's *Dictionary*, $3; lot of old books, $2. *RB 26, 181, 182*.

Edward Barnes, 14 Dec. 1829—one lot of books, $2. *RB 26, 186*.

Elisha H. Gill, account of sales, 8 March 1830—one lot old books sold to Thomas Davis, 41¢. *RB 26, 235*.

Mrs. Catherine Blackerby, account of sales, 8 March 1830—four books sold to Thomas Blackerby, 88¢; balance of books sold to Thomas K. Hurst, $1. *RB 26, 239*.

Thomas Lamkin, 10 Aug. 1830—one lot books, $1. *RB 26, 352*.

Charles Marsh, 8 Nov. 1830—parcel of books, 12 1/2¢. *RB 26, 410*.

Jeduthan Moore, 14 March 1831—a parcel of books, $4.50. *RB 26, 466*.

Samuel Hughlett, 15 March 1831—one lot of books, $3.25. *RB 26, 472*.

Thomas W. Hughlett, account of sales, 10 May 1831—one lot of books, 6 1/4¢; one lot of books, 25¢; one lot of books, 25¢; *Gospel History*, 6 1/4¢; another lot, 6 1/4¢; one lot school books, 15¢; Henning's *Justice*, 6¢; *Medical Companion*, 40¢; three books, 8¢; four books, 6 1/4¢; *Rousseau*, 13¢; Clerk's *Magazine*, 65¢; *Buckannon*, 7¢; three books, 13¢; *Concordance*, 35¢; Yorick's *Sermons*, 29¢; F.

[*Family?*] Checks, $3; F. [Family?] *Bible*, $4.75; M. *Magazine*, $3.25; *Wesley's Sermons*, $4.16. *RB 26, 495.*

Ester Hughlett, 10 May 1831—lot of books, $1. *RB 26, 502.*
John Robinson, 13 June 1831—one lot of books, 13¢. *RB 26, 523.*
Hezekiah Gill, 14 Nov. 1831—parcel books, 30¢. *RB 26, 576.*
Edward Barnes, 14 Nov. 1831—*Walker's Dictionary*, 56 1/4¢; one lot old books, 60¢. *RB 26, 581.*

Fleming Bates, 14 Nov. 1831—*British Encyclopedia*, twenty volumes, $100; *Gunther's Geography*, two volumes, $2; *History of Man*, two volumes, $1.50; *Lee's Memoirs*, two volumes, $2; *Leo the Tenth*, four volumes, $4; *Burk's War in India*, $4.50; *American Biographer*, $2.50; *Naval Monument*, $1.50; *Monroe's View*, $1.50; *Masonic Laws*, $1.50; *Volney's Ruins*, $1.75; *Constitutions*, $2.50; *Smith's History of Virginia*, $2.50; *Biographical Dictionary*, $2.50; *Journal of the Convention*, $3.50; *Boscoe's Lorenzo*, three volumes, $3.50; *Burk's Reflections*, $3.75; *Hume's Essays*, two volumes, $3.75; *Stewart's Philosophy*, $1.75; *Public Characters*, $1.75; *Receptor*, two volumes, broken, $1.50; *Rumford's Essays*, two volumes, $2.50; *Bacon's Essays*, two volumes, $2.50; *Stephen's Wars*, two volumes, $2.50; *American Gazetteer*, $2.50; *Pursuits of Literature*, $1.50; *Hume's History of England*, eight volumes, $12.50; *Yoonama*, two volumes, $2.50; *Goldsmith's Animated Nature*, $3.50; *Botanic Garden*, $3.50; *Biographical Dictionary*, eight volumes, $12.50; *Nile's Weekly Register*, thirty-eight volumes, $100.50; *Laseasse's Napoleon*, three volumes, $2.50; *Hallam's Middle Ages*, two volumes, $2.50; *Lady Morgan's Italy*, two volumes, $1.50; *Frederick the Great*, $1.50; *Universal Magazine*, broken, $1.50; *British Magazine*, broken, $1.25; *Woodward on Fossils*, $1.25; *Cullin's Practice*, $2; *State Papers*, $2.50; *Payne's* [Paine's?] *Writings*, $1; *Annual Register*, $1.25; *Addison's Freehold* [*Freeholder*], $1.25; *Doctor Priestly's Pamphleteer*, $1.25; *Beatlie's Essays*, $1.25; *Schrevile's Lexicon*, $1.25; documents, $1.50; *Rollin's Ancient History*, eight volumes, $8; *British Classics*, (there should have been thirty-nine volumes, but there are only thirty-six), $27; *Monastery*, two volumes, $1; *Court of St. Clon*, $1.50; the book, $1.50; *Mavor's Plutarch*, $1.50; *Park's Travels*, $1.50; *Washington Guide*, $1.25; *Byron*, two volumes, $1.50; *Don Rodorio*, $1.38; *Johnson and Collins*, $1.38; *Queen's Wake*, $1.38; *Marion*, $1.50; *American Constitution*, $1.50; works of Ossian, $1.50; *Female Monitor*, $1.25; *Turkish Spy*, eight volumes, $2.25; *Locke's Essays*, three volumes, $2.25; *Thompson's* work, four volumes, $2.25; *Voltaire*, (should have been twenty-four volumes but there are only eighteen), $9.25; *Voltaire's History*, $2.25; *Modern Chivalry*, two volumes, $1.25; *Pope's Iliad*, four volumes, $3.25; *Cowper's*

Poems, (there should have been three volumes but there are only two volumes), $1.25; *Horace* translated, four volumes, $3.25; Addison's works, two volumes, $1.25; Harris's *Discourses,* $1.25; *Elements of Criticism,* three volumes, $1.50; *History of England,* quarto, three volumes, $2.50; *Medical Companion,* $2.75; *Virginia Convention,* $4.50; Johnson's *Dictionary,* two volumes, $2.50; *Philosophy of a Future State,* $1.50; *Pastor's Fireside,* two volumes, $1.50; *Edinburg Medley,* $1.25; *Revolution of Portugal,* $1.25; *Comparative View,* $1.13; Shakespeare, eight volumes, $4; Duncan's *Logic,* $4.50; *Life,* $4.50; Hutton's *Measures,* $4.25; *Virtue and Happiness,* $4.13; *New York Mirror,* seven volumes quarto, $7; *British Spy,* 75¢; *Alfred,* 25¢; Barrow's work, two volumes quarto, $2.25; novels and old miscellaneous works, sixty volumes, $30; Robinson's *Forms,* $2.50; *Journal of the Law Schools,* $1.30. RB 26, 585–587.

Lindsey Davis, account of sales, 13 March 1832—one trunk and old books sold to Fanny Reyon, $1.23. RB 27, 44.

Francis Vanlandingham, account of sales, 13 March 1832—a parcel of books sold to William Blincoe, $1.32. RB 27, 51.

Willis Ingram, account of sales, 14 May 1832—one lot of books sold to George W. N. Berryman, 85¢. RB 27, 68.

Mary Hughlett, account of sales, 14 May 1832—parcel of old books sold to Leroy Harcum, $1.55. RB 27, 91.

Hiram Blackwell, articles at the academy, 14 May 1832—Johnson's *Dictionary,* $1.25; *American Nepos,* $1.50; *Wonders of Creation,* one volume, $1.25; Harris's *Discourse,* $1.25; *Masonic Laws,* $1.75. RB 27, 95. [Word *Discourse* determined by looking at account of sales.]

Leroy McCave, account of sales, 14 May 1832—*Saints Rest* and one other book sold to Maximillian Haynie, 52¢. RB 27, 107.

Robert Conway, account of sales, 14 May 1832—Clarke's *Commentaries,* $2.63; *Josephus,* $1.30; Wesley's *Notes,* $1.27; *Wisdom's Voice,* $1.10; Brown's *Concordance,* $1.20; *Common Prayer,* $1.08. RB 27, 117.

William Crowder, 11 June 1832—parcel books, $1. RB 27, 141.

John Mealey [also spelled Maley, Maily], account of sales, 9 July 1832—parcel old books sold to Thomas Dawson, $1.51; one large *Bible* sold to Harriot Mealy, $1.50. RB 27, 154, 155.

Elisha Fallin, account of sales, 9 July 1832—one lot books sold to Brodie L. Hull, $4.50. RB 27, 160.

Everard M. Stith, 12 Dec. 1832—Watt's *Logic,* one volume, $5.25; Murphy's *Lucean* [*Lucian*?], one volume, 6 1/2¢; Boncastle's *Algebra,* 6 1/4¢; Quenton

Durward, two volumes, 25¢; *Peregrine Pickle* [*The Adventures of Peregrine Pickle*], four volumes, 50¢; *Children of Abby*, three volumes, 50¢; Ewing's *Synopsis*, 35¢; *Horace Delphini*, 50¢; *Caesar*, 25¢; Simson's *Euclid*, 50¢; Gipson's *Surveying*, $1; Ferguson's *Lectures*, two volumes, 50¢; Matthew's *Population*, 50¢; McCauley's *England*, broken, 0; *French Dictionary*, 6 1/4¢; Young's *Night Thoughts*, 50¢; Byron's works, eight volumes, $2; Byron's *Conversations*, 12 1/2¢; Shakespeare, eight volumes, $2; *Ossian*, two volumes, 50¢; *Paradise Lost*, 50¢; Homer's *Iliad*, two volumes, 50¢; *Telemachus*, two volumes, 50¢; Homer's *Odyssey*, two volumes, 50¢; Aitkinson's *Poems*, 25¢; Rollin's *Ancient History*, ten volumes, $2.50; *History England*, two volumes, 50¢; *Roman History*, 25¢; Goldsmith's *Essays*, Lasscass's *Napoleon*, two volumes, 50¢; *Spectator*, eight volumes, $2; Andrew's *Rhetoric*, $2.25; *Memoirs of Alexander*, $2.25; works of nature, $2.25; Mavor's *Voyages*, fifteen volumes, $1; Philip's *Speeches*, 12 1/2¢; *British Spy*, 25¢; *Francis Marion*, 12 1/2¢; Ewel's *Medical Companion*, $1; *Greek Lexicon*, 50¢; lot of old books, 25¢. *RB 27, 211*. [Some titles determined by looking at account of sales.]

Kenner Cralle, 10 Dec. 1832—parcel old books, $1.50; family *Bible*, $1.25. *RB 27, 234*.

Thomas E. Harding, 11 Feb. 1833—a parcel of books, $10. *RB 27, 282*.

Francis Pickering, 13 May 1833—one desk, one lot of books, and one looking glass, $3. *RB 27, 366*.

Richard Toulson, 11 June 1833—a parcel of books, 25¢. *RB 27, 399*.

Austin Hall, account of sales, 11 June 1833—one lot of books sold to Mrs. Hall, $1. *RB 27, 409*.

James G. Beacham, 9 Sept. 1833—a lot of old books, 6 1/4¢. *RB 28, 1*.

William Ball, 13 Jan. 1834—one *Dictionary*, 75¢; a lot of books, 85¢; one family *Bible*, $3.75; three books, $1.15; one book, 75¢; one book, 25¢. *RB 28, 76, 77*.

Isaac Hurst, 12 March 1834—one lot of books, $4. *RB 28, 119*.

John Rice, 11 March 1834—one lot of books, 12 1/2¢. *RB 28, 131*.

William Sydnor, account of sales, 12 May 1834—one *Biographical Dictionary* sold to Thomas Ball, $1. *RB 28, 176*.

James Barrett, 12 May 1834—parcel old books, $2. *RB 28, 183*.

William Harding, account of sales, 9 June 1834—*Encyclopedia*, eleven volumes, $1.50; one-half dozen books, different sorts, 38¢; one-half dozen books, different sorts, $1; one lot books, different sorts, 22¢; three *Prayer Books*, 50¢; one-half dozen other books, $1; one dozen other books, 12 1/2¢; one-half dozen other books, 2¢; eight other books, 12 1/2¢; one lot pamphlets, 8¢. *RB 28*,

220, 223.

William I. Sebree, 14 July 1834—one lot of books, 12 1/2¢. *RB 28, 253*.

Ann D. Claughton, 13 Oct. 1834—one lot books, $2.25. *RB 28, 303*.

John F. Prosser, account of sales, 13 Oct. 1834—a parcel of books sold to Alexander Rock, 25¢. *RB 28, 308*.

Nancy Davis, account of sales, 10 Nov. 1834—one lot of books sold to William E. Jett, 65¢. *RB 28, 323*.

Joseph C. Edwards, account of sales, 8 Dec. 1834—Johnson's *Dictionary*, 85¢; Buckan's *Domestic Medicine*, 20¢; *Roderick Random*, 25¢; *Life of Dr. Cook and Fletcher*, 25¢. *RB 28, 354*.

Elizabeth Foulks [also spelled Fulks], account of sales, 13 April 1835—one-half dozen old books sold to John Claughton, 40¢. *RB 28, 403*.

Edwin Nelms, account of sales, 11 May 1835—lot of old books sold to Edwin Nelms, 25¢. *RB 28, 425*.

Joseph Ball, 11 May 1835—family *Bible*, $3; *Biographical Dictionary*, $1.50; a parcel of old books, $4. *RB 28, 448*.

John Hull, 9 June 1835—one lot of books, $2. *RB 28, 466*.

George Y. Beane, account of sales, 13 July 1835—lot of old books sold to Milton G. Beane, 6¢. *RB 28, 513*.

Lindsey O. Davenport, account of sales, 13 July 1835—one lot of books sold to Judith Davenport, 1¢. *RB 28, 514*. [Word books determined by looking at appraisement of estate.]

Elizabeth Doulin, account of sales, 13 July 1835—one lot of books sold to Samuel Hull, 40¢. *RB 28, 524*.

John S. Tapscott, 13 July 1835—one lot of books sold to Henry Beale, 50¢. *RB 28, 529*.

Samuel Cralle, 14 Sept. 1835—*United States Laws*, 50¢; *Wesley's Notes*, 50¢; *Revised Code*, 50¢; *Dictionary*, 50¢; *Bible*, 50¢; *Family Instruction*, 25¢; *Poor Laws*, 12 1/2¢; large family *Bible*, $1. *RB 28, 563*. [Some titles determined by looking at account of sales.]

Dr. John McAdam, 12 Oct. 1835—eight volumes Hume's *History of England*, $3; eleven volumes of medical works, $4; six volumes Bell's *Surgery*, $3; two volumes *Principal of Health and Surgery*, 50¢; Scott's *Life of Napoleon*, $3; *Horace and Cicero*, $1.50; Chapman's *Ruins* [?], 75¢; Quincey's *Lexicon*, $1; *Elements of Philosophy*, 50¢; Armstrong on *Fever*, 50¢; Cullin's *Materia Medica*, 75¢; lot of old books in case, $2; *Life of Cumberland*, 50¢; eight volumes *Spectator*, $2; *History of Greece and Rome*, 50¢; work on *Botany*, $3; Cullin's *Practice*, two volumes, $1;

Lenad [?] on *Fever*, 75¢; *American Dispensatory*, $1.50; sermons in two volumes, 25¢; Gay's *Fables*, 50¢; *Vicar of Wakefield*, 50¢; *Beauties of Kirkwhite*, 50¢. RB 28, 590.

David T. Ball, 12 Oct. 1835—Clarke's *Comments on New Testament*, $4.01; Burket's *Comments on New Testament*, $1.62 1/2; Buck's *Theological Dictionary*, $1.25; *Methodist Magazine*, 91 3/4¢; Setcher's *Sermons and Lectures*, 50¢; mathematical works, 25¢; *Travels in America*, 15¢; *Wisdom's Voice*, 12 1/2¢; Cook's *Voyage*, 40¢; *Sketches of Sermons*, 37 1/2¢; [?] *Sermons*, 1¢; Garrot's [?], 2¢; Fletcher's *Checks*, 40¢; lot of books, 41¢; one singing book, 1¢; Smith's *Sermons*, 1¢; Baxter's *Saints Rest*, 2¢; *Much Ado About Nothing*, 1¢; old tracts, 1¢; *Lorenzo Don*, 32¢; singing book and *Bible*, 37 1/2¢; Simpson's *Plea*, 6 1/4¢; one large lot of books, 4¢. RB 28, 613, 614.

Charles Harcum, 12 Oct. 1835—one lot of books and scissors, 50¢. RB 28, 620.

William Tellis, 14 Dec. 1835—one ciphering book and *Testament*, 12 1/2¢. RB 28, 650.

John Tapscott, 8 Feb. 1836—a parcel of old books, $2. RB 29, 25.

Griffin Edwards, 8 Feb. 1836—parcel books, $1. RB 29, 26.

Sally Maith, account of sales, 8 Feb. 1836—one lot of books sold to Daniel Laws, 19¢. RB 29, 30.

Kenner Cralle, 14 March 1836—one old trunk and lot of old books, $1.50. RB 29, 71.

Thomas Brown, 10 May 1836—Clarke's *Commentary*, $10; Wesley's works, $7; other books, $15. RB 29, 106.

John Booth, 12 Sept. 1836—one lot of books, $1. RB 29, 208.

William France, 15 Nov. 1836—one lot of books, 25¢. RB 29, 246.

Willis Haydon [spelled Hayden in appraisement], account of sales, 15 Nov. 1836—*A* [*American*?] *Biography*, 50¢; *Hymn Book* and two pamphlets, 31¢. RB 29, 259.

Hardeaia Dameron, 13 Feb. 1837—one large *Bible* and a parcel of other books, $2. RB 29, 301.

George S. Corbin, 13 Feb. 1837—all books, $2.50. RB 29, 317.

Harriet Fallin, 8 May 1837—bag and corn, lot books, $9.70. RB 29, 371.

Kenner Cralle, account of sales, 10 July 1837—one lot of books sold to Littleton Cockarill, 37 1/2¢. RB 29, 406.

William Sydnor, account of sales, 13 Nov. 1837—*Life of Franklin*, $6.25; two military books, $6.25; balance of books, $6.50. RB 29, 471.

Elizabeth L. Carter, 13 Nov. 1837—fifteen small books (old), $1.25; six Watt's works, $3; one lot old books in draw, 25¢. *RB 29, 487.*

Lindsey Barnes, 13 Nov. 1837—two volumes Wesley's *Sermons*, $2; six volumes Clark's *Commentaries*, $15; *History of the United States*, and map, $2; *American Biography*, $2; McGavin's *Protestant*, two volumes, $5; *Revolution in Europe*, $2, Burk's *Discovery*, $1.50; five books, 75¢. *RB 30, 32.*

George I. Hughlett, 13 Nov. 1837—two Webster's *Spelling Books*, 40¢; one book as No. 3, 25¢; one book as No. 4, 30¢. *RB 30, 70, 73.*

Thomas Bell, 12 Feb. 1838—parcel books, $2.75. *RB 30, 126.*

Samuel G. Dawson, 12 March 1838—one parcel of books, 37 1/2¢. *RB 30, 156.*

William T. Polk, 12 March 1838—one bookcase and books, $25. *RB 30, 157.* [In account of sales, the bookcase was sold to Benedict Burgess for $5.65, p. 159.]

John N. Webb, 12 March 1838—two glasses and old book, 25¢. *RB 30, 168.*

John Blackwell, 15 May 1838—parcel of books, $4. *RB 30, 178.*

William B. Kent, 11 June 1838—books, $3. *RB 30, 220.*

Yarrett Hughlett, 8 Oct. 1838—one lot old books, 38¢. *RB 30, 270.*

Ann B. Dungan, account of sales, 12 Nov. 1838—a parcel of books sold to John Bryant, 40¢. *RB 30, 292.*

Joel Robinson, 11 Feb. 1839—one family *Bible*, $3. *RB 30, 339.*

Samuel Blackwell, 11 Feb. 1839—Payne's *Universal Geography*, four volumes, $2; Winter Botton's *America*, four volumes, $2; Marshall's *Washington*, five volumes, $10; *Biographical Dictionary*, $1.50; *British Encyclopedia*, twelve volumes, $10; *Biographical Dictionary*, $1.50; *British Encyclopedia*, twelve volumes, $10; Locke on Gibbs, $1; Hume's *England*, nine volumes, $15; Lockhart's *Burns* [*Life of Burns*?], $2; Bryon's works, $2; Junius's *Letters*, 50¢; Thompson's *Seasons*, 25¢; *Beauties of Stirne*, 50¢; *Hudibras*, 50¢; Homer's *Iliad*, four volumes Harper's *Family Library*, $2; *Natural History*, two volumes, $2.50; Deck's works, two volumes, $4.50; *History United States*, $1.50; *American Biography*, $1.25; Ossian's *Poems*, two volumes, $1.50; Blair's *Lectures on Rhetoric*, three volumes, $2.50; Locke on *Understanding*, two volumes, $1.50; West's *Life of Patrick Henry*, $1.25; one set of Shakespeare in six volumes, $2.40; *Spectator* in twelve volumes, $5; Pender's works, three volumes, $1.50; Sterne's works, five volumes, $2.50; Burk's *History of Via* [*Virginia*?], two volumes, 75¢; Jefferson's *Notes on Virginia*, 75¢; one lot miscellaneous works, $12; Macnalley's *Evidence*, two volumes, $2; Washington's *Reports*, two volumes, $2; Cole's *Reports*, three volumes, $3.50; Bacon's *Abridgment*, seven volumes, $15; Stark's on *Evidence*, three volumes, $9;

Chetty's *Pleadings*, thirty volumes, $7.50; *Equity Draftsman*, $2.50; Harrison's *Chancery*, two volumes, $3; Bullir's *Nici Prias*, $1; *Revised Code and Supplement*, three volumes, $6; *Laws of Virginia*, four volumes, $2; *Virginia Reports*, [no price given]; Randolph's *Reports*, six volumes, $15; Lee's *Reports*, six volumes, $20; Chetty's *Equity Digest*, two volumes, $8; Chetty's *Blackstone*, $4.50; Robinson's *Practicle*, second volume, $5; Toller on *Executions*, $2.50; Blackstone's *Commentaries*, old edition, four volumes, $2; Forblauque's *Equity*, $3; *Maxims in Law and Equity*, $2; Henning's *Justice*, $2; Mumford's *General Index*, $2.50; Powel on *Contracts*, $1.50; Wattel's *Law of Nations*, $3; Allyn's *Reports*, two volumes, $3; Yates's *Digest*, $2.50; Clark's *Commentaries*, six volumes, $10; book of nature, $3; Sally's *Memoirs*, five volumes, $3; *Virginia Convention Debates*, $2; Webster and Walker's *Dictionaries*, $4; parcel miscellaneous pamphlets and magazines, etc., $15. RB 30, 348.

Elizabeth R. Shearly, account of sales, 11 March 1839—lot of books sold to John Edwards, 13¢. RB 30, 388.

Sally Hull, account of sales, 8 July 1839—one box and books sold to George W. Way, 50¢. RB 30, 449.

Randal R. Kirk, account of sales, 8 July 1839—one lot old books sold to Thomas Beatley, 76¢. RB 30, 459.

Job Slacum, account of sales, 8 July 1839—books and secretary sold to Ann Slacum, $2; *Farmer's Register* and *American Farmer* sold to Alfred Hudnall, $11.80. RB 30, 465, 466.

John Bramble, account of sales, 12 Aug. 1839—two books sold to William F. Bramble, 7¢. RB 30, 498.

Betsy Winstead, 14 Oct. 1839—one lot of books, 50¢. RB 30, 531.

George Christopher, account of sales, 12 Nov. 1839—lot of books sold to John H. Jett, 12 1/2¢. RB 31, 12.

Brodie S. Hull, account of sales, 12 Nov. 1839—lot of books sold to Benedict Burgess, $1. RB 31, 16.

Samuel Hull, account of sales, 12 Nov. 1839—*Bible* sold to Paul Hull, 29¢; *Dictionary* sold to Benedict Burgess, $1.29; lot books sold to John T. Lackey, $3.29. RB 31, 19.

John Hughes, account of sales, 12 Nov. 1839—one *Bible* sold to John Hughes, $1; one lot old books sold to Richard Bell, 13¢. RB 31, 27.

George Robinson, 12 Nov. 1839—one parcel of old books, 50¢. RB 31, 32.

John Rice, 12 Nov. 1839—one *Testament* and books, 18¢. RB 31, 35.

Susan Hill, 12 Nov. 1839—one lot old books, 25¢. RB 31, 42.

William E. Hughlett, 9 Dec. 1839—one lot of old books, 25¢; *Saints Rest* and *Perseverance*, 25¢; one volume *A Clark's Life*, 25¢; *Methodist Preachers* and *Surveyors*, 25¢; *Moral Sketches* and *Christian Pattern*, 25¢; Bottas's *History*, two volumes, $1; *Theological Institutes*, 75¢; *Theological Colloquies*, $1.50; *Methodist Magazine*, two volumes, $1.50; *Biographical Dictionary*, 50¢; Gibson's *Surveying*, 50¢; *Celebrated Travels*, 75¢; Walker's *Dictionary* and slate, 25¢; family *Bible* and *Hymn Book*, $2. *RB 31, 55*.

Charles Curtis, 10 Feb. 1840—one desk and a parcel of books, $5. *RB 31, 84*.

James Pasquith, 10 Feb. 1840—one *Testament* and *Hymn Book*, 50¢. *RB 31, 96*.

Royston B. Covington, 13 April 1840—parcel of books, $1. *RB 31, 141*.

Hiram Forbush, 13 July 1840—one looking glass and old books, 62¢. *RB 31, 207*.

John Swift, 13 July 1840—parcel of books, $1. *RB 31, 231*.

Robert P. Betts, 8 March 1841—lot of books, 6¢. *RB 31, 359*.

Richard Rice, 8 March 1841—five old books, 50¢. *RB 31, 361*.

Peter Coles, account of sales, 8 March 1841—one book sold to Mrs. Coles, 25¢. *RB 31, 364*.

Richard Headley, 10 May 1841—some books, $5. *RB 31, 395*.

George Wheatley, account of sales, 10 May 1841—one *Bible* and *Almanac*, 75¢; *Testament* and *Gulliver's Travels*, 16¢; Murry's *Grammar* and *Reader*, 26¢; *Dictionary* and *Memoir of Washington*, 12 1/2¢. *RB 31, 401, 402*.

Col. Samuel Downing, 11 May 1841—one lot books, $1. *RB 31, 406*.

Thomas G. Rains, 12 July 1841—one books, 50¢. *RB 31, 439*.

William Walker, 12 July 1841—one book case and old books, $6. *RB 31, 452*.

Richard Coles, 13 Sept. 1841—one large *Bible*. *RB 31, 488*.

Thomas Hughlett, account of sales, 13 Sept. 1841—*Testament*, $1.56 1/4; five receipt books, 31 1/4¢; two *Catechisms*, 8¢. *RB 31, 512*.

Samuel McCave, 14 Feb. 1842—lot of books [no price given]. *RB 32, 77*.

John Dawson, account of sales, 14 Feb. 1842—one family *Bible* sold to John C. Luttrell, 15¢; one lot small books sold to Benjamin Smith, 6 1/4¢. *RB 32, 96*.

B. M. Leland, 13 March 1842—parcel books in book case, $5. *RB 32, 133*.

Joseph Rice, 9 May 1842—one lot books, $1. *RB 32, 163*.

Martha Hall, 8 Aug. 1842—one desk, book case, and books, $2. *RB 32, 249*.

Samuel E. Hall, 14 Nov. 1842—one lot of books, $1.50. *RB 32, 361*.

Mary P. Glascock, 14 Nov. 1842—one lot books, 50¢. *RB 32, 383*.

Edward Anderson, 14 Nov. 1842—one lot old books, 50¢. *RB 32, 385*.

Thomas Blackwell, 13 Feb. 1843—one pair drawers, book case, and books, $10. *RB 32, 521.*

Peter McVicar, 13 March 1843—books in library, $100. *RB 32, 564.*

George S. Walker, 14 Aug. 1843—lot books, $2. *RB 33, 69.*

William H. Gaskins, 14 Aug. 1843—two books, 50¢. *RB 33, 88.*

Alexander Dameron, 14 Aug. 1843—one book, 25¢. *RB 33, 102.*

Edward Chamberlin, 14 Aug. 1843—lot of old books, 50¢. *RB 33, 107.*

Austin W. Dungan, 9 Oct. 1843—one lot of books, 25¢. *RB 33, 126.*

Benedict M. Williams, 9 Oct. 1843—one lot of books, $1. *RB 33, 135.*

William Douglas, 11 March 1844—lot of books, $3.72. *RB 33, 268.*

Nancy Blackwell, account of sales, 11 March 1844—lot of books sold to Cuthbert Harcum, $2.90. *RB 33, 276.*

Thomas Oldham, account of sales, 11 May 1844—one lot of old books sold to John T. Beacham, 6¢. *RB 33, 325.*

Ann C. Tomblin, 12 Aug. 1844—*History of France*, three volumes, $1; Roberson's *Talmert*, $1.50; Adam Clarke, $1.25; Titus's *History*, 6¢; Blair's *Lectures*, 20¢; Simson's *Euclid*, 6¢; Mosses's *Geography*, 1¢; *Modern Europe*, five volumes, $2.15; Stern's *Travels*, 20¢; Hume's and Smollett's *History of England*, twelve volumes, $5; Henry's *History of England*, six volumes, $3; Miller's *General History*, fifty-eight volumes, $3; Robertson's *History of Scotland*, two volumes, $2; Robertson's *History of America*, twenty-eight volumes, $2; Rollin's *Ancient History* in ten volumes, $1; *History of Rome* in three volumes, $1; *History of Spain* in three volumes, $1; *History of the East and West Indies* in six volumes, $2; *History of England*, 50¢; Montesquieu's *Spirit of Law with a Commentary Therein*, 50¢; Delano on *The Constitution of England*, 50¢; Smith's *Wealth of Nations* in three volumes, 50¢; *American State Papers* in twelve volumes, $6; Stewart's *Mental Philosophy*, $1; Paylus's *Moral Philosophy* in two volumes, $1; Hume's *Essays* in two volumes; Dufus's *Nature Displayed* in two volumes, Goldsmith's *Animated Nature* in four volumes, $3; Addison's works in three volumes, 50¢; *Tatler* and *Zimmerman*, 25¢; Cowper's *Poems*, 50¢; Pope's works in eight volumes, $1.50; Johnson's *Lives of English Poets* in four volumes, $2; Thomson's *Seasons* and *Mackakimon* [?], 25¢; Byron's *Poems* in three volumes, 50¢; Shakespeare's plays in eight volumes, $2.50; *British Theatre* in eleven volumes, $3; *Divine* in three volumes, 50¢; *Tales of Fashionable Life*, 50¢; two books of letters, 25¢; *Connoisseur* in four volumes, $1.25; *Peregrine Pickle* in three volumes, 50¢; Murray's *Grammar*, 50¢; Gurthey's *Geography*, $2; Webster's *Dictionary*, $1; Ainsworth's *Latin Dictionary*, 50¢; *Treatise on Fruit Trees* and *Housekeeping*, 25¢; *Practice Physic*, 25¢;

Spirit of Missions, 25¢; Latin books, 25¢; old books, 25¢; Ferguson's *Lectures*, 52¢. RB 34, 10, 11. [Some titles determined by comparing account of sales.]

George Rice, 12 Aug. 1844—one large *Bible*, 50¢; lot of old books, 6¢. *RB 34, 23.*

Alexander Rock, 9 Sept. 1844—one lot of old books, 75¢. *RB 34, 48.*

Henry B. Marsh, 9 Sept. 1844—lot of books, $1. *RB 34, 57.*

Thomas H. Lansdell, 9 Dec. 1844—family *Bible*, $2; Clark's *Commentary*, four volumes, $10; Moshein's *Church History*, $3; *Josephus*, two volumes, $2; Cooper's *Sermons*, two volumes, $1.50; McGavin's *Protestant*, two volumes, $3; *Revolutions in Europe*, $3.50; Snithen on *Representation*, $3.50; Williamson on *The Lord's Supper*, 10¢; *Farmer's Register*, one volume bounded and two not bounded, $2; *Life of Perry*, 25¢; *Cornelius Nepos*, 25¢; *English Exercises*, 10¢; *Conversation in Chemistry*, 25¢; *Saints Rest*, 10¢; Dabott's *Arithmetic*, 10¢; Murray's *Grammar*, 10¢; *Female Friend*, 10¢; *Key to Pike's Arithmetick*, 5¢; Blair's *Lectures*, 10¢; Milton's *Paradise Lost*, 50¢; *Natural Philosophy*, 25¢; *French Grammar*, 10¢; *French Dictionary*, 10¢; *Telemaque* [*Telemachus*?], 10¢; parcel of old books in the sideboard, 50¢. *RB 34, 95, 96.*

Henderson Haynie, 11 March 1845—one lot old books, 12¢. *RB 34, 167.*

Samuel Cralle, 18 July 1845—*United States Laws*, 50¢; Wesley's *Notes*, 50¢; *Revised Code*, 50¢; *Dictionary*, 50¢; *Bible*, 50¢; *Family Instruction*, 25¢; *Poor Laws*, 13¢; one large family *Bible*, $1; two books [no price given]. *RB 34, 227.*

Nancy Williams, 11 Aug. 1845—lot old books, 6¢. *RB 34, 246.*

Nancy B. Kent, 8 Sept. 1845—lot old books, 22¢. *RB 34, 264.*

William Blackerby, 9 Feb. 1846—lot of books, $1. *RB 34, 334.*

William C. Wheeler, account of sales, 10 Aug. 1846—one lot of books sold to William Perciful, 25¢. *RB 34, 437.*

Leroy Harcum, account of sales, 10 Aug. 1846—old books sold to William Coles, 25¢. *RB 34, 456.*

Griffin H. Foushee, 10 Aug. 1846—one table, bookcase, and books, $5. *RB 34, 478.*

John B. Kenner, 8 March 1847—one lot books, $4.25. *Estate Book A, 8.*

George Gill, 12 July 1847—lot of old books, 13¢. *Estate Book A, 47.*

Thomas L. P. James, 12 July 1847—one lot of books, 51¢. *Estate Book A, 52.*

Septimus Cralle, 9 Aug. 1847—five books, $1. *Estate Book A, 67.*

John Bryant, 13 Sept. 1847—one hat and case and book, $7.50. *Estate Book A, 95.*

Leven M. Harris, account of sales, 14 Feb. 1848—first lot of books sold to

James L. Lamkin, 57¢; second lot of books sold to H. H. Hughes, 57¢; third lot of books sold to George Vanlandingham, 25¢. *Estate Book A, 112.*

Walter Morrison, 13 March 1848—books, $1. *Estate Book A, 151.*

George Wilkins, account of sales, 13 March 1848—first lot of books sold to William H. Benson, 12¢; second lot of books sold to Leroy O. Dameron, 33¢. *Estate Book A, 160.*

Thomas Norman, account of sales, 10 April 1848—lot books sold to Frederick Downing, 6¢. *Estate Book A, 168.*

Richard C. Luttrell, 10 April 1848—one lot of old books, 25¢. *Estate Book A, 199.*

John R. Winstead, 10 April 1848—books, $5. *Estate Book A, 205.*

John Frances, account of sales, 14 Aug. 1848—one lot of books sold to John Tucker, $2.25. *Estate Book A, 232.*

George W. Booth, 11 Sept. 1848—one lot books, $1. *Estate Book A, 241.*

Hiram Claughton, 9 April 1849—one set Comp [?] *Commentareies*, $10; fourteen volumes Evl [?] Library, $5; one lot books, $3. *Estate Book A, 290.*

Robert Pinckard, 9 July 1849—Clarke's *Commentaries* in six volumes, $10; Wesley's works in six volumes, $3; Blackstone's *Commentaries*, $1; McGavin's *Protestant* in two volumes, $1; *Theological Colloquies, Josephus,* and Buck's *Dictionary*, $2; Jess's *Surveying*, 25¢; Sicker's and Blaire's *Sermons* in two volumes each, $2; one volume Westley's works, Jay's *Sermons*, and selections from Westley, Bayler's *Dictionary*, 30¢; lot old books, $1. *Estate Book B, 3.*

John Smith, account of sales, 18 July 1849—lot books sold to John Ayres, 51¢. *Estate Book B, 27.*

William Basye, account of sales, 10 Sept. 1849—lot of law books, $100; one volume Peak's *Evidence*, 37¢; Highonord on *Bail*, 6¢; *Espinasse Nici Prices*, $1; Harrison's *Chancery*, $1.37; Bacon's *Abridgment*, $3.50; Montesquieu's *Spirit of Laws*, 25¢; Stub's *Crown Circuit*, 12¢; four volumes Blackston's *Commentaries*, $2.60; Beccavir on *Crimes*, 30¢; Anslaw *Nisi Prices*, 17¢; Powell on *Contracts*, $1; Powell on *Mortgages*, $1.31; *Clerk's Magazine*, 26¢; *Principles of Health*, 26¢; *Revised Code 1803*, 18¢; two volumes *Revised Code*, $1.10; Rollin's *Belles Letters*, 80¢; Josephus's works, $1.28; Cooper's *Naval History*, $1.61; Botta's *History*, $1.75; Adam's *Lectures*, 63¢; Simpson's *Euclid*, 6¢; Curran's *Speeches*, $1.25; Oneq's *Pliny*, 60¢; Muir's *Trial*, 12¢; Crabb's [?], $2.19; Rollin's *History*, $4.47; Meshiem's *Church History*, $1.51; Nich's *Encyclopedia*, $8.10; *History of the United States*, 69¢; Brook's *Gazeteer*, 87¢; Paley's *Philosophy*, 43¢; Barrou's *Travels*, 25¢; Burns's works, $1; Byron's works, $1.60; *British Poets*, $1.25; Shakespeare, $1.75;

Mason's *Farrier*, 57¢; *Beauties of Scotl* [*Scotland*?] and Moore, 75¢; Greg's *Poems*, 14¢; *Salled Rook* [?], 51¢; Mrs. Heman's *Poems*, 42¢; *Spectator*, 20¢; Pope's *Poems*, 52¢; Homer's *Odyssey*, 42¢; Marvis's *Voyages*, 64¢; *Bible Dictionary*, 34¢; Hervey's *Meditation*, 26¢; Montgomery's works, 7¢; Milton's *Paradise Lost*, 50¢; *Beauties of Shakespeare*, 20¢; [?] *Letters*, 16¢; *Federalist*, 80¢; Garrett's *Lectures*, 12¢; Thornton's works, 62¢; *History of the World*, 27¢; Erskine's *Speeches*, 27¢; *Catholic Christian*, 7¢; Marsh's *Epitome*, 26¢; *Antiuniversalism*, 13¢; Addison's *Poems*, 6¢; *Boston Spectator*, 63¢; Clarke on *Promises*, 6¢; Clarke on *Commentaries*, $6.62; two volumes *The Entail*, 40¢; two volumes *The Pirate*, 50¢; *Memoirs of Luther Rice*, 50¢; Spark's *Washington*, 50¢; *Life of Abram Clarke*, 44¢; Volney's *Views*, 27¢; *Virginia Baptist Minister*, 50¢; *Prayer Book*, 27¢; Turnbrell's *History*, 6¢; *Bio* [*Biographical?*] *Dictionary*, 14¢; *Common Prayer*, 7¢; Dicer on *Baptism*, 41¢; *Bible*, 27¢; *Geography*, 1¢; *History of England*, 2¢; *Geography*, 3¢; lot of miscellaneous books, $1.20. *Estate Book B, 58–60*.

John Christopher, 8 Oct. 1849—one lot of books, 10¢. *Estate Book B, 69.*

Christopher Heartley, 10 Dec. 1849—one lot old books, 12¢. *Estate Book B, 80.*

Mottram B. Cralle, 11 Feb. 1850—lot of books, $15; bookcase, desk, and books, $5. *Estate Book B, 123.*

Frances K. Grinstead, 11 March 1850—three volumes Bunyan's works, $1.50; two volumes Clarke's *Commentaries*, $3; four volumes sermons, $1.50; two volumes Newton's works, $1.50; *Revolutions in Europe* [no price given]; *American Biography of United States*, $1.50; *Theological Colloquies*, $1; Buck's *Theological Dictionary*, 75¢; one lot miscellaneous books, $2. *Estate Book B, 147.*

Benedict Burgess, 8 April 1850—one lot of books, $5. *Estate Book B, 170.*

Robert J. Dameron, account of sales, 13 May 1850—one lot of books sold to William Hudnall, 55¢. *Estate Book B, 201.*

William R. Blackwell, 13 May 1850—set china glass, books, and brushes, $10. *Estate Book B, 211.*

Hiram Ingram, 10 June 1850—one lot books, $1. *Estate Book B, 235.*

Thomas Weymouth, 12 Aug. 1850—lot books, $1. *Estate Book B, 261.*

Robert S. Cox, 12 Aug. 1850—lot books, $25. *Estate Book B, 269.*

Mary S. Eustace, account of sales, 9 Dec. 1850—lot of old books sold to James Ewell, $1.25. *Estate Book B, 305.*

Dr. John T. Basye, 13 Jan. 1851—one lot medical books, $25. *Estate Book B, 307.*

James A. Palmer, 10 Feb. 1851—one lot medical books, 50¢; Frost's *Pictorial*

World, three volumes, $3; *Revised Code* and Henning's *Justice*, $1; Brook's *Gazeteer*, 50¢; one lot of books, *Lives of the Apostles*, 50¢; one lot of books, Mason's *Farrier*, 50¢; one lot of small books, 50¢; one lot of medical works, No. 2, 50¢; one lot old books, 50¢. *Estate Book B, 312.* [Some titles determined by account of sales.]

William Wallace, 10 March 1851—one lot of books, $1.10. *Estate Book B, 333.*

William Lewis, account of sales, 10 March 1851—*Bible* and hymn books sold to J. B. Lewis, $2.25. *Estate Book B, 347.*

Thomas Ball, 14 April 1851—lot books, $2. *Estate Book B, 358.*

Elizabeth Rice, 14 April 1851—one lot books, 50¢. *Estate Book B, 367.*

Robert Howerth, account of sales, 11 Aug. 1851—lot of books sold to William Gill, 35¢. *Estate Book B, 406.*

Mrs. Ann Eskridge, 11 Aug. 1851—lot of old books, 6¢. *Estate Book B, 409.*

Griffin Garner, 8 Sept. 1851—one family *Bible*, 75¢; lot of books, 50¢. *Estate Book B, 424.*

Thomas W. Hughlett, 10 Nov. 1851—one lot books, $2.50. *Estate Book B, 458.*

Dr. Joseph Basye, 10 Nov. 1851—lot of miscellaneous books, $25. *Estate Book B, 474.*

Nathan Moore, 10 Nov. 1851—one lot of books, 25¢. *Estate Book C, 4.*

Index

All Northumberland County residents mentioned in the text have been indexed. However, people outside of Northumberland County as well as authors and titles have not been.

Abbay
   John 75
Adams
   John 57
Agnew
   Margaret 36
Airs
   Samuel 74
   Thomas 74
Alexander
   Ann 45
   Ewell 58
   James 67
   John 39, 57
   Dr. Lawrence 32
   Rawleigh 83
   Robert 36, 100
Allen/Allin
   John 24, 83
   Teag 22
   William 86
Allmond
   Ann 83
Anderson
   Andrew 51
   Edward 110
   Izates 93, 100
   John 78
   Walter 12, 92
Andrews
   Thomas 13, 77
Angel/Angell
   Robert 48
   William 8, 60, 89

Angle
   George 51
Appleby/Applebay
   John 22, 40
   Norman 74
Arledge
   Sarah 24
   William 21
Ashburn/Ashburne
   George 79, 98
   George C. 100
   Peter 40
   Thomas 21, 40, 50, 91
   William 94
Ashton
   John 43
Aublin
   Henry 23
   Peter 24
Austin
   John 42
Ayres
   John 113

Bacon
   William 16
Bailey
   William 59
Baker
   Corbin 93
   Mary 3

Ball
  Anna 71
  David 13, 90, 91
  David Jr. 50, 57
  David T. 15, 107
  Elizabeth 97
  Fanny 101
  George 83
  George Jr. 76
  Capt. George 5, 6, 36, 59
  Grace 2, 43
  James 74
  Capt. John 41
  Joseph 21, 68, 85, 101, 106
  Kilkiah 92
  Mottrom 89
  Richard 71, 84, 86
  Sarah 96
  Thomas 89, 92, 105, 115
  William 35, 92, 105
Banks
  Mrs. Elizabeth 20
  Robert 24
Barecroft/Bearcroft
  Alexander 65
  George 67
  John 34, 72
  Lucretia 35
  Mottrom 82
  Peter 5, 37
  Richard A. 78
  Thomas 23, 38, 87
  William 72
Barns
  Edward 39, 102, 103
  Edwin 81
  Henry 75
  Lindsey 15, 108
  Linsey F. 100
  Neddy 76
  Samuel 100
  Samuel G. 94
  William 39, 94
Barr
  John 65

Barrat/Barret
  George 38, 95
  James 105
  John 63
  William 4, 32, 52, 63, 76
Basey/Baisey/Basie/Basye
  Edmond 22, 79
  Elismond 45
  Isaac 28
  Jesse 57
  John 70
  Dr. John T. 114
  Dr. Joseph 115
  William 15, 50, 113
Bates
  Fleming 15, 103
Bayless
  Thomas 46
Beacham/Beachum
  Daniel 30, 80
  James G. 97, 105
  John T. 111
  John W. 80
  Samuel L. 12, 85, 86
  Thomas 12, 75, 79, 81, 98
  Trussel 81
Beale
  Henry 106
Bean/Beane
  George 84
  George Y. 106
  John 44
  Milton G. 106
  Peter 75, 79
  William R. 84
Bearcroft see Barecroft
Beatley/Beetley
  Francis 46
  John 46
  Thomas 109
Bedmon
  Caleb 90
Beekley
  John 40
Beland
  Mary 76

Bell
    John 95
    Col. John 57
    Mary 31
    Richard 109
    Thomas 93, 108
    William 34
Bennet
    John 17
Benson
    William H. 113
Bentley
    John 20
Berry
    George 45
    John 71
    Samuel 97
    Thomas 32
    William 22, 51
    Winefred 64
Berryman
    George W. N. 104
    Willoughby 85
Betts
    Charles 49, 50, 51
    Daniel 74
    John 54
    Jonathan 49
    Mary Ammy 53
    Robert P. 110
    Roysten 72
    Royston Jr. 96
    Thomas 100
    William 42, 45
Billins
    Soloman 72
Blackerby
    Mrs. Catherine 102
    Thomas 64, 68, 102
    William 92, 112

Blackwell
    George 70, 97
    Hiram 104
    John 108
    Joseph 60, 67
    Nancy 65, 111
    Samuel 5, 6, 15, 32, 51, 57,
        75, 92, 101, 108
    Thomas 111
    William 68, 70
    William R. 114
Blincoe
    James 49
    John 22, 70
    William 104
Blundall/Blundal
    Elijah 50
    John 48
    William 79
Blundon
    John 102
    Samuel 90
    William 83
Boaze
    John 18
Boggess/Bogges
    Henry 25
    Mary 32
Bonum
    Thomas 29, 43
Boolock
    Edward 43
Booth
    Adam 48
    George W. 113
    James 41
    John 81, 107
    Richard 28, 44
Booze
    William 35
Boswell
    John 62
Bowen
    John 37
Bowley
    William 35

Boyd
   David 69, 70
   Mrs. Frances 52
   John 30
   Robert 5, 18, 37
Boyer
   Henry 51
Bradley/Bradly
   Elizabeth 27
   John 2
   Robert 2, 25
   William 17
   __ Widow 2, 17
Bramble
   John 109
   William F. 109
Brann
   Nicholas 80
Bransdon
   John 42
Brent
   Elizabeth 60
   William 5, 27
Bridgman
   Thomas 48
   William 46
Broughton
   John 57
   Thomas 17
Brown
   Charles 81
   George McAdam 12, 87
   John 44
   Mandley 42
   Phillip C. 62
   Thomas 27, 107
Bryan
   John 94
Bryant
   John 99, 108, 112
   Wilfrey 45
Buckley
   John 73
Burberry
   Malachi 20

Burbury
   James 25
Burch
   John 32
Burgess
   Benedict 108, 109, 114
   Samuel 101
Burn
   John 22
   Thomas 4, 7, 29
Burton
   Richard 71
Bussell
   Jack 78
   Matthew 49
Butcher
   Catherine 22
   William 56
Butler
   James 49

Campbell
   Pryce 81
   Thomas 24, 34
   William 62
Carter
   Charles 70
   Elizabeth L. 108
   John 61
   Peter 79, 92
   Thomas 76
Cartey
   John 35
Catchmay
   Henry 16
Chamberlin
   Edward 111
Champion
   James 75
   Joshan 55
   Moses 46
   William T. 82, 85

Chilton
    Andrew 49
    Mary 62
    Stephen 54
    William 60
Chocalat
    Richard 26
Christall
    Rev. Henry 7, 8, 33
Christee
    John 44
Christopher
    Dolly 82
    George 38, 109
    Henry 2, 25, 73
    John 43, 114
    John Jr. 68
    Robert 82, 93
    William 25
Churchill
    Joseph 22
    Willoby/Willoughby 64, 68, 71
Clark/Clarke
    Charles 80
    Jane 50
    Robert 34, 73, 91
    Samuel 98
Claughton
    Ann D. 106
    Griffethells 64
    Griffith 70
    Hannah 82
    Hiram 113
    James 16, 25, 65
    Jane 64
    John 42, 64, 80, 106
    Nancy 83
    Pemberton 62, 64, 94
    Richard 64, 94
    Thomas 71
    William 13, 87, 92
Clayton
    John 23
Clutton
    John 88, 97

Coan
    John 50
Cockarill/Cockrell
    John 34, 68, 91, 101
    Littleton 97, 107
    Peter P. 95
    Richard 100
Cole/Coles
    Edmond 42, 43
    Edward 53, 100
    John 45, 63, 101
    Peter 110
    Richard 86, 95, 110
    Richard P. 97, 100
    Robert 26
    William 72, 112
    William Jr. 91
Coleman
    Charles 66
    John 34
    Mary 52
    Thomas 74
Colston
    Travers 42
Colton
    John 28
Connally/Connolly
    George 89
    John 83
    Mary 89
Conway
    Anne 25
    Dennis 21, 67
    Edwin 68, 89
    George 39
    James 57
    John 4, 25, 44
    Joseph 91
    Peter 29
    Robert 104
    Thomas 102
    Capt. Thomas 72
Coodrak/Coolrick
    Joanne 63

Cooke
  John 16
  William 48
Cookman
  George 89
Copedge/Coppedge
  Benjamin 21
  Charles 8, 40, 74, 77
  James 29
  John 24, 36, 50
  Lazerus 51
  Patience 50
  William 53, 54
Corbell
  Hiram 100
  John 18, 67
  Richard S. 81
  Spencer 60, 63
  William 67, 92
Corbin
  George S. 107
Cornish
  Richard 40, 74
  William 25, 26, 72, 74
Cottrell
  Elizabeth 25
  John 24, 25, 102
  Sarah 24
  Thomas 59
Courtney
  James 58
  John 49
Coutanceau
  John 19
  Peter 18
Covington
  Royston B. 110
  Thomas D. 96, 98
Cox
  George 51
  Peter 77
  Robert S. 114
Crain
  Stephen 58

Cralle
  Mrs. Ann 98
  John 13, 46, 52, 62, 67, 89, 90, 97
  Capt. John 25
  Kenner 76, 101, 105, 107
  Mrs. Mary 100
  Mottram B. 114
  Rodham Kenner 50
  Samuel 15, 106, 112
  Septimus 112
  Thomas 10, 23
Crane
  James 58
Craven
  Charles 29
Creal/Creel
  Charles 24
  Elizabeth 23
Crockett
  Robert 81
Crossfield
  Winefred 76
Crowder
  Jesse 82, 100
  Thomas 99
  William 104
Crowther
  Robert 58
Crute
  Rebecca 45
  Richard 36
Cundiff
  Benjamin 73
  Henry 82
  Richard 22
  Thomas 100
Cunningham
  Thomas 25
Curtice/Curtis
  Benjamin 50
  Charles 110
  George 26
  Hillary 76
  John 57
  William 72

Dameron
    Alexander 111
    Bartholomew 88
    Bledsoe 59
    George 20
    Hannah 67
    Hardeaia 107
    John 4, 6, 10, 35
    Joseph 49
    Josias 24
    Leroy O. 113
    Onisephorus 51, 70
    Robert J. 114
    Sarah 2
    Thomas 2, 42, 45, 54
    William 62, 72
Danks
    George 57
Daughity/Doarthy/Dorty/Doherty
    James 60
    Neale 27
Davenport
    Elizabeth S. 99
    John 13, 98, 99
    Judith 106
    Lindsey O. 106
    William 13, 76, 81, 98
Davis
    Barbee 63
    John 79, 93
    Judith 78
    Lindsey 104
    Linszey 98
    Nancy 106
    Robert 41
    Samuel 52
    Thomas 39, 101, 102
    William 45
Dawkins
    George 4, 23, 26
    Jesse 75, 81
    Pendley 71

Dawson
    David 71, 80
    John 4, 19, 83, 110
    Samuel G. 108
    Thomas 104
Deacon
    William 73
Demmeritt/Demerrit/Demerit
    Alice 98
Dennis
    John 16
    John Jr. 16
Denny
    Edmund 19
    John 56
    Richard 33
    Samuel 41
    William 72
Dermott
    Hugh 19
Derrick
    Thomas 60
Dodson
    Archibald 94
    Charles 12, 86
Doggett/Dogget
    Benjamin 53
    John 28
    Judith 89
Dollin/Dollins
    Hannah 53
    John 22, 50
Donaway
    John 31
Dotton
    John 88
Douglas
    Edward 77
    William 111
Doulin
    Elizabeth 106

Downing
    Betty 84
    Charles 29
    Edward 28
    Mrs. Frances 28
    Frederick 113
    John 77
    Samuel 45
    Col. Samuel 110
    Sarah 80
    Thomas 21
    Capt. Thomas 80
    Col. Thomas 84
    Col. Thomas D. 92
    Thomas F. 93
    William 30, 71
Downman
    Grace 2
    Harris 2
    William 101
Doxey
    John 75
Dudley
    Winnifred 68
Dungan
    Ann B. 108
    Austin W. 111
Dunlap
    James 23

Earle
    John 17
Easton
    John 70, 74
Edenton/Edington
    David 9, 59
Edmonds
    Elias 32, 34
    William 48
Edward
    John 48

Edwards
    Ellis 94
    George 82, 87
    Griffin 107
    Haynes 95
    Isaac 2, 43, 54
    John 29, 81, 109
    Jonathan 65
    Joseph C. 106
    Leroy 81
    Richard 65, 89, 91
    Robert 65, 91
    Capt. Robert 82
    Thomas 58
Efford
    John 70
    Lewis 90
    Zachariah 36, 77
Elleston
    Jervace 29
Eskridge
    Mrs. Ann 115
    Samuel 61
    William 101
Eustace
    John 75, 91
    Capt. John 18
    Mary S. 114
    William 82
    Capt. William 10, 28
Evans
    Soloman 98
Everett/Everitt
    Nancy 76, 79
    Thomas 57
Eves
    George 27
Ewell
    James 114

Fairweather
    Patrick 35

Fallin
  Ann 33
  Charles 43, 62, 70, 83
  Dennis 24, 61
  Elisha 74, 92, 104
  Harriet 107
  John H. 82
  Tygner 57
  William 24, 84
Farnid
  Edwin 39
  James 39
Fauntleroy
  Mrs. Ann 50
  Capt. Griffin 45
  Maj. Griffin 40
  Judith 63
Fielding
  Ambrose 40, 53
Fitzmorris
  James 46
Fletcher
  William 36, 46
Flint
  John 44, 74, 83
Floyd
  Nathaniel 28
Fluker
  David 50
Flynt
  John 100
  Richard 17
  Richard Sr. 101
  Thomas 20
Fogg
  Israel 49
Fontaine
  James 36
Foot
  Henry 13, 66
Forbush
  Hiram 110
Forrest
  Benjamin 36

Forrester
  Griffin 80
  James 90
  Robert 81, 97
Fossett
  William 51
Foster
  Edward 35
Foulks/Fulks
  Elizabeth 106
  John 86
  Richard 25
Foushee
  Griffin H. 93, 112
  John H. 76
France
  John 50
  Thomas 57
  William 107
Frances
  John 113

Gaines
  Daniel 45
Garlington
  Capt. Christopher 43
  Elizabeth 58
  John 38, 58
  Maurice 52
  Samuel 28
  William 45, 46, 83
  William Jr. 46
Garner
  Edward 57, 72
  Elizabeth 80
  Griffin 115
  James 23, 42
  John 41
  Mary 54
  Samuel H. 93
  Vincent 45, 62
  William 41, 43, 64
  William P. 80

Gaskins
   Edwin 38, 86, 89
   Francis 28
   Henry L. 83, 86
   Henry Lee 13, 14, 94
   H. L. 92
   Jesse 46
   John 40, 48, 52, 62, 69
   Josias 46
   Samuel 33
   Thomas 10, 23, 82
   Col. Thomas 79
   William 82
   William H. 111
Gater
   Mathew 22
Gatley
   Elinor 49
Gator
   John 43
Genn
   James 20
George
   Balaam 82
   Betty 90
   John 100
   Nehemiah 79
   William 88
Gervis
   James 41
Gibbons
   John 72, 78
   Morris 36
Giddings
   William 82
Gilbert
   William 20

Gill
   Eli 90
   Elisha H. 102
   Ellis 68
   Capt. Ellis 50
   George 112
   Hezekiah 103
   John 53
   Thomas 28, 53
   William 37, 68, 115
Glascock
   Mary P. 110
   William 64
Gordon
   William 89
Gouch
   Jeffrey 25
   John 37
   Samuel 49
Gough
   Benjamin 74
Graham
   John 18
   William 77
Greenstreet
   William 52
Greenwood
   William 61
Grinsted/Grinstead
   Adam 25
   Frances K. 114
   John 79
   Richard 83

Hack
   John 8, 37
   Peter Spencer 49, 52
   Spencer 24
   Tunsall 46
Hadwell
   Jane 50
   John 23

Hall
    Austin 105
    John 47, 65, 76, 82, 90, 97
    Martha 110
    Mrs. __ 105
    Samuel E. 110
    Stephen 24, 71, 77
    Thomas 27, 30
Hammon
    Peter 19
Hammond
    Gedion 53
    John 48
    Peter 3
Hammonds
    L. 98
Hammontree
    David 58
Hampton
    John 4, 16
Harcum
    Charles 107
    Cuthbert 111
    Elisha 81
    James 90, 100
    John R. 97
    Leroy 95, 104, 112
    P. I. 97
    Samuel 97, 100
    Thomas 48, 81, 88
    William 19, 51, 91
Harden
    Thomas 23
Harding
    Cyrus 83
    Hopkins 12, 88
    Mark 64
    Mrs. Sarah 52
    Thomas 51
    Thomas E. 105
    William 53, 73, 105
Hardwick/Hardige
    Joseph 64
Harford
    John 45

Hargrove
    John 29
Harper
    Joshua 70
Harris
    John 19
    Leven M. 112
Harrison
    George 34, 65
    James 75
    John R. 79
Hart
    John 37
Hartly
    John 26, 74
Harvey
    George 52
    John 35
    Onesiphorus 83
    Sukey 99
    Thomas Jr. 96
    W. 99
Hayden/Haydon
    Ezekiel 75, 87
    George 83, 99
    John 98
    Leanah 76
    Samuel 58
    Thomas 76
    Willis 107
Hayes
    John 100
    Peter 45, 46
    Sally 100
    Sarah 42
    Thomas 52
Haynes
    Thomas J. 96

Haynie
    Alexander 99
    Bridgar 80, 96
    Charles 68
    Daniel 78
    Davenport 98
    David 98
    Mrs. Eleanor 44
    Harriet 96
    Henderson 101, 112
    Henry 63, 72
    Hiram 99
    Holland 100
    Isaac 10, 58
    James 84
    Jeadethan 80
    John 6, 22
    John Sr. 78
    Mrs. Lucy 97
    Martin 12, 82
    Maximillian 27, 79, 100, 104
    Ormsby 10, 33
    Peter 66
    Richard 38, 40, 43, 44, 67
    Capt. Richard 10, 22
    Sally 94
    Samuel 99
    Sarah 10, 34, 39, 48
    Stephen 48, 89, 93, 99
    Thomas 29, 62
    William 74
    Capt. William 51
Hays
    George 71
Hazard
    Henry 81
Headley
    Luke 78
    Randel 101
    Richard 91, 110
    William 88
Heartley
    Christopher 114
Heath
    George 8
    John 71
    Samuel 31
    Thomas 24
    William 20
Henderson
    Col. W. 100
Henry
    Edward 90
Hester
    Isaac 62
    Joseph 51
Hickmas
    Thomas 38
Higgins
    Hannah 53
Hill
    Britain 35
    Charles 57
    Enoch 2, 20
    Ezekiel 37
    Hannah 30
    John 30, 51
    Joseph 72
    Luke 40
    Sarah 6, 43
    Spencer 60, 62
    Susan 109
    William 35
Hobson
    Clark 32
    John 51
    Judith 53
    Thomas 2, 23
    William 28
Holliday
    Frances 100
Hopkins
    Thomas 17
Hopwood
    Mary 47
Hornsby
    John 43

Hoult
    John 44
    Joseph 19
Howard
    William 23
Howerth
    Robert 115
Howson
    Hannah 34
    Mrs. Hannah 35
    Judith 62
    Richard 34
Hubbard
    William 72
Hudnall
    Alfred 109
    Ann 86, 88
    Ellis 64
    John 43, 95, 99
    Joseph 9, 31
    Nanny 82
    Partin 21
    Rebecca 52
    Richard 6, 42, 49, 58, 82, 101
    Thomas 13, 83, 86, 98
    Warner 89
    William 77, 84, 114
    Willis W. 13, 93, 102
Hudson
    John Corbin 79
    Presly 100
    Robert 46
    Rodham 49, 76
    Thomas 65
Hughes
    H. H. 113
    John 109

Hughlett
    Ann 100
    Mrs. Elizabeth 87
    Ephraim 24
    Ester 103
    George I. 108
    Holland H. 101
    John 80
    John Jr. 79
    John H. 89
    Mary 18, 104
    Nicholas 53
    Roger W. 89, 90
    Samuel 78, 102
    Thomas 2, 3, 13, 59, 92, 102, 110
    Thomas W. 102, 115
    William 78, 102
    William E. 110
    Winny 78
    Winter 78
    Yarrett 42, 80, 81, 108
Hull
    Broadie 101
    Brodie L. 104
    Brodie S. 109
    John 106
    Maj. John 90
    Paul 109
    Richard 19, 20, 65
    Sally 109
    Samuel 106, 109
Humphlet/Humphlett
    Edward 91, 100
    Nancy 100
Humphris/Humphriss
    Elias 76
    George 45, 71
    Joseph 57, 74
    William 26
Hunt
    George 35, 45
    John 38

Hunter
  Allen 39
  John 23
  Robert 29
Hurst
  Henry 62, 83, 85
  Isaac 77, 92, 98, 105
  James 99
  John 35, 36, 39, 74, 89
  Joseph 79
  Kemp 45
  Thomas 13, 14, 47, 83, 93, 97, 99
  Thomas Jr. 83
  Thomas K. 102
  Mrs. Winefred 99
  Winnifred 92
Husk
  John 18
Hutchings
  Richard 79

Ingram
  Charles 5, 49
  George 39
  Capt. George 8, 80
  Hiram 114
  John 21, 92
  Samuel 34
  Thomas 89
  Willis 104

James
  Cathran 82
  John 44
  Joshua 35
  Margaret 22, 46
  Moses 49, 62
  Partin 30
  Thomas 43, 81
  Thomas L. P. 112
  William 58
Jaques
  William H. 77
Jeffries
  Edmund R. 101

Jett
  John H. 109
  Joseph H. 102
  Thomas H. 98
  William E. 106
Johnson
  William 27
Johnston
  Dr. Archibald 28
Jones
  Maj. Catesby 81
  Charles 8, 31, 44, 67
  Mrs. Elizabeth 31
  George 98
  Joshua 71
  Judith 4, 6, 7, 30, 31
  Lemore 51
  Loftis 81
  Robert 41, 78
  Samuel 95, 99
  Sarah 5, 20
  Dr. Walter 92
  William 38, 39, 83

Keble
  Cary 2, 26
Keene
  Mrs. Anne 65
  John 31, 76
  Newton 62
  William 10, 22
Keeve
  Beverly 58
Kellum
  Elizabeth 97
  Richard 51
  William L. 83
Kennedy
  Elizabeth 65
  Richard 49
  William 64

Kenner
    Capt. Francis 26
    John B. 101, 112
    Capt. Matthew 33
    Richard 23
    Rodham 9, 32
    Col. Rodham 13, 73
    Capt. William 62
    Winder 52, 83
    Col. Winder 73
Kent
    John 6, 17
    John Jr. 54
    John Sr. 54
    John C. 96
    Nancy B. 112
    Warner 99
    William B. 108
Kerr
    Edward 6, 54
    George 5, 6, 54
    John 8
Kesterson
    George 53
    John 42
    Quilla 52
    William 27
Kilpatrick
    Edward 18
Kirk
    John 70
    Randal R. 109
Kirkley
    George 53
Knight
    Francis 24
    Hannah 74
    John 65, 66, 77
    Joseph 22, 26
Knott
    James C. 83
    Peter 65
    Richard 47
    William 38

Lackey
    John T. 109
    Mrs. Mary 83
Lamkin
    George 81
    Griffin 94, 97
    James 29, 67
    James L. 113
    John 42
    Lewis 28, 58, 64
    Matthew 100
    Peter 71
    Thomas 102
Lancaster
    John 27, 35
    Joseph 34, 42
    William 53
Langley
    William G. 83
Langsdale
    John 24
Lansdell
    Benjamin 72, 92
    John 102
    John Sr. 102
    Mary 98
    Thomas 89, 98
    Thomas H. 112
    William 71, 76
Lathrom/Lathrum
    John 43, 44
Lattimore
    Charles 58, 82
    David 57, 58
    Joanne 58, 67
    Richard 10, 26
    Sally 67
    William 47, 60, 86
Laurence
    John 19
    Susanna 21
Laws
    Daniel 107
Leach
    John 45, 62

Leazure
  Bartholomew 21
Lecompt
  Edmond 102
Ledford
  Elizabeth 45
  James 71
Lee
  Charles 5, 31, 36
  Col. Charles 72
  Maj. Charles 4, 6, 29
  Elizabeth 31
  George 101
  Hancock 2, 3, 4, 5, 6, 7, 18
  Mrs. Judith 29
  Kendall 68
  Mrs. Leanna 50
  Richard 7, 28, 29, 30, 99
Leland
  Miss Ann H. 84
  B. M. 110
  Charles 12, 13, 91, 93, 95
  John 2, 36, 95
  Rev. John 13, 66
  Lucy 2
Lewis
  James 37, 41, 78, 79
  J. B. 115
  John 36, 37, 81, 92
  Jordan 101
  Peter 40, 41
  Sarah Ann 75
  William 44, 45, 115
  William B. 79
Lindsey
  Henry 23
Little
  William 17
Littrell/Luttrell
  John 50
  John C. 110
  Richard 73, 94
  Richard C. 113
  Thomas 90
Lork
  John 49

Love
  Alexander 25
Low
  Abraham 32
  Samuel 89
Lowry
  Elias 53
  Sarah 57
Lowther
  Thomas 49
Lucas
  Samuel 67
  Thomas 22
Lunsford
  Alexander 40
  John 51
  Lewis 77, 79
  Moses 76
  Richard 46
  Samuel 28
  Swanson 48

Mahane/Mahanes
  Deborah 46
  John 60, 63
  Meredith 25
  Samuel 28, 41
  Thomas 36
Maith
  Sally 107
Maley
  James 75
Marsh
  Charles 71, 93, 102
  Edward 86
  Gideon 84, 88
  Henry B. 112
  James 57
  Richard 78
  William 44
Marshall
  Richard 41
Mason
  Edward 36
  John 46
  Peter 48

Maudley
    Edmund 3
    Rebecca 3
Mayes/Mays
    Henry 40
    John 40, 71
McAdam
    Dr. John 106
McCally/McCollis
    Charles 51
McCave
    John 83, 92
    Leroy 104
    Samuel 110
McClanahan
    Elizabeth 100
    James 80
    Peter 79
    Thomas 83, 94
McCurdy
    Samuel 89, 90
McGoon
    John 62
McNaughton
    Rev. Duncan 12, 85
McQuhae
    Anthony 63
McVicar
    Peter 111
Mealey/Maily/Mealy
    Harriot 104
    John 104
    Patrick 24
Menzies
    Rev. Adam 9, 55, 63
    George 68
    Mrs. Phebe 4, 5, 8, 9, 63, 68
    Samuel Peachey 68
Metcalf/Metcalfe
    Henry 54
    William 23, 57
Middleton
    John 92, 93
    William 93
Millard
    Joseph 28

Miller
    Elizabeth 47, 57
    Henry 38
    Jane 29
    John 13, 14
    John Jr. 84
    Thomas 89
Mitchell
    William 91, 100
Moltimore
    William 77
Moon
    James 30, 36
    Mary 96
    William 90
Moor/Moore/More
    David 21
    Col. James 90
    Jeduthen 90, 102
    Joseph 51
    Nathan 100, 115
    Robert 45
    Mrs. Sarah 12, 90
Moorhead
    Alexander 34, 37, 44
Morgain
    David 59
Morris
    William 48
Morrison
    Richard 81, 101
    Walter 113
    William 87
Mott
    Mosley 4, 5, 46
    Randolph 32, 74, 75
    William 53, 74
Mottrom
    Col. John 2, 16
Murphey
    Thomas 43
    William 41
Muse
    Daniel 82
    William 75

Nash
   William 16, 40
Neale
   Christopher 9, 24, 36
   Capt. Christopher 21
   Daniel 25
   Ebenezer 3, 19
   John 73
   Mrs. Judith 35
   Matthew 10, 24, 34
   Capt. Matthew 68
   Peter 26
   Presley 72
   Richard 26, 72
   Shapleigh 37
   William 74
Nelms
   Aaron 43
   Charles 64, 79
   Eben 81
   Edwin 89, 101, 106
   Elizabeth 5, 50
   Hiram 98
   Richard 6, 27
   Samuel 50
   William 20, 43, 50, 98
Nelson
   Rev. Joshua 34
Newton
   Christopher 21
Nichols/Nicholls
   John 25
   William 16
Nicken
   Amos 83
Nicoll/Nicolls
   William H. 12, 13, 14, 96
Norman
   Thomas 62, 113
Norris
   Joseph 66
Norton
   Mr. ___ 81

Nutt
   Ann 19
   Benjamin 26, 29
   Elizabeth 43
   Farnefold 51
   John 56
   Joseph 54
   Moseley 82, 88
   Richard 19, 65, 88
   William 19, 38
O'Daughity
   Neale 22
Oldham
   Edward 96
   George 46, 75
   James 19
   John 43
   John Jr. 43
   Mary 50
   Thomas 111
   William 76, 80, 81
Oliver
   Mrs. Elenor 20
   Lowry 67
Ollard
   Judith 71
Opie
   Anne 21
   Capt. John 22
   Lindsey 10, 37, 73
Overzee
   Symon 17
Owens
   William 47

Palfry
   Mary 31

Palmer
   Charles 97
   Isaac 38
   James A. 114
   Joseph 89
   Nargail Sharezer 58
   Robert 70
   Robert D. 89
   Rodham 77
   Thomas 39
   William 53
Parker
   James 19
   Jane 23
   Jonathan 17
   Mary 31
Parrott
   Lawrence 37, 38
   William 67
Parsons
   James 44
Partridge
   John 70
Pasquith
   James 110
   William 95
Patterson
   Eli L. 101
Payne
   George 58
   John 25
Peachey
   Judith 44
Pearce
   Richard 28
Pearse
   John 17
Peart
   Rev. Francis 32
Peed
   Isaac 71
Percifull/Percivall
   Thomas 19
   William 112
Pery
   Jane 6, 16

Pew
   James 32
Phillips
   George 79, 81
   William 81
Pickering
   Francis 105
Pickrell
   William H. 81
Pickren
   David 58
   George 41
   Spencer 63
   William 80
Pierce
   Joseph Jr. 76
Pinckard
   Cyrus 101
   Elizabeth 88
   Robert 74, 113
Pitman
   Burgess 81
   Robert 62
   Susanna 85
   Thomas 32
   William 67, 81
Polk
   William T. 108
Poole
   Samuel 3
Pooley
   William 82
Pope
   John 22
   Joseph 54
   Nicholas 65
Potts
   Ezekiel 70
   Robert 70
Power
   John 31
   Joseph 67, 82
   William 72
Presly
   Capt. Peter 20

Price
  Mary 23
  Richard 23
  William 20
Pritchard
  Charles 68
  Swanson 28, 32
Prosser
  John F. 106
Pullen/Pullin
  Henry 81
  Leroy 89
  Nathan 75
  Thomas 68, 97
Pullum
  Thomas 49

Quaram/Quarom/Quarson
  Mary 44
  Thomas 39

Rains
  Thomas G. 110
  William 77, 90
Ramsey
  Robert 58
Reade
  Thomas 16
Reason
  John 20, 37
Reed
  Andrew 22
Reeves
  Thomas 27
Reyon
  Fanny 104

Rice
  Charles 88
  Charles Jr. 89
  Elizabeth 115
  George 112
  Isaac 90
  John 52, 74, 105, 109
  John Sr. 91
  Joseph 110
  Milley 90
  Peter C. 13, 93
  Richard 31, 110
  Sarah 93
  William 73, 76
Richardson
  Elizabeth 21
  Isaac 70
Rider
  Henry 25
  John 28, 40
Roberson
  Joseph 45
  Joseph Jr. 47
Robertson
  Rev. Moses 9, 37
Robinson
  Benjamin 22
  George 109
  Jeremiah 98
  Jesse 53
  Joel 108
  John 95, 103
  Thomas 20
Robuck
  Robert 41
  William 52, 75
Rock
  Alexander 94, 97, 106, 112
Rogers
  Edward 44
  George 71
  Dr. James 19
  John 12, 74, 81
  William 101
Rosson
  William 77

Rout/Routt
    John 48
    Richard 75, 94
    Thomas 67
Rush
    Richard 19
Russell
    Richard 18
    Thomas 75
Ryan
    Edward 48

Sacheveril
    Timothy 20
Sampson
    Joseph 70
Sanders
    William 18
Sandford/Sandiford
    Thomas 5, 9, 21
    William 86
Schrever
    Bartholomew 20, 26
    Elizabeth 27
Sebree
    James 56
    John 74
    Moses 75
    Richard 32
    William 71, 75
    William I. 106
Sedgrave
    Robert 16
Self
    James 65, 77
    Matthias 82
    Samuel B. 80
    Thomas 48
    Walter 101
    widow 101
    William 60
Shadock
    John 36
Shapleigh
    Thomas 18

Shaw
    John 17
Sheverall
    Allen Long 76
Shirley/Shurley/Shearly
    Daniel 56
    Elizabeth 101
    Elizabeth R. 109
    John 27, 30
    Richard 25
Short
    Benedict 71
    Robert 39
    Thomas 37, 41
    William 32
Sims
    Thomas 29, 52
Singer
    John 37, 38
Slacum
    Ann 109
    George 85, 86
    Job 109
Smith
    Baldwin Matthews 6, 52
    Benjamin 110
    Edwin 40
    Mrs. Hannah 32
    John 38, 52, 113
    Lazarus 31
    Col. Philip 34
    Richard 8, 38
    Robert 17
    Samuel 29, 41
    Thomas 5, 8, 47, 60, 67
    William 43, 65
    Wooldridge 52, 60
Smither
    George 74, 75
    John 71
Smoot
    Charles 74
Snow
    Elisha 73
    Elizabeth 95
    Samuel 35

Span
    Capt. Cuthbert 44
    John 21
    Capt. Richard 26
    Samuel 26
Speke
    Mr. __ 16
Spence
    David 23
    John 25
Spriggs
    Joseph 72
Stanly/Stanley
    John 23
    Joseph 41
Steed
    Thomas 17
Steel
    Jane 74
    Samuel 62
Stepto/Stoptoe
    John 30
    William 40
Stewart
    James 35
Stith
    Everard M. 15, 104
Stott
    Stephen 46
Stowell
    Ann 4, 23
Straughan
    James 29, 30
    John C. 92
    Richard 67
    Samuel 93, 94
    Samuel L. 96
    Winifred 36
Sullevan/Sullivant/Sullivan
    Charles 56
    Cornelius 50
    Dennis 75
    Moses 56
    Peter 37

Sutton
    Mrs. Catroun/Caty 82
    Elizabeth 70
    Isaac 73, 74
    James 79, 97
    John 31, 41, 71
    Lazarus 61
    Moses 82
    William 6, 44, 71, 101
Swain
    Joseph 77
Swanson
    Aaron 56
    Ann 35
    Benjamin 41
    Chloe 46
    Dennis 44, 49
    Jesse 83
    John 42, 45, 46
Swift
    John 64, 110
Sydnor
    Anthony 12, 67, 97
    William 15, 105, 107
Symmons
    Elizabeth 17
Taite
    William 54
    Maj. William 6, 9, 61
Tapp
    William 20
Tapscott
    James 57
    John 107
    John S. 106
Tarkleson
    Tarkle 30

Taylor
    Aaron 37
    Argail 48
    John 4, 5, 6, 26, 42, 57, 62
    Joseph 70
    Judith 64
    Lazarus 34
    Michael 60
    Moses 81
    Thomas 21, 46, 79, 81
    William 37, 39, 70, 95
Tellis
    William 107
Thomas
    James 86
    John 20, 65
    Peter 34, 75
    Richard 30
    Sarahann 34
Thompson
    Frances Ann 40
    James 44
    Simon 18
Thomson/Tomson
    Barbary 43
    Frances Ann 39
    Richard 22, 37
Thornton
    John 71
    Peter Presley 68
    Hon. Presly 9, 58
Throp/Tropp
    Richard 85
Tignor
    Elizabeth 3
    James 65
    Martha 41
    Phillip 3, 64, 84
Timberlake
    Francis 52
Tobin
    Thomas 35
Toby
    Jane 27

Tolson
    John 35
    Mary 30
Tomblin
    Ann C. 111
Tomson
    James 32
Toulson
    Mary 42
    Richard 105
    Thomas 27
    William 28
Towles
    Thomas 92, 93
Townsend
    Elizabeth 72
    Joshua 62
    William 60
Travers
    Henry 79
    William 79
Treakle
    James 97
    William 90, 95, 97
Troop
    William 53
Trussel
    John 44
    Col. John 16
    William 39
Tucker
    John 113
Tullos
    John 31
Turner
    Benjamin 93
    Charles 82
    Edward 27
    George 36
    Hannah 43
    Henry 42
    John 30, 78, 79

Urguhart
    Thomas 19

Vanlandingham
  Frances 91
  Francis 28, 43, 104
  George 63, 113
Waddy/Waddey
  Benjamin 7, 8, 29, 31, 41, 70
  George P. 88
  James 22, 62
  John 39, 64
  Mrs. Sarah 39
  Shapleigh 84
  Shapleigh N. 89
  Thomas 28, 79
  William 83
Waide
  Richard 91
Walkden
  James 27
Walker
  Francis 75
  George 75, 76
  George S. 111
  Jane 40
  Jesse 90
  John 65
  Joseph 42, 71
  Leonard 42
  Manuel 46
  Nathaniel 26
  Richard 63, 80
  Risdon 72
  Thomas 16, 34, 76
  William 49, 99, 110
Wallace
  William 115
Waller
  James 34
Wallis
  Hugh 19
Warrick
  Richard 26
  William 40
Watson
  Hugh 55
  Margaret 62

Watts
  Edward A. 100
  Richard 65
  Robert 23
  Thomas 40
Waughop
  John 2, 8, 40
Way
  Betsy 76
  Davenport 76
  George W. 109
  John 80
  Richard 67
  William 94
Weaver
  Richard 48
Webb
  Aaron 49
  Benjamin 72
  Edward 100
  Elizabeth 46
  Ewell 91
  Francis 25
  Giles 60
  Hannah 74
  John 18, 61, 72
  John N. 108
  John Span 74, 77
  Joseph 53
  Leanna 72
  Thomas 17, 21, 71, 72
  William 34, 37, 51, 52, 80
  Miss Winefred 92
Welch/Welsh
  Benjamin 72
  Betsy 94
  Elinor 22
  Mary 77
  Silvester 43
West
  John 50
Wetherstone
  Alexander 3
Weymouth
  Thomas 114

Whaley
   Thomas 77
Whealor/Wheeler
   John 79
   Moses 77
   William C. 112
Wheatley
   George 15, 110
Whiddon
   John 35
White
   Edward 52
   Robert 38
Whitehead
   Thomas 20
Wildey/Wildy
   Jane 49
   Joseph 7, 38, 58
   Motley 38
   Sarah 94
   William 22, 31, 38, 49, 83, 94
Wilkins
   Charles 31
   Daniel 56
   Dorothy 76
   George 113
   Haynie 92
   Jane 42, 53
   John 31, 56
   Peter 90
   Thomas 48
   William 75
Wilkinson
   William 97
Williams
   Aron 41
   Benedict M. 111
   James 90
   John 49
   John Sr. 102
   Capt. John 57
   Nancy 112
   Thomas 34, 65, 80

Wilson
   Jane 41
   Nathanael 79
   Robert 4, 25
Winstead/Winsted
   Betsy 109
   Daniel 77
   Elizabeth 53
   George 52
   James 72
   John 50
   John R. 113
   Samuel 24, 63
   William 97
Winter
   Betty 65
   Roger 48
   Thomas 52
   William 56
Wise
   Spencer 53
Woddrop/Woodrop
   Robert 8, 56
Wood/Woods
   John 2, 28, 48
Wornom
   Jane 32
   John 60
   Thomas 32, 57, 75
   William 89
Wright
   John 80
   Richard 20
   Capt. Richard 17

Yerby
   Charles 78
   Thomas 39, 78
Young
   Mary 27

www.ingramcontent.com/pod-product-compliance
Lightning Source LLC
Chambersburg PA
CBHW070451090426
42735CB00012B/2511